The Sociolinguistics of Sign Languages

This is an accessible introduction to the ... they relate to sign languages and Dea... ... brings together a team of leading experts in sign linguistics to survey the field, and covers a wide range of topics including variation, multilingualism, bilingualism, language attitudes, discourse analysis, language policy and planning. The book examines how sign languages are distributed around the world; what occurs when they come in contact with spoken and written languages; and how signers use them in a variety of situations. Each chapter introduces the key issues in each area of inquiry and provides a comprehensive review of the literature. The book also includes suggestions for further reading and helpful exercises.

The Sociolinguistics of Sign Languages will be welcomed by students in Deaf studies, linguistics and interpreter training, as well as spoken language researchers, and researchers and teachers of sign languages.

CEIL LUCAS is Professor of Linguistics at Gallaudet University. She is the co-author of *The Linguistics of ASL* and of *Language Contact in the American Deaf Community* (both with Clayton Valli), both published in 1992.

The Sociolinguistics
of Sign Languages

Edited by

Ceil Lucas

UNIVERSITY PRESS

PUBLISHED BY THE PRESS SYNDICATE OF THE UNIVERSITY OF CAMBRIDGE
The Pitt Building, Trumpington Street, Cambridge, United Kingdom

CAMBRIDGE UNIVERSITY PRESS
The Edinburgh Building, Cambridge CB2 2RU, UK
40 West 20th Street, New York, NY 10011-4211, USA
10 Stamford Road, Oakleigh, VIC 3166, Australia
Ruiz de Alarcón 13, 28014 Madrid, Spain
Dock House, The Waterfront, Cape Town 8001, South Africa

http://www.cambridge.org

First published 2001

Printed in the United Kingdom at the University Press, Cambridge

Typeface Times 10/12 pt.   *System* LaTeX 2_ε [TB]

A catalog record for this book is available from the British Library.

Library of Congress Cataloguing-in-Publication Data
The sociolinguistics of sign languages / Ceil Lucas, editor.
p.   cm.
Includes bibliographical references and index.
ISBN 0 521 79137 5 (hardback) – ISBN 0 521 79474 9 (paperback)
1. Sign language.   2. Deaf – Means of communication.   3. Sociolinguistics.
I. Lucas, Ceil.
HV2474 .S62   2001
306.44′087′2 – dc21

ISBN 0 521 79137 5 hardback
ISBN 0 521 79474 9 paperback

For Joel Sherzer, who, in 1975,
got me started in sociolinguistics

Contents

Figures

Tables

Contributors

JEAN ANN is an Assistant Professor at SUNY, Oswego. She teaches in the Department of Curriculum and Instruction and the Program in Linguistics. Her recent publications include joint work on sign languages (Ann and Peng, 2000) and spoken languages (Peng and Ann, 2001).

BEN BAHAN is an Associate Professor and Chair of the Deaf Studies Department at Gallaudet University. Ben is a deaf son of deaf parents who grew up in New Jersey. He attended and graduated from a residential school in West Trenton, NJ: Marie Katzenbach School for the Deaf. He then went on to Gallaudet University and furthered his education at Boston University where he earned an M.A. in Deaf Education and a Ph.D. in Applied Linguistics. Today he is a renowned American Sign Language (ASL) storyteller, linguist, researcher, author and presenter on issues related to ASL and Deaf Studies. Ben has produced a number of videotapes and books. Most recently he co-authored *The Syntax of American Sign Language* (Neidle *et al.*, 2000).

ROBERT BAYLEY is an Associate Professor of sociolinguistics at the University of Texas at San Antonio. His publications include *Second Language Acquisition and Linguistic Variation* (Bayley and Preston, 1996), *Sociolinguistic Variation in American Sign Language* (Lucas *et al.*, 2001) and numerous articles on sociolinguistics and second language acquisition.

SARAH BURNS is a Senior Speech and Language Therapist at Lucena Clinic, Dublin, Ireland and co-coordinator of the Fulbright Scholarship in Deaf Studies. She graduated with a B.Sc. (1991) and M.Sc. (1995) from the University of Dublin, Trinity College, and spent one year (1996–97) at Gallaudet University, Washington, DC as a Fulbright Scholar. She previously lectured at the School of Clinical Speech and Language Studies, Trinity College. Areas of special interest include sociolinguistics of Deaf communities (attitudes and language planning) and bilingual–bicultural models of education for deaf children. Previous publications include: *Irish Sign Language: Ireland's second minority language* (Burns, 1998).

FRANCES ELTON is a Lecturer in Sign Language and Deaf Studies at City University in London and teaches the only advanced British Sign Language (BSL) linguistics course for BSL tutors and Deaf Professionals in the UK. She was a Teaching Fellow at Durham University and has played a key role in the training of BSL tutors since 1987. From 1990 to 1996 she was a Director of the Tutor Training Course as well as teacher of Advanced Certificate, Postgraduate Diploma and M.A. courses offered by the Deaf Studies Research Unit. She was a member of the editorial team which produced the first and only BSL/English Dictionary in 1992 (Brien, 1992). As a member of the British Deaf Association's (BDA) sign language task force, she helped draw up the BDA's Sign Language Policy and founded the Institute of British Sign Language. She was also closely involved with the making of City University/CACDP's Introduction to the Linguistics of BSL video in 1999. Her interests include sign linguistics, sociolinguistics, cross-cultural linguistics and research into London Sign Variation.

CEIL LUCAS is Professor of Linguistics in the Department of ASL, Linguistics, and Interpretation at Gallaudet University, where she has taught since 1982. Her main area of interest is the structure and use of sign language, and she has co-authored and edited numerous articles and books in this area, the main ones being *Linguistics of American Sign Language* (Valli and Lucas, 2000), *Language Contact in the American Deaf Community* (Lucas and Valli, 1992). She is the series editor for a series entitled *Sociolinguistics in Deaf Communities*, of which Volume 7 is a co-authored volume entitled *Sociolinguistic Variation in ASL*, a book which describes the findings of a National Science Foundation project of which she is the director.

PATRICK A. MATTHEWS is a researcher/lecturer on Deaf studies and an interpreter trainer who runs his own company, Irish Sign Language (ISL) Studies. Having obtained a Certificate in Social Sciences in Deaf Studies at the University of Bristol, a Diploma in Sign Language Teaching from NUI, Maynooth, he received an M.Phil. in Applied Linguistics at Trinity College, Dublin. Patrick has a wealth of experience working in the Deaf community teaching ISL to deaf people as first-language learners and to non-deaf second-language learners at a variety of proficiency levels. He has also worked in broadcasting, research and curriculum development. His published work includes a major demographic study and a linguistic description of ISL. Patrick has a particular interest in pedagogy and the influence of culture in language teaching and learning.

MELANIE METZGER currently works as an Associate Professor in the Department of ASL, Linguistics, and Interpretation at Gallaudet University. Recent publications include a journal article on gesture in American Sign Language

(Liddell and Metzger, 1998) as well as the book *Sign Language Interpreting: Deconstructing the Myth of Neutrality* (Metzger, 1999). She also served as guest editor for Volume 6 of Lucas' Sociolinguistics in Deaf Communities series, *Bilingualism and Identity in Deaf Communities* (2000).

EVELYN NOLAN-CONROY is a registered qualified interpreter, having studied Deaf Studies and interpreting at Trinity College, Dublin, Ireland and the University of Bristol, UK. She also obtained a Masters in Applied Linguistics at Trinity College. An experienced interpreter in a wide range of settings, Evelyn has made a significant contribution to the development of the profession of sign language interpreting in Ireland. Her work includes lecturing on interpreting, curriculum development, and she has developed a particular interest in Discourse Styles and Translation. She is now gaining wider recognition through her writings and has several published articles and contributions to chapters on language and the Deaf community.

TIMOTHY REAGAN is Professor of Educational Linguistics and Associate Dean of the Neag School of Education at the University of Connecticut. He has published extensively on issues of language planning and language policy, and his work has appeared in journals such as the Harvard Educational Review, Educational Theory, Language Problems and Language Planning, Foreign Language Annals, the Northeast Conference on the Teaching of Foreign Languages Review, Sign Language Studies, Multicultural Education and Educational Foundations.

MARY ROSE holds a Master's degree in Linguistics from Gallaudet University and is currently a doctoral student in Linguistics at Stanford University. She has co-authored papers on linguistic variation in ASL and on discourse analysis in medical contexts. She has presented papers at the conference on Theoretical Issues in Sign Language Research and at the American Dialect Society and is a collaborator on a volume entitled *Sociolinguistic Variation in ASL*, an account of a six-year project funded by the National Science Foundation.

RACHEL SUTTON-SPENCE is a Lecturer in Deaf Studies at the Centre for Deaf Studies at the University of Bristol, UK. She is co-author of the introductory text book *The Linguistics of British Sign Language* (Sutton-Spence and Woll, 1999).

CLAYTON VALLI completed his doctoral degree in Linguistics and ASL Poetics at the Union Institute in Cincinnati, Ohio in 1993. He is a freelance teacher, linguistic consultant, editor and ASL poet and now resides in Miami, Florida. He is co-author of the text *Linguistics of American Sign Language* (Valli and Lucas, 2000), of *Language Contact in the American Deaf Community* (Lucas and Valli, 1992), of *Sociolinguistic Variation in ASL* (Lucas *et al.*, 2001) and of the videotape *ASL Poetry: Selected Works by Clayton Valli* (Valli, 1995).

BENCIE WOLL joined the Department of Language and Communication Science at City University, London in 1995 to take up the newly created Chair in Sign Language and Deaf Studies, the first chair in this field in the UK. After studying linguistics in the USA and Britain, Bencie Woll pioneered Deaf Studies as an academic discipline in the UK; research and teaching interests embrace a wide range of subjects related to sign language, including the linguistics of British Sign Language (BSL) and other sign languages, the history of BSL and the Deaf community, the assessment of sign language, and sign language and the brain. She currently holds research grants from the Leverhulme Trust, the Wellcome Trust, the Commission of the European Union and the Medical Research Council. She is co-author of the introductory text book *The Linguistics of British Sign Language* (Sutton-Spence and Woll, 1999).

ALYSSA WULF holds a Master's degree in Linguistics from Gallaudet University and is currently a student in the doctoral program in Linguistics at the University of California at Berkeley. She has presented papers at the American Dialect Society and at the conference on Theoretical Issues in Sign Language Research, and is a collaborator for the volume *Sociolinguistic Variation in ASL* (Lucas *et al.*, 2001).

Foreword

Walt Wolfram

No topic within sociolinguistics reflects the growth of the field more symbolically than the study of the sociolinguistics of sign languages. Less than half a century ago, the fundamental debate centered on the rightful place of sign languages with a complete set of linguistic structures and full range of natural language entitlements. Such debates were, of course, framed by the ideology of linguistic subordination, in which difference was equated with deficit and legitimacy was defined by dominance. Happily, but not without continued vigilance, the study of sign languages has now developed a full-course sociolinguistic menu, with ample offerings in all of the major areas of specialization now subsumed under the general rubric of sociolinguistics.

The essays in this collection represent a full complement of sociolinguistic topics, including both macro-variables that relate to broader situations external to the community and micro-variables that focus on specific factors affecting particular language events and interactions. On a macro-level, we witness concern for the distribution and roles of sign languages throughout the world, and the influence of political, economic, social and ideological conditions on their existence. Familiar sociolinguistic topics include issues related to multilingualism, language choice and shift, language policy and planning and language ecology. The issues are at once both basic and complex. On the most fundamental level, we still find the existence of an assumed correlation between sign language and national boundaries and/or spoken-language families manifested in the nomenclature of sign languages: a continuing reflection of a legacy of erroneous assumptions and underlying language ideology about sign languages. On a descriptive level, however, there are complex issues related to documenting the sign languages of the world, sorting out historical and comparative relationships and arriving at valid typological classifications of different sign languages.

On a micro-level, we see increasing attention to interactional sociolinguistics and language variation, two of the most prominent subfields within sociolinguistics. The various dimensions of discourse analysis, for example, seem to come of age in this volume. While there is still a paucity of research on the full range of discourse topics, we have seen an encouraging burst of activity on the discourse of sign languages in the last decade. This trend bodes well for the future of discourse analysis in the study of sign languages. At the same time, much insight can be gained about the universal basis of discourse construction from a research perspective that focuses on a visual modality vis-à-vis one confined to an oral–aural modality.

The same can be said for the examination of systematic variation in sign languages. Although we may assume that variation in sign languages is sensitive to both internal, linguistic structures and external, social variables, describing and explaining the intersection of these constraints is challenged – and enriched – by comparing specific sign language communities and communities of practice. The analysis of systematic variation in sign languages is, however, hardly immune to ongoing debates about the fundamental components of the sign; these controversies impact the definition of the "linguistic variable" and the determination of the fluctuating variants that comprise its empirical reality. In fact, one of the most exciting aspects of variation analysis set forth in this book is the comparison of the ways in which sign language variation both parallels and contrasts with systematic variability in spoken languages.

In an important, positive sense, this volume reveals the exacting challenge for the sociolinguistics of sign languages: to be informed by the perspective and the insights from general sociolinguistic inquiry and description without being confined to the search for parallels between sociolinguistic situations representing different language modalities. This concern is not meant to denigrate the numerous parallels that certainly exist in the sociolinguistic worlds that affect the global collective of language communities regardless of language modality; nor is it intended to marginalize the examination of the social context in which sign languages are embedded as these situations compare with other sociolinguistic circumstances. My point is simply that we deprive ourselves of comprehensive insight into the human capacity for language, and the social context in which it is embedded, if we do not take full advantage of the rich sociolinguistic resources afforded by research into differential modalities of language expression. Volumes such as this can only enrich the general study of sociolinguistics as well as inform the specific study of sign languages in their social context.

WALT WOLFRAM, William C. Friday Professor
North Carolina State University

Preface and acknowledgments

This book grew directly out of my experience in teaching a graduate-level course entitled Sociolinguistics in Deaf Communities at Gallaudet University in Washington, DC, and out of my frustration at not having one unified self-contained text to use for the course. I have been teaching this course since the early 1980s. When I first taught the course, the readings that pertained specifically to Deaf communities came mostly from work on diglossia by Stokoe, work on variation and language contact by Woodward and others, and work on conversational structure by Baker. All this material was published in the late 1960s and early 1970s. However, since the early 1980s, with the ever-growing recognition and acceptance of sign languages as real languages and with the continuing empowerment of deaf people, the field of sign language sociolinguistics has virtually exploded. There is work to report on from all of the major areas of sociolinguistics: multilingualism, bilingualism and language contact, variation, discourse analysis, language planning and policy, language attitudes, and work that reports on Deaf communities all over the world. It is definitely time for a volume such as this one: a text for use in upper-level undergraduate and graduate sociolinguistics courses, a text which will be of interest also to sign language researchers, sociolinguists both deaf and hearing and interested laypersons.

I am very grateful to my co-contributors for their excellent and prompt work and, as a group, we express our deep gratitude to Ms. Jayne McKenzie, Department Secretary for the Department of ASL, Linguistics, and Interpretation at Gallaudet University, who patiently and cheerfully prepared the final manuscript, and to Mrs. Ethylyn DeStefano, Administrative Secretary in the same department, who provided invaluable technical support. We also acknowledge Andrew Winnard, Brenda Burke and Martin Mellor of Cambridge University Press, for their hard work on the volume. We are also grateful to Lois Lehman-Lenderman for the drawings in Chapter 4 and to M. J. Bienvenu for serving as the sign model. Finally, we give a collective and hearty thank you to our families, partners and friends for their support and encouragement.

Abbreviations

AAVE	African American Vernacular English
ASL	American Sign Language
Auslan	Australian Sign Language
BDA	British Deaf Association
BSL	British Sign Language
DASL	Dictionary of American Sign Language
DGS	German Sign Language
FSL	Filipino Sign Language
EUD	European Union of the Deaf
IPSL	Indopakistan Sign Language
ISL	Irish Sign Language
JSL	Japanese Sign Language
LIS	Italian Sign Language
LOVE	Linguistics of Visual English
LSF	French Sign Language
LSQ	Langue des Signes Quebecoise
MCE	Manually Coded English
NAD	National Association of the Deaf (USA)
NCJD	National Congress of Jewish Deaf (USA)
NFSD	National Fraternal Society of the Deaf (USA)
NZSL	New Zealand Sign Language
PSE	Pidgin Sign English
SASL	South African Sign Language
SEE-I	Seeing Essential English
SEE-II	Signing Exact English
SLN	Sign Language of the Netherlands
SSS	sign-supported speech
TSL	Taiwan Sign Language
tty	teletypewriter, a text telephone device
WFD	World Federation of the Deaf

1   Introduction

Ceil Lucas

Recent history has included some major events in both the American Deaf community* and around the world, and many of the events have been fundamentally sociolinguistic in nature. For example, 13 years ago, in March 1988, the campus of Gallaudet University erupted into a week of protests stemming from the selection of Elizabeth Zinser as the seventh president of the 124-year-old institution. The outcomes of the Deaf President Now (DPN) movement are history: the resignation of the newly appointed president and of the chairman of the Board of Trustees, the reconstitution of the board to contain a majority of deaf people, the selection of a deaf president and the promise of no reprisals against the protesters.

In *The Sociolinguistics of Society*, Ralph Fasold (1984) observes that the essence of sociolinguistics depends on two facts about language: first, that language varies, which is to say that "speakers have more than one way to say more or less the same thing" (p. ix); and, second, that language serves a broadly encompassing purpose just as critical as the obvious one of transmitting information and thoughts from one person to another. Namely, language users use language to make statements about who they are, what their group loyalties are, how they perceive their relationship to interlocutors and what kind of speech event they consider themselves to be involved in. Critical to an understanding of the events at Gallaudet University is the critical purpose that language serves in defining one's identity, group loyalty, relationship to interlocutors and understanding of the speech event.

The major demand of the protest was for a deaf president, and the issues underlying that demand are fundamentally sociolinguistic in nature. On the one hand, it was repeatedly declared with disdain during the protest that Dr. Zinser could not sign and had only just begun learning sign language. On the other hand, in remarks following her resignation, Dr. Zinser stated that signing is important symbolically to the Deaf community, and that it is important for members of the board to "learn a little sign . . . just a few basic phrases, some

* I have adopted the use of "deaf" (with lower case *d*) as an adjective referring primarily to hearing loss and the use of "Deaf" (with upper case *D*) as an adjective referring to social collectivities and attitudes arising from interaction among people with hearing losses. This distinction is employed throughout the volume.

1

warm sentences when they meet people around the school" (*Washington Post*, 12 March 1988). For deaf people and their supporters, Dr. Zinser's lack of knowledge about the Deaf community was directly linked to and symbolized by her lack of knowledge of American Sign Language (ASL). The reality of her linguistic repertoire and the language choices at her disposal made clear and inevitable statements about who she was, what her group loyalty was, and how she perceived her relationship to her interlocutors. And those statements simply could not be reconciled with the qualifications that the Deaf community required of the next president.

With her observation that signing is important symbolically within the Deaf community and her recommendation that board members "learn a little sign", Dr. Zinser focused on the symbolic role of signing while ignoring the fact that signing is, first of all, a communication system. The high symbolic value of sign language derives in part from the fact that signing allows people to communicate unhindered, with a focus not on the medium but on the message. To suggest patronizingly that board members "learn a little sign ... some warm sentences" was to patently misunderstand the sociolinguistic reality of Deaf communities and to misperceive the particular form of interplay between communicating information and defining the social situation in Deaf communities. The protest was fundamentally a sociolinguistic event because of the central role of that interplay: *How* information is communicated – with ASL, with some manual code for English, with spoken English – inevitably defines the social situation and one's place in it. The place that Dr. Zinser was proposing to define for herself was simply unacceptable.

Related to the issue of sign language being first of all a communication system that allows unhindered communication is another event in recent history having sociolinguistic import. This is the publication in February 1989 of a paper entitled *Unlocking the Curriculum* written by Bob Johnson, Scott Liddell and Carol Erting. The paper takes a critical look at Deaf education in the USA. The authors state that the failure of Deaf education is due to "deaf children's fundamental lack of access to curricular context at grade level and from the general acceptance of the notion that below grade-level performance is to be expected of deaf children" (p. 3), and that the problem of access is largely a language-related issue. It is fair to say that the paper has been a catalyst for a vigorous and ongoing debate among teachers, administrators and parents of deaf children all over the world. It has been translated into French, Spanish, German, Thai, Japanese and Italian and has provided part of the inspiration and theoretical support in many locations for the implementation of programs that use the natural sign language of the community as the medium of instruction (e.g. the Learning Center for Deaf Children in Framingham, MA; the Indiana School for the Deaf in Indianapolis; and the California School for the Deaf in Fremont).

It has been followed by insightful work on the nature and consequences of language policy and planning in Deaf communities (see, for example, Ramsey, 1993; Nover, 1995). Language policy and planning in any situation are by definition sociolinguistic activities, and they necessarily include an examination of the functions of language in society and attitudes to language and are not limited to a description of language forms. Insofar as *Unlocking the Curriculum* gets to the heart of language policy and planning as it pertains to Deaf education, its publication and the debate surrounding it are sociolinguistic events.

The third event is the Deaf Way conference held in Washington, DC in July 1989. It was the first conference of its kind focusing on the language, culture and history of deaf people, at which over 5,700 deaf people from all over the world were in attendance. Quite apart from the vast sharing of information that took place about the numerous and diverse Deaf communities around the world, the conference was a sociolinguistic event in that it had the effect of reinforcing the reality of a Deaf cultural identity, an identity that is shaped in part by the use of natural sign languages. As Carol Erting (1994) states in the introduction to the Deaf Way Volume, "The Deaf Way has become a reference point . . . even for Deaf people who did not attend. It set a standard for accessibility, respect, pride, and perhaps most of all, celebration of a rich heritage and the determination to improve life for Deaf people around the world" (p. xxx).

Sociolinguistically, then, the Deaf community is currently very active. Issues of empowerment and self-awareness are closely tied to issues of language use, as are the practical changes being proposed and implemented all over the world – in some cases rapidly – in the education of deaf children. It may be useful to examine where we have been and where we are going, as far as sociolinguistics of sign languages is concerned.

Studies of sociolinguistic issues in the American Deaf community find their beginning in the late 1960s, with Stokoe's (1969) characterization of language use as diglossic, following Ferguson's (1959) model. Subsequent studies included examinations of the linguistic outcome of contact between ASL and English, with claims that the outcome was a pidgin (e.g. Woodward, 1973c; Woodward and Markowicz, 1975; Reilly and McIntire, 1980), studies of variation within ASL (e.g. Battison *et al.*, 1975; Woodward and Markowicz, 1975; Woodward and DeSantis, 1977a; 1977b), studies of language maintenance and choice (Lee, 1982), studies of language attitudes (Kannapell, 1993 [1985]) and studies of language policy and planning (e.g. Johnson *et al.*, 1989; Ramsey, 1989; Nover, 1995). It is fair to say that all the major areas of sociolinguistics have been examined to some extent as they pertain to the Deaf community. These include areas such as regional and social variation, bilingualism and language contact phenomena, language maintenance and choice, language attitudes, language policy and planning, and language and social interaction.

Research certainly has not been limited to the American Deaf community, but has been carried out as well in countries all over the world. However, even though each of the major areas has at least been touched on, the earliest sociolinguistic research in the Deaf community was shaped and perhaps limited by at least four interrelated considerations:

1. the relationship between the spoken language of the majority community and the sign language, particularly in educational settings;
2. limited knowledge of the linguistic structure of the sign language;
3. doubts as to the actual status of the sign language as a "real language";
4. application of spoken language sociolinguistic models to sign language situations.

As concerns the first, it is interesting to notice that the bulk of early sociolinguistic research in the American Deaf community, for example, had to do with the interrelationship between English and ASL. A lot of attention was given to one outcome of language contact, traditionally known as PSE (Pidgin Sign English) and to characterizations of the sociolinguistic situation as diglossic or as a continuum and so forth. I suggest that where linguistic research energy has been directed is a reflection of where societal energy has gone. For example, the focus in American Deaf education since its inception in 1817 has been largely on how to teach English to deaf children, with a variety of philosophies and methodologies. Not until recently has there been any focus on the use of ASL in educational or other social settings. And the same is true for Deaf communities around the world. Research on language contact, for example, is by and large research on the contact between spoken languages and sign languages. It is not that contact does not occur between sign languages; it is simply that this kind of contact is only now beginning to receive research attention.

The second and the third considerations contribute to this state of affairs. For one thing, it is probably safe to say that the sociolinguistic studies of a language accompany or follow linguistic descriptions of a language, but they do not precede those descriptions. That is, it is difficult to describe what sociolinguistic variation looks like in a language until we have at least some basic understanding of the structure of the language. In fact, some early descriptions of variation in ASL describe as variable features that in fact are not variable at all (Lucas, 1995). Of course, sociolinguistic research will be hindered by notions that what we are investigating might not really be a language.

The fourth consideration has to do with the application of models developed for spoken languages that may not be entirely suitable for sign languages. My research with Clayton Valli illustrates how these considerations can affect sociolinguistic research. We have investigated a kind of signing that results from the contact between English and ASL and has features of both languages (for a full description of the project, see Lucas and Valli, 1992). Our description of what we call contact signing naturally led us to a review of language contact phenomena in spoken language situations, but it also made us see the necessity for a very basic distinction between contact between two sign languages and contact between a sign language and a spoken language. Clearly this distinction is motivated by the presence of two modalities, so that what happens when two sign languages are in contact will probably be different from what happens when a sign language is in contact with a spoken language. It was in trying to illustrate the distinction with examples that we realized where the focus in language contact studies has been. That is, although we were able to think of and casually observe examples to illustrate the outcome of contact between two sign languages, our search for empirical research on lexical borrowing, code switching, foreigner talk, interference, pidgins, creoles and mixed systems – all as they result from the contact between two sign languages – turned up practically nothing.

Sign languages borrow from each other; bilingual signers code-switch between two sign languages; a native signer of one sign language uses a reduced form of that language with a non-native signer or demonstrates interference when using another sign language; and pidgins, creoles and mixed systems could conceivably come about given the right sociolinguistic conditions. It is not that these things do not happen, but rather that researchers have only just begun to look for them and describe them. Early research attention turned elsewhere, to focus on the relationship between the spoken language and the sign language. The Deaf community has been looked at all too often within the framework of spoken language sociolinguistics, and labels from spoken language situations have been applied too hastily to sign language situations. One problem with this is that it leaves the impression that the situation has been adequately described, when in fact it turns out to be a lot more complex than we thought. For example, the term "pidgin" as applied to the Deaf community needs to be re-examined. Not that pidgins cannot occur; they probably can. Many other terms used in sociolinguistics to describe oral language use such as "lexical borrowing", "code mixing", "code switching" and even "bilingualism" also merit re-examination. Indeed, some researchers have already re-examined some terms; for example, Lee's (1982) re-examination of the term "diglossia" and Cokely's (1983) re-examination of the term "pidgin".

It is fair to say that each of the four considerations that seem to have governed the study of sociolinguistics in Deaf communities is changing. Our knowledge of the basic linguistic structure of sign languages is increasing every day, and the notion that sign languages are not "real languages" is happily an endangered one. Research is being undertaken in all areas of sociolinguistics, including multilingualism, bilingualism and language contact, variation, discourse analysis, language policy and planning, and language attitudes. Much of this current work is discussed in this volume. Studies on all aspects of the sociolinguistics of Deaf communities are currently in a period of rapid development. The focus is being extended beyond the relationship between sign languages and spoken languages to the relationship between sign languages, and research on sign languages is beginning to provide crucial insights into the nature of spoken languages as well. For example, work on the differences between signing and gesturing (e.g. McNeill, 1992) has provided insight into the role of gesture in spoken language discourse.

The answer to "Where are we going?" seems to be in three parts. First, we are in the process of studying all aspects of the sociolinguistics of Deaf communities all over the world, and I anticipate that with these studies we will be able to show strong parallels between the sociolinguistics of spoken languages and the sociolinguistics of sign languages. Second, at the same time, mainly because of the fundamental difference in modality – that is, a verbal–aural system compared to a visual–manual one – I anticipate that studies on the sociolinguistics of sign languages will show that the models developed for spoken languages cannot be automatically applied to sign language situations, and that phenomena unique to sign languages will be revealed. We already see this in the contact phenomenon of fingerspelling (the unique contact between the writing system developed to represent a spoken language) and sign languages. I expect that other such unique phenomena will also emerge. Moreover, there is also a current focus on cross-linguistic studies that compare sign languages to each other and to spoken languages. Third, extensive studies of the socio-linguistics of Deaf communities will no doubt provide insights into aspects of spoken languages, aspects that may have been overlooked. The issue here is that sociolinguistic studies will become a two-way street, on which spoken language and sign language studies inform each other.

I close this chapter with some reflections on the importance of sociolinguistic research for Deaf communities. In discussing what guided him in the preparation of the dictionary of American Sign Language (DASL) as early as 1957, Stokoe cited the thinking of George Trager and Henry Lee Smith: "They insisted that language could not be studied by itself, in isolation, but must be looked at in direct connection to the people who used it, the things they used it to talk about, and the view of the world that using it imposed on them" (Stokoe *et al.*, 1965: 333). This sociolinguistic perspective clearly guided the inclusion of Croneberg's appendices in the DASL, appendices that showed "how language and culture as well as deafness formed a special community" (1965: 334). The importance of studying the sociolinguistics of sign languages is two-fold. First, the recognition that ASL has a sociolinguistic life like other systems that we recognize as languages reinforces the status of ASL as a real language. And as we see in this volume, the study of sign language sociolinguistics has also contributed to our understanding of spoken language sociolinguistics. Second, the study of sign language sociolinguistics has had a direct impact on the lives of deaf people in terms of educational and employment opportunities. Indeed, it seems fair to say that this impact has been very tangible. Research on sign language sociolinguistics has helped lead to the recognition of sign languages as real languages and has had the effect of legitimizing them. This legitimization has allowed for the discussion of what the medium of instruction should be in Deaf education and to the question as to why it should not simply be sign language. This discussion has led to the improvement of Deaf education at all levels and to, as Johnson, Liddell and Erting said in 1989, the unlocking of the curriculum, at least for some deaf students. It has led to the improvement of services for deaf people, such as interpreting, and has opened up new career paths for deaf people as teachers both of deaf children and adolescents and as teachers of sign language. The research on sign language structure and sign language sociolinguistics which Bill Stokoe initiated has ultimately contributed to the continuing empowerment of deaf people all over the world.

2 Multilingualism: The global approach to sign languages

Bencie Woll, Rachel Sutton-Spence and Frances Elton

A language is a dialect with an army and a navy.

Anon

And the whole earth was of one language and of one speech.

Genesis 11:1

Sign language is sometimes called gesture speech as it is a method of conversing by means of gestures or signs. It is a form of speech in use among civilised and savage races, which is perfectly understood, and although greatly limited in its forms of expression by those who have spoken language, rich in its vocabulary and possessed of an extensive literature.

John Maclean, 1896

This chapter provides an overview of the occurrence and distribution of sign languages around the world. Every year, the existence of more sign languages and more signing communities is being recognized. Lexicography (the making of sign language dictionaries) and analyses of the structure and use of these languages follow recognition and play a key role in the empowerment of deaf people. This chapter provides an estimate of the number of sign languages in existence and describes the diversity of Deaf communities using sign languages. It outlines the different factors we need to consider when describing the existence of any language and shows why it is so difficult to provide an exact description of the distribution of sign languages.

Sign languages are used by deaf people around the world. In the past, many people believed that signing was an international form of communication (e.g. Bulwer, 1644; see also Mirzoeff, 1995 and Rée, 1999 for descriptions of eighteenth- and nineteenth-century beliefs about the international nature of "gesture languages"). This was based on the erroneous belief that sign languages are nothing more than gesture and that gesture is universal. However, linguists now know that sign languages use conventionalized signs and that these conventionalized signs vary from language to language. It is also not true that gestures are internationally understood. Many gestures made by users of spoken languages are specific to a given culture.

It is very clear that there is not one single internationally understood sign language. It is now widely accepted that Deaf communities around the world use different sign languages. In much of this chapter, we refer to some of the difficulties that occur when we try to describe the sign languages of the world. However, we may accept as a starting point that deaf people in communities in different parts of the world use many different sign languages. We should note, however, that many deaf people do not have contact with other deaf people and are not part of a Deaf community in any way. These people may develop their own system of communicating with hearing people, using their own gestures. These gesture systems are characteristically very limited and are referred to as "home sign". We do not count them as sign languages in the sense of those complex, well-developed sign languages used by members of Deaf communities.

Sign languages used by hearing people

While it is usually members of Deaf communities who use sign languages, we should acknowledge that hearing people also use complex sign systems that are not sign languages of deaf people. These "secondary" sign languages are outside the main remit of this chapter but are nevertheless of interest.

The Plains Indian Sign Language of North America has been described in some detail. Plains Indian Sign Language was used as a lingua franca among the tribes of the North American plains who spoke many different languages. Tomkins described it as "The first and only American universal language" (Tomkins, 1969: 7). In 1885, it was estimated that there were over 110,000 "sign-talking Indians", including Blackfoot, Cheyenne, Sioux and Arapahoe. By the 1960s, there remained a "very small percentage of this number" (p. 7). This sign language had its own syntactic rules and Tomkins makes it clear that it differed from the American Sign Language (ASL) used by deaf people at that time, both lexically and grammatically. There is evidence, however, that deaf American Indians used this Plains Indian Sign Language, rather than ASL. Tomkins refers to a Mr. J. L. Clark, a Blackfoot Indian who "has the misfortune to be deaf and dumb, and this has developed him greatly as a sign talker" (p. 9).

Other communities of hearing people who use spoken languages use sign languages for social reasons. Kendon has documented the sign language of the Warlpiri people in Australia (Kendon, 1988). The Warlpiri use this language at points in their life when speech is not allowed. Religious orders that seek to limit the use of speech also use sign languages. Barakat (1987) has researched the sign language used by Cistercian monks in the USA, Banham (1991) has described signs used in Anglo-Saxon monasteries and Quay (1998) has reported on signs used by Trappist monks in Japan and China.

In some cases only hearing people use a sign language, but in other situations deaf and hearing people form part of a signing community. While the incidence of congenital deafness is approximately 1 in 2,000 in Western Europe, in some more isolated communities around the world there is a higher than average incidence of congenital, hereditary deafness as a result of consanguineous marriage.

One of the most well-known examples is the community which lived on the island of Martha's Vineyard off the East Coast of the United States. In the seventeenth century, a group of settlers arrived there from the Weald area of Kent (see also Chapter 3). Although none of the original settlers was deaf, the population carried genes for deafness and deaf children were born to the settlers. By the eighteenth century, as many as 10 percent of the people in some villages on the island were deaf. The unusually high incidence of deafness continued until the late nineteenth century when the islanders' isolated lifestyle ended. The consequence of the large number of deaf people, according to one older islander interviewed in the 1970s, was that "everyone here spoke sign language" (Groce, 1985). Groce's anthropological study of the situation on the island showed that hearing and deaf people signed together, although hearing people usually spoke English while they signed. The form of the sign language used on Martha's Vineyard is not clear from Groce's research. It clearly existed before modern ASL was established in 1817, and it may even have influenced modern ASL. There has been the suggestion that the sign language would have been some form of "Old Kentish Sign Language". This needs to be treated with caution because no deaf people were part of the original migration from Kent, and nothing is known about any specific variety of signing used in Kent.

Today, there are still communities where an unusually high proportion of deaf people results in a sign language used by both deaf and hearing people. Washabaugh (1981) has described the situation of deaf people on the island of Grand Cayman in the Caribbean. The sign language was not as well developed as it is in some larger communities, and deaf people in the community had a lower status than hearing people. Both deaf and hearing people considered the sign language to be inferior to the spoken language, but it was still used by deaf and hearing members of the community. A similar situation has been found on the Yucatan peninsula of Mexico and among the Bedouin Arabs living in Israel (Johnson, 1994a; Scott *et al.*, 1996; Kisch, in preparation).

Branson *et al.* (1996) have described the situation of the deaf people living on the island of Bali in Indonesia (see also Chapter 3). As in the other cases mentioned above, the incidence of genetic deafness has created a "deaf village" where the population of deaf people is unusually large. Branson *et al.* have described the social standing of the deaf people in this village and their language, showing that it has features common to other complex extended sign languages. Importantly, again, the sign language is used by both deaf and hearing people in the village, and the deaf people are able to participate in the daily life of the village because they do not suffer from barriers to communication.

There are relatively few situations where a community of hearing and deaf people all use a sign language. There are also relatively few sign languages used primarily (or exclusively) by hearing people. Although new examples are occasionally described, these languages are of peripheral importance to the general description of the world's sign languages. Next, we address the question of the number and distribution of sign languages used by Deaf communities around the world. In order to do this, we need to ask the seemingly simple question "How many languages are there?"

How many languages are there?

This would seem to be a fairly simple question for the world's scholars to answer. Surely, linguists can supply the number of languages in the world. All they need to do is organize one great language census. Yet, answers to this seemingly simple question are surprisingly varied. Some sources quote a figure of 6,000–7,000 (e.g. Branson and Miller, 1998b); others suggest 4,000 (Fromkin and Rodman, 1998) and another source quotes 3,000 (Ong, 1982). David Crystal (1997: 287) claims that a total of 6,000 should be "a safe estimate for the 1990s". Voegelin and Voegelin, in their work *Classification and Index of the World's Languages* (1977) give over 20,000 language and dialect names which have been grouped into approximately 4,500 languages. Perhaps the most reliable up-to-date source for the number of languages in the world is the Ethnologue database collected by the Summer Institute of Linguistics (Ethnologue database, 1996). This gives a figure of 6,703 languages.

Part of the problem is that the number of known languages in use is not stable. Languages can become extinct, sometimes very rapidly. Some of the languages listed in the Ethnologue database are already extinct or may have never been distinct languages (for example Manx or Old Kentish Sign Language). Languages die when their speakers die. At the start of the twenty-first century, there are about 150 languages with over one million speakers, and it is highly unlikely that these could become extinct in the near future. On the other hand, about half of all the world's languages have fewer than 1,000 speakers. A single outbreak of disease or another cataclysmic event could easily mean that the people and their language disappear. It is even more likely that the speakers cease to use that language because the younger generation grows up to use a more socially and economically powerful language. Crystal (1997) has estimated that of over 1,000 languages used in Brazil two hundred years ago, now only 200 remain. It is very likely that some languages become extinct without linguists ever knowing of their existence.

Although languages are dying out, languages can also be added to the list of known languages. Each year a few more languages are added to the Ethnologue database. Occasionally people living in very remote regions are contacted for the first time and their language is recorded by linguists. More often, the speakers of the language are known but their language is not recognized. Over the last three hundred years in particular there have been dramatic movements of populations around the world, especially through colonization, mass migration of labor and through the forced relocation of many people through slavery. These have caused new languages to emerge. These new languages, called pidgins and creoles, are not always recognized however. They are sometimes ignored altogether. Other times they are dismissed as being dialects of another language, usually some sort of "inferior" dialect. They might not even be considered "language" at all. If we count the large numbers of pidgins and creoles that have emerged in the last three hundred years, the number of languages in the world might be seen to be very much bigger. The Ethnologue database lists 79 creole and pidgin languages but it is likely that there are many more that could be added to this list.

Sign languages are an example of languages that have emerged only over the last three hundred years. Just as all languages need a community of users, sign languages need a Deaf community. Deaf communities can only exist where there is a large enough concentration of deaf people. In Europe this only happened with the development of large towns in the industrial revolution. Before that, signers were scattered across villages and small towns and any signing must have been widely varied. The development which triggered the creation of large Deaf communities and sign languages as we know them today came when schools were set up for deaf children, starting in the late-eighteenth century in Europe. At these schools, children were able to use a single form of a language, developed out of the signed languages that were being used by educators. In many countries today, education for deaf children has only recently begun and, in turn, has provided an environment in which sign language can develop. Linguists (e.g. Kegl *et al.*, 1999) have described how the establishment of the first school for deaf children in Nicaragua in the 1980s led to the beginnings of a national sign language.

Counts of the world's languages almost always exclude sign languages. This may be because of the relative newness of sign languages. We should also be aware that many people still mistakenly believe that sign languages are simply forms of spoken languages. Other people do not consider sign languages to be languages at all but merely non-linguistic systems of gesture and pantomime. All these factors might explain why sign languages have been ignored, along with many spoken languages of disempowered communities.

The Ethnologue database, however, does include sign languages. It lists 103 known sign languages. This figure almost certainly underestimates the number of sign languages in the world, but it is an initial figure to work with.

In this chapter we look at a possible count of sign languages. It is not a simple question of listing one sign language for every spoken language. Sign languages are independent of the spoken languages that surround them, so we cannot assume that for every spoken language there will be a sign language. In many cases there is no single community using a sign language within a particular spoken language community. There are also deaf people who use different sign languages even when the surrounding hearing communities use the same spoken language. For example, hearing people in Ireland, the USA and the UK all speak English, but the deaf people living in these countries use three different sign languages.

A major problem in a language count (discounting the practical fact that linguists have never managed a single worldwide, day-long language census of the world's six billion populace) is that it is remarkably difficult to define "a language". We see in this chapter what the problems are for the definition of "a language" and how sociolinguists have tried to overcome them.

Mutual intelligibility

The simplest way to identify two languages as different is to consider if their speakers understand each other. If they do not, their language forms are "mutually unintelligible" and we can claim that they are two different languages. If there is some degree of understanding, however, we might claim that the two languages are dialects of the same language. This approach can be used to count the number of sign languages as well as spoken languages. If an Estonian signer watched two Thai signers or a Thai signer watched two Estonians signing, they would not understand the others' language. We would say that the two language forms were mutually unintelligible and that we were seeing two different sign languages.

We will see, however, that mutual intelligibility is not a clear-cut marker for defining either spoken or sign languages. Some forms of language may be very different, to the extent of appearing to be mutually unintelligible, yet the language users consider them to be the same language. What we call "Chinese" is a linguistic phenomenon made up of hundreds of dialects, grouped into eight "macro-dialects" which are to some extent mutually unintelligible. Yet, for social and political reasons Chinese people consider all these forms to be the same language. Crystal (1997) mentions that the same is true for the three "dialects" of Lapp which, although mutually unintelligible, are seen by Lapp speakers as forms of the same language. In the former Yugoslavia, the Serbian and Croatian languages that made up Serbo-Croat were only partially mutually intelligible, yet – although they use different scripts – they were treated as dialects of the same language in order to foster a sense of a single nation. It is possible that some national sign languages are made up of dialects that are to some extent mutually unintelligible. They are considered to be single languages by Deaf communities or hearing people working with Deaf communities because there are social, political or economic reasons for doing so (Branson and Miller, 1998b).

The idea that each nation should have its own language is a recent one. In the nineteenth century, nationhood and language became linked for political reasons. Although at this time there was considerable language variation in countries such as France, Germany, Britain and Spain, as well as the USA, governments pursued policies to encourage a single language for a nation (Baynton, 1996). In Europe and North America, we are now used to the idea that each country has a single national language. However, in most nations of the world the use of more than one language is common.

The idea that there should be a national sign language has arisen in part because we understand the idea of a national spoken language. We are able to talk about Sign Language of the Netherlands, Japanese Sign Language (JSL), Hungarian Sign Language and so on, because we know that these countries are committed to single spoken languages. We are not surprised to learn that there are two sign languages in Canada: a language very close to ASL, used by those living in Anglophone communities and Langue Des Signes Québecoise (LSQ) used by those living in Francophone communities. The Ethnologue database lists "Canadian Sign Language" as a separate language, although the signing used by most signing Americans from Canada and from the USA is a form of ASL and is fully mutually intelligible.

For many countries, however, it might not make sense to refer to a single national sign language. We should not assume, for example, that a single Indian Sign Language or one South African Sign Language exists. Deaf communities may well have a sense of national identity but different forces may affect their language choices. Branson and Miller (1998b) have drawn attention to a dictionary of South African signs, drawn from 12 distinct communities with distinct differences in their signing. The preface to this dictionary refers to the "diversity of South African Sign Language" and the "South African Deaf Community". Branson and Miller claim that such statements indicate that there are 12 different sign languages in South Africa, and they criticize politicians, linguistic rights activists and linguists for accepting without reason or justification that these 12 languages and communities are merely subdivisions of one overall language and community.

However, linguists working in South Africa disagree with their claims. Aarons and Akach (1998) have argued that South Africa does have a single sign language. They acknowledge that the divisions imposed by apartheid created considerable lexical variation in signing used in South Africa, but they dispute the conclusion that there are many different sign languages used in South Africa. They report that their findings show mutual intelligibility among the sign dialects. Aarons and Morgan (1998) further conclude that, based on uniformity of handshapes, classifier constructions, syntax and facial expressions, there is only one South African Sign Language (SASL).

The number of sign languages in India and Pakistan is also unclear. Jepson (1991) describes Rural Indian Sign Language and Urban Indian Sign Language. Even these two terms cover many different sign languages used by different communities in cities and rural areas. The names carry a powerful implication, however, that these two forms are merely dialects of a single form.

Zeshan (2001) has argued that India and Pakistan have only one sign language, which she terms Indopakistani Sign Language (IPSL). Her research shows that the political border of India and Pakistan does not create a language border and that the same sign language is used in Karachi and New Delhi. She also acknowledges that there is dialectal variation in North-Western and Central India and that the sign language used in rural areas is different from that used in the cities. People in Pakistan speak of Pakistani Sign Language and people in India speak of Indian Sign Language, but deaf people who cross the border between the two countries find the signing to be intelligible. Lexical variation for the whole Indian subcontinent clusters around 75 percent, with a range of 85 percent to 60 percent in different areas. Given these percentages of lexical variation, it might be appropriate in some cases to say that we have languages belonging to the same family, rather than dialects of the same language (see the discussion of Swadesh and Woodward below). This, however, does not detract from Zeshan's central assertion that there is, based on the intelligibility criterion, only one sign language used in India, Pakistan and Nepal.

Even where a national sign language is understood to exist, there may be great variation within the language. Irish Sign Language (ISL) is considered to be a single national sign language, used by the Irish Deaf community. However, up until the 1950s, two very lexically distinct forms of language were used in the Dublin schools. The sign language used in the girls' school was different from that used in the boys' school, to the extent of mutual unintelligibility (Matthews, 1996). Research in South Africa has shown that differences in signing do not match the differences in the spoken languages surrounding the Deaf communities. Instead, the signing used depends upon the nationalities of the foreigners who funded and ran the schools for different groups of deaf children (Aarons and Morgan, 1998). In Britain, there is no special dialect of British Sign Language (BSL) used by deaf people living in Welsh-speaking areas or areas using Scots Gaelic. However, in Northern Ireland, although

English is the dominant language, the dialect of BSL is very different from that used by signers in other parts of Britain.

Some languages may appear to be very similar and yet the communities of users consider them to be two different languages. Again, this may be for political, social or historical reasons. Hindi and Urdu are essentially one language, written in two different scripts, used by people of different religions, with different literatures. Swedish, Danish and Norwegian are similar enough to be mutually intelligible, as are Portuguese and Spanish, yet national identity serves to give them different names. BSL, New Zealand Sign Language and Australian Sign Language (Auslan) are mutually intelligible, but their different names show the different national identities of their users.

The problem of nomenclature for sign languages

The issue of what defines a sign language has been debated since linguists first started describing and naming sign languages. Before linguists gave names to sign languages – such as BSL, ASL or French Sign Language (LSF) – signers simply called their languages "sign", "Deaf sign" or "Deaf language". The use of the term "language" on its own as a label for one's own language is also found in spoken languages, for example, Bahasa in Indonesia and Malaysia.

Because sign languages generally do not have distinctive names, the International Standard Organization lists them by country in most cases. This creates the misleading impression of a one-to-one correspondence between sign languages and national boundaries.

Linguistic research around the world has led to the identification and description of various forms of signed languages. With so many descriptions and labels of systems and languages in use by deaf people, it is hard to know what may be included within the definition of a particular sign language and what may not. It is possible that the problem of "different sign languages" is caused by the "naming" acts of linguists. Once something is named, it appears to be distinct from something with a different name. Linguistic philosophers and politicians who see language identity as part of national identity often believe that languages are discrete entities which may be defined and distinguished from other languages. This attitude may also have served to create confusion in relation to BSL, because of the use of terms like Pidgin Sign English, Signed English and Sign Supported English, as well as BSL, to describe the variety of communication forms in use by deaf people.

This issue was debated in a book entitled *Communication Issues Among Deaf People* (Garretson (ed.), 1990). The prevailing opinion of the American Deaf contributors to that monograph was that deaf people consider ASL to be a broader term than a linguist might, with the prevailing opinion being that as long as deaf people understood the signing, the language was satisfactory.

Linguistic descriptions of ASL emphasize its difference from English and often ignore the aspects of ASL that are influenced by English. One result of this is that some deaf people whose language has been influenced by English are not comfortable with saying that they use ASL. One Deaf contributor in the Garretson monograph, Bernard Bragg (Bragg, 1990), rejects the exclusion of English influences on ASL. He accepts that "traditional ASL" is hardly influenced by English at all, but maintains that some ASL (termed by him as modern ASL and Englished ASL) is heavily influenced by English. Both of these forms, however, are still "ASL" to him.

Stewart's view exemplifies a broad approach to the definition of ASL:

The reality is that most Deaf folks have had to use whatever was at hand at the time, theory be damned, including SEE-1, SEE-2 [manual representations of English used in education in which each English morpheme is represented by a sign], SEE Heinz 57, Siglish [also called "Sign Supported English" or "keyword signing"], the Rochester method [communication through fingerspelling], Cued Speech [a system which uses hand configurations to disambiguate words which appear similar on the lips], gestures, ... eye-blinking, face twitching, head nodding, ear wiggling, and just about anything else that might possibly help to bridge the vast gulf that normally separates us deaf people from one another. (cited in Garretson, 1990: 118)

In their study of contact signing Lucas and Valli (1992) reported one experiment that demonstrates how important social attitude is in deciding when a variety of language is ASL. Two groups of signers were shown a video-recording of a person signing. One group was told that the signer came from a deaf family, and the other group was told that the signer came from a hearing family and only learned ASL late in life. Both groups were then asked if they considered the signer to be using ASL. The responses from the two groups were different, demonstrating that judgments are made as much by what one knows about a signer's cultural identity as by the linguistic evidence.

One of the criteria recently suggested for deciding if a sign language should be included in a list of world languages is that it should be an "established signed language that is taught in schools, standardised at times and studied by others" (Sutton, 1999). It is necessary to have some criteria to ensure that every "home sign" system used by a lone deaf villager is not included as a "sign language". However, this definition is unusually tight, given that most spoken languages are neither taught in schools nor standardized. The idea that to be "a language" the language must have been studied again suggests that the interests of linguists defines a language. One of the sign languages in the Ethnologue database is Rennellese Sign Language. This was the language used by the only deaf person in a community on the Solomon Islands to communicate with family members (Kuschel, 1973). The language was described by a linguist and this was, by itself, enough to justify inclusion in the list. There are anecdotal reports that, for example, the sign language used by Peruvians in Lima is very different from that used by Peruvians in the mountainous rural regions. However, this has never been formally studied and consequently there is still only one "Peruvian Sign Language" listed, not two.

"Planned" signed languages that are not used by Deaf communities

Another problem for counting sign languages lies in the decision of what constitutes a "sign language" at all. This chapter does not focus on "artificial" sign languages devised by hearing people for the sole purpose of representing spoken languages visually to deaf people. This group is a large one and it would be possible to set criteria allowing us to include them in the count. Some forms of signed language are clearly not to be classed as separate sign languages. They are merely different ways of representing a spoken language. Examples include manual systems designed to clarify ambiguous lip patterns (such as cued speech used in the USA and Britain or the Forchhammer hand–mouth system used in Denmark). Manual alphabets, which vary widely around the world, also should not be treated as separate languages since they are systems for representing the orthography of written languages.

Other artificial systems have their own vocabulary independent of spoken or written language. The Paget–Gorman Sign System is a signed language used in Britain that cannot be understood by English speakers or BSL signers as its signs are unrelated either to English or to BSL, although the syntax and morphology of Paget–Gorman signing largely match that of English (Paget and Gorman, 1976). Some sign languages have been used for the creation of a variety of languages that match the spoken language of the hearing community. These are difficult to categorize. In these language variants (for example, Signed Dutch, Irish Signed English or Signed French) the grammar is derived from that of the spoken language but the vocabulary is derived from the signed language. It is worth noting that a decision to include these language variants in a language count would make a big difference to the final total.

From the discussion above, we can see that, as Romaine (1989) has remarked, "the recognition of a linguistic system as an autonomous language is ultimately a socio-political matter" (p. 283). What is considered a language and what is merely seen as a "dialect" of another language or even not as a language at all are decisions intricately linked to attitudes and power in a language community. As we study and attempt to identify the variety of sign languages seen in the world, we realize that this holds as true for sign languages as it does for spoken languages.

The "standard" and the importance of dictionaries

To identify languages as distinct from dialects, we usually refer to the "standard form". The standard form of a language is frequently used as a defining marker for a language's identity. This idea of a "standard form" has, however, arisen in literate communities and we must bear this in mind when we consider sign languages.

The standard form of a language is usually the form with the highest prestige, and it is considered the form that exemplifies the essential features of the language, even though – since it is an abstract ideal – there is no one who actually uses the standard. As an abstract ideal, it is not a dialect that can be observed in any individual. Most importantly, the form likely to be closer to the standard form of a language is the one that is prescribed for writing. Haugen called this form the "grapholect" (1971).

The grapholect is used in writing and especially in printed texts. It is described in grammars, printed in books and taught in schools and to second language learners. It is used by the social and political elite of the language community and broadly cuts across "regional" dialects of that language. It is used in prestigious situations, such as schools, universities, the national broadcast media, and courts and civil services. Its vocabulary is to be found in dictionaries and it includes words no longer in regular use. To a great extent, certainly in the past, the contents of dictionaries have been based on words used in written language. Languages that do not have a written form do not usually have dictionaries. Dictionaries of predominantly unwritten languages can be made, of course, for the purposes of language teaching or for "preservation" of the language, but the language communities using these unwritten languages do not have the same immediate need as literate communities for dictionaries.

When we seek to define languages and think of standard dialects as a means to this end, we need to be aware that we are living in a highly literate society and that we cannot expect most of the world's languages to be defined in a similar way. According to Ong, of the several thousand spoken languages used today, only 78 have a written literature (Ong, 1982). For these 78, there might be a way of defining the standard form in terms like "Standard English" or "Standard French", but for other languages this is not so.

There are no widely used written forms of sign languages and no sign language has a body of written literature, so any "standard" form of a sign language would have a very different function from a standard spoken language with a written literature. There is work now to encourage the written form of some sign languages (for example, ASL and Nicaraguan Sign Language;

see www.signwriting.org). However, it will be many years, if at all, before we see these written forms of sign language having the same status and function as written forms of spoken language.

As members of literate language communities we see a dictionary as a symbol of authority that gives linguistic status to a language variety or a word used in that variety. We can see this, for example, in the game of "Scrabble" where the simple solution to the question "Is that a word in this language?" is to check for its appearance in a dictionary. There are increasing numbers of sign language dictionaries and we might assume that they would hold the same authority for questions about signs. These sign dictionaries, however, are generally very different in structure and function from spoken language dictionaries. Unlike many spoken language dictionaries, for example, sign language dictionaries cannot be researched by analyzing large numbers of written texts. Usually, they are not even created as a result of an analysis of thousands of hours of signing on a wide range of topics by a wide range of signers. To do so would be beyond the current technological and financial capacities of any sign lexicographer. The result is that sign language dictionaries do not cover the vocabulary of sign languages in the depth that we might expect in well-researched dictionaries of written forms of spoken languages. Regional dialect signs may be excluded from the dictionaries simply because the dictionary-makers have limited knowledge of regional variants. Signs used by older people may be excluded merely because older people are not involved in the dictionary-making process. The identification of shortcomings in many sign language dictionaries is not a criticism of their lexicographers (who frequently struggle to do the best possible job in very difficult circumstances). However, as sociolinguists we must understand the implications of the differences between these dictionaries and those of languages such as English.

Sign language dictionaries are usually created to allow others to learn the language or to collect and preserve the vocabulary items of the language. Such dictionaries have existed for several centuries (see, for example, Bulwer, 1644; Pelissier, 1856). We should be aware that such functions are very different from the sort of English dictionaries we are used to, which define words, give their correct spellings, pronunciations and explain their origins. Almost all so-called "dictionaries of sign language" are really bilingual dictionaries (or phrase books) in which the sign is "defined" by providing a translation into a written language. Sign origins may be referred to in the context of the visual motivation of the sign, as part of the description of the articulation of a sign, but not from a historical perspective. It should be noted that the formal provision of definitions is not a common feature of linguistic interaction. Members of a non-literate language community have no need to check the pronunciation of a word or sign because they always have first hand experience of it. The origin of a word or sign is usually irrelevant, since if a form has never been written down, there is no way of checking when and where it was first used. Sign language dictionaries, therefore, are not created for fluent users of the language to consult in order to check the meaning, pronunciation or origin of the sign.

Despite the great differences between the functions and uses of signed and spoken language dictionaries, the fact remains that sign language dictionaries can have substantial impact upon the status of sign languages and what is accepted as a distinct sign language. Signs that are included in dictionaries are more likely to be accorded high status and be in more widespread use than those that are left out. This is because appearing in a dictionary has been traditionally regarded as having received a validation of status. Learners of a sign language as a second language who use these dictionaries often become educators or interpreters and may ultimately have considerable power within a sign language community.

Although sign languages are unwritten, videotape is becoming an increasingly common way of recording and transmitting the languages. In developed countries, the use of videotape effectively allows all members of the language community to record, transmit, store and review their sign language. Popular commercially produced sign language videotapes may be seen by hundreds or thousands of people, in a way never possible before. In cases where these videotapes contain teaching materials, the impact on the language of second language learners could be considerable. In the future, videotape or computer graphics and digital video might have the same function as written language, as a standardizing tool for sign languages.

Television broadcasts of sign language are another example of the electronic media impacting on sign languages. In Britain, the first regular magazine program for deaf people using BSL was broadcast in 1980. The effect of 20 years of British broadcasting of BSL has been to expose large numbers of people (deaf and hearing) to the language of a small number of signers from the BSL elite. Signers across the nation can now see regional signs and new signs for new concepts. It is too early to tell what impact this will have upon the emergence of a standard form of BSL, but there is evidence that signing on television does influence the signing of the community at large (Woll, 1991).

Statistical approaches to the definition of languages

It is recognized that different modern languages may share a common ancestor. As people using a given language disperse, their language dialects become separated and language variants develop and change in their own way to become new languages. One technique which linguists use to research the relationship between languages is "glottochronology" (Gudschinsky, 1956). This is based on the principle that the rate of language change is relatively constant over time. The longer the time that two languages have been apart, the fewer vocabulary items they will have in common. Two languages descended from the same "parent" language should have approximately 86 percent of their vocabulary in common after 1,000 years of separation.

The same method can be applied to defining languages as either separate languages or as dialects of the same language. If 80 percent or more of the words or signs are similar, then the variants are dialects of the same language. If 36 percent to 80 percent of the words or signs are similar, then the two languages belong to the same family. If the similarity is 12 percent to 35 percent, then the languages belong to families of the same stock. If it is under 12 percent then they are unrelated.

Although all languages are ultimately socially and politically defined, some linguists have recognized that this detached, mathematical approach can cut through the complications of social attitudes. A simple comparison of the words used for certain items in different languages might be enough to determine if the variants of the language studied belong to the same language or are different languages. The greater the percentage of similar words, the more likely that the language variants are mutually intelligible and considered the same language.

Swadesh (1972) created a word list for collecting vocabulary in the field that could be used for this method of comparing languages. The list contained 100 core items considered to be common to all societies (there is an extended list of 200 items, although this is less widely used). Linguists could find the words for each of these 100 core items in any set of languages and then compare them. Languages with a high number of items in common were more closely related, or had split apart more recently, than languages with a small number of items in common.

The strength of the glottochronological approach is that it is free from social attitude judgments. However, sign linguists trying to use the Swadesh list to describe the relationships between sign languages have found problems. Some of the Swadesh list is inappropriate for modern sign languages in the developed world. It contains words (like "louse" and "dung") which are not core words in all sign language cultures, and certainly not in urban European or North American settings. It also contains items that we might expect to be similar in sign languages because of the use of visually motivated signs, such as DRINK (Pizzuto and Volterra, 1996). Sign linguists have therefore had to adapt the Swadesh lists. For example, the list used by Kyle and Woll was based on the Swadesh list, but with additional items that were especially relevant to deaf people, such as "deaf", "fingerspelling" and "signing" (Kyle and Woll, 1985).

It is important to remember that glottochronological comparisons of sign languages use a very different scale from comparisons of spoken languages. The spoken languages cited in most studies are known to have been in existence for thousands of years, but most sign languages have only existed for centuries at most, and in some cases only for decades. The degree of similarity seen between languages because of visual motivation in signs (as mentioned above) also makes it necessary to shift the time scale devised for calculating differences between spoken languages. Another source of problems for glottochronological approaches is the extent to which language mixing can take place between signed and spoken languages. We discuss this further in the next section.

Woodward (1978) applied a glottochronological analysis to ASL and LSF, finding a similarity score of 60 percent. Given that historical records demonstrate that ASL as we know it was only formed after LSF was introduced to America in 1816, 60 percent is a very low figure (this figure would be consistent with two spoken languages that had diverged at least 1,700 years ago). Woodward concluded that ASL must have mixed with other sign languages that were already used in America and must be some sort of creole.

Kyle and Woll (1985) looked at BSL, Sign Language of the Netherlands (SLN), Italian Sign Language (LIS) and Walloon (Francophone Belgian) Sign Language. They deliberately chose these because they were not believed to be related to each other. This appeared to be borne out by data from terms for family members, which are often similar in related languages. When Kyle and Woll looked at signs for family members, they found no similarities. Yet over 40 percent of the signs in the four languages were closely similar or identical. The researchers noted that this figure would be remarkable in unrelated spoken languages and suggested that this high degree of similarity was caused by the presence of visually motivated (iconic) signs in the languages which exhibited similarity independently of historical links. This feature of sign languages will always cause problems for the classification of sign languages, unless such examples can be factored out.

McKee and Kennedy (1998) have compared ASL, Auslan, New Zealand Sign Language (NZSL) and BSL using a modified version of the Swadesh list of vocabulary items. They found that Auslan, NZSL and BSL had a similarity of about 80 percent, when using the Swadesh list. However, this fell to about 64 percent when they used a semi-random selection of signs. They found that Auslan and NZSL were more similar to each other than they were to BSL. Anecdotal observations suggest that many Auslan signs that were "different" from BSL were similar to old BSL signs that are no longer commonly in use in Britain. We can see here the dangers of comparing a small list of signs and the importance of the need to recognize that some dialects of different sign languages may be more similar to each other than other dialects.

Sign languages in Europe

The idea that each nation might have more than one sign language is implied by the European Union's commitment to "recognise sign languages as used by

Deaf people in each member state". To make a statement such as this implies that deaf people within each member state might use more than one sign language.

In Europe, many deaf people believe that each country has a single national sign language. However, this is not always the case. In a study commissioned by the European Union of the Deaf (EUD), deaf people around Europe were asked what they called their communication (Kyle and Allsop, 1997). Respondents from 14 countries replied with a single name, and these (with the exception of Finland) all contained the name of the country in their sign language name. However, Belgium, Luxembourg and Spain each provided two names. Both Belgium and Spain had names for sign languages based not only on the country's name but also on a specific region of the country. The report comments that "each language name has different origins depending on culture, experience and recency of naming. The World Federation of the Deaf has developed the policy of accepting the name used by each national Deaf association without question or comment" (p. 46).

The report also assumes that there is one national Deaf association for each country which in turn might lead to the idea of one sign language. However, this is clearly not the case. Within a national boundary there may be more than one clearly identifiable language or cultural group. The Walloon and Flemish communities of Belgium identify their sign languages differently. In Spain, there is a Catalonian sign language that is considered separate from Spanish Sign Language.

We have already seen that one rule of thumb for distinguishing between different languages is that of mutual intelligibility. If two variants of a language are mutually intelligible then they can be called dialects of the same language. If they are mutually unintelligible then they should be considered two separate languages. In the EUD study, European signers were asked "Do you always understand someone from a town 100 kilometers away?" The first column of figures in Table 2.1 shows the extent to which signers claimed that they could understand someone living 100 kilometers away.

These figures are not necessarily concrete, irrefutable evidence of the degree of mutual intelligibility. Signers may have been particularly cautious when answering this question and answered "no" where they only understood partially. This is particularly possible when we consider answers to the question "Do you always understand someone from your town?", shown in the second column of figures in Table 2.1.

The low figures for intelligibility in a signer's own town imply that signers are remarking not on a general ease of intelligibility but on something more specific. As a comparison, 10 hearing people who had lived in Bristol, UK, for a minimum of 15 years were asked similar questions. When asked if they could always understand someone from Bristol, only 70 percent said they could. Despite this, 100 percent said that they could always understand someone from towns

Table 2.1 *Percentages of signers in various European countries who replied they could always understand another signer from (a) a town 100 kilometers away and (b) their own town*

Country	100 kilometers away	Own town
Austria	69	88
Belgium	40	88
Denmark	82	100
Finland	67	67
France	66	65
Germany	81	94
Greece	42	83
Iceland	n/a	38
Ireland	25	58
Italy	60	90
Netherlands	25	63
Norway	33	50
Portugal	44	69
Spain	44	62
Sweden	89	100
UK	58	84

approximately 100 kilometers away. Much of this needs to be interpreted cautiously. Bristol residents were more aware of strong "Bristol" dialects that they might not understand but only considered the speech used in other towns in a more general way. A similar interpretation may need to be made of the EUD data.

We should also note that signers sometimes underestimate their ability to understand sign dialects. Another study showed that British signers were frequently able to understand the content of video clips of signers from around the UK with relative ease, despite claiming that they did not understand other dialects (Woll, 1991). Clearly, lexical variation counts are not necessarily perfect guides to mutual intelligibility in languages.

Historical relationships

One of the great achievements of comparative linguistics over the last 200 years has been the construction of language "family trees". Using clues from similar words and grammars and available knowledge of a language's history, linguists have placed languages into families and described their relationships to each other. The relationship of sign languages can also be traced, but the relationships are different from those of spoken languages. Anderson (1979) is one of the few linguists to have attempted to create "family trees" for sign languages. Figure 2.1 shows Anderson's suggestions for relationships

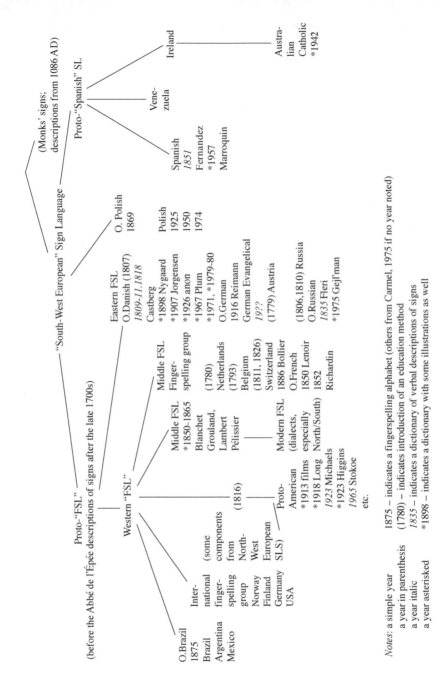

Fig. 2.1 *Proposed relation of "South-West European Sign Languages"*
Source: Anderson, 1979

Notes: a simple year — 1875 – indicates a fingerspelling alphabet (others from Carmel, 1975 if no year noted)
a year in parenthesis — (1780) – indicates introduction of an education method
a year italic — *1835* – indicates a dictionary of verbal descriptions of signs
a year asterisked — *1898 – indicates a dictionary with some illustrations as well

between many of the world's sign languages. By comparing signs and manual alphabets from different sign languages he attempted to group languages together. He suggested that there may have been one ancestral "South-West European" sign language, from which many other languages are descended, claiming that three main families of languages were descended from the original ancestor: "Proto-French Sign Language", "Old Polish Sign Language" and "Proto-Spanish Sign Language". The "Proto-French Sign Language", according to Anderson, gave rise to sign languages now used in Brazil, Argentina and Mexico, as well as languages now used in the USA and various European countries. The "Proto-Spanish Sign Language" gave rise to modern Spanish Sign Language, as well as sign languages now used in Venezuela and Ireland. Anderson claimed to have evidence that there was a separate ancestor for other sign languages, the "North-West European" sign language, which ultimately gave rise to British, German and Swedish Sign Languages, and their descendants (see Figure 2.2). He accepted that the two groups of languages interacted, as when both groups contributed to the development of ASL.

There are some problems with Anderson's charts. For example, it is well documented (e.g. Matthews, 1996) that Irish Sign Language is descended from French, not Spanish, Sign Language. The evidence for some of the relationships between languages is also sometimes rather thin. However, his charts are a useful first attempt to categorize sign languages according to their history.

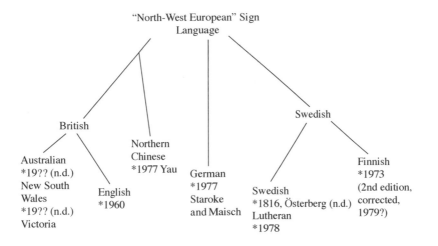

Fig. 2.2 *Proposed relation of "North-West European Sign Languages"*
Note: a year asterisked indicates a dictionary with some illustrations as well
Source: Anderson, 1979

Spoken languages are believed not to arise independently, spontaneously and rapidly. Some linguists believe that spoken language only emerged once, and that all spoken languages are descended from a single ancestor. Others believe that it arose independently in several locations around the world. In general, however, the spoken languages we see today are all assumed to have histories of many thousands of years. Sign languages, on the other hand, clearly arise spontaneously and independently in many parts of the world.

Although we cannot divide sign languages into families in the same way that we can look at spoken languages, we can, nonetheless, find patterns and relationships between sign languages. Specifically, we can see how both world politics and situations specific to the Deaf community, especially education and other "welfare" arrangements, affect sign languages.

World politics

Colonialism of different kinds has greatly shaped world history for millennia, and one major impact of colonialism has been on language. The languages of the great colonial powers (for example, English, French, German, Japanese, Russian and Spanish) are very powerful world languages. Colonial politics have greatly affected the spread of languages around the world and have also affected sign languages. One major difference is that variants of the spoken languages of colonial powers are considered to be a single language even when they vary enough to be called dialects of that language (e.g. English in Britain, North America and Australia or Portuguese in Portugal, Brazil and Angola). The sign languages that arose in colonies are, however, often considered to be separate languages.

The sign languages of Germany, Austria and Hungary are closely related, as part of the legacy of the Hapsburg Empire. Teachers of the Deaf were trained in Germany, and they influenced Deaf communities throughout that Empire (McCagg, 1993). Britain's history of Empire and Commonwealth has meant that sign languages thousands of miles apart may be very similar. Deaf children from all over the former British Empire were educated in Britain and returned to their own countries, bringing their signs with them. Even more significantly, deaf adults joined other immigrants to the colonies, bringing BSL (e.g. Flynn, 1984). Consequently today Auslan, NZSL and certain dialects of Indian and South African sign languages are intelligible to BSL users.

The first Irish Deaf school was set up by Dr. Charles Orpen in Dublin in 1816. The first headmaster of the school trained at the Braidwood Schools in Britain and for several decades BSL was used by the pupils there (Matthews, 1996). Today, despite subsequent radical changes in the Irish Deaf education system which resulted in ISL being more closely related to LSF, some ISL signs are similar to BSL. Much of this may be accounted for by later borrowing but other signs are considered by ISL signers to be well established signs that are not seen as loans (Matthews, 1996). As a result of the Japanese occupation of Taiwan, some dialects of sign language in Taiwan are very similar to JSL. Since Japanese withdrawal, however, and with the influx of large numbers of people from the Chinese mainland, another form of Taiwan Sign Language (TSL) has developed, which is more similar to the sign language used in Shanghai (Ann, 1998a; 1998b).

World politics has also influenced Israeli Sign Language. In the early years of Jewish settlement in Palestine, most deaf people came from Germany, Hungary and other central European countries. These deaf people were relatively well educated and were fluent signers. They had considerable influence in the education system and in the production of the Israeli Sign Language dictionary. Israeli Sign Language today contains many signs similar to those in German Sign Language (Namir et al., 1979).

Educational systems

Another very strong influence on sign languages has come not from political domination but from educational systems being shared between nations. Frequently educators from one country have had a religious or missionary agenda when bringing education and their own sign language to other countries.

The language which has had the most profound influence on other sign languages, especially in Europe and North America, has been French Sign Language (LSF). The powerful influence of French Sign Language over the world's sign languages should not be underestimated. Influence from LSF can be seen clearly in Irish Sign Language (ISL) (Burns, 1998), ASL (Lane, 1984), Russian Sign Language (Mathur et al., 1998) and on some dialects of BSL (particularly where BSL has been influenced by ISL). In each case, educators were influenced by the French Deaf education system and brought LSF back to their own countries. Other sign languages have also had this sort of influential role. For example, Swedish Sign Language has influenced Portuguese Sign Language through its use of the manual alphabet, after a Swedish educator, Per Aron Borg – who had established a private school for the Deaf in Stockholm in 1808 – helped to found a Deaf school in Lisbon in 1824 (Eriksson, 1998).

ISL, originally heavily influenced by LSF, has also had considerable impact on sign languages around the world. Irish nuns and Christian brothers have taught in Catholic schools for deaf children in countries including India, South Africa and Australia, and the influence of ISL is noticeable in the sign languages in these countries (Aarons and Morgan, 1998).

ASL, also heavily influenced by LSF in the past, now has a major impact on sign languages around the world. Gallaudet University is able to offer scholarships to foreign deaf students who take ASL back to their own countries. The

USA has been especially generous in providing teacher training for teachers in many countries of the developing world. Andrew Foster, a deaf African-American, led a movement for the establishment of schools in African countries where ASL was introduced as the language of tuition (Lane *et al.*, 1996). In Nigeria today, ASL taught in schools is mixing with the indigenous sign languages (Schmaling, 2000). Even when ASL is not deliberately taught in schools in other countries, the presence of fluent signers of ASL can exert an influence. The American presence in Nicaragua has led to an influence of ASL on Nicaraguan Sign Language. Scandinavian sign languages have also influenced African and Asian sign languages as aid programs use foreign nationals to help set up schools in developing countries.

In summary, we have seen that the question "How many sign languages are there?" is not an easy one to answer. We may base our estimates on either linguistic judgments about lexical or structural similarities, or on social attitudes to the languages. Many of the tools we can use for such studies come from research conducted on spoken languages. We have seen that any ideas we might have, based on spoken languages (particularly the more "powerful" European languages) must be applied with caution to sign languages. The more "detached" approach using numerical comparisons of vocabulary lists needs to be used in conjunction with considerations of identity of the deaf people using the sign language. It will probably never be possible to reach an agreed figure for the number of sign languages in the world. Attempts to find that number, however, can lead to a much greater understanding of the structure and standing of many of the world's sign languages.

Suggested Readings

David Crystal's (1997) *The Cambridge Encyclopaedia of Language* gives an excellent description of the languages of the world and their relationships. For up-to-date lists of the languages of the world, including some sign languages, the Summer Institute of Linguistics' web site is very useful (www.sil.org/ ethnologue). Nora Groce's (1985) book *Everyone Here Spoke Sign Language* describes the social and historical situation that led to a community of hearing people using sign language with deaf people. It is more anthropological than linguistic, so it does not give a detailed description of the form of the sign language, but it is clearly written and useful to read. Branson *et al.*'s (1996) chapter describes a similar present day society in Bali and focuses more on the language used in such a situation. The papers in the volumes *Multicultural Aspects of Sociolinguistics in Deaf Communities* (1996), and *Pinky Extension and Eye Gaze* (1998) – both edited by Ceil Lucas – address a range of issues related to a wide variety of different sign languages.

Exercises

1. We are used to the idea that British and American English are dialects of the same language. Although they are essentially mutually intelligible, there are some noticeable differences in pronunciation, vocabulary, semantics and grammar. Find examples of 20 lexical differences between the two dialects (e.g. "tap" in British English vs. "faucet" in American English). Find examples of three grammatical differences between the two dialects (e.g. "I have already seen him" in British English vs. "I already saw him" in American English).

2. We are used to the idea that within our own country there are dialects of the same language. Although they are essentially mutually intelligible, there are some noticeable differences in pronunciation, vocabulary, semantics and grammar. Find examples of 20 lexical differences found in regional dialects in your country (e.g. "bap" or "bun" in British English). Find examples of three grammatical differences in the dialects used in your country (e.g. "Where is it?" or "Where is it to?" in British English).

3. In this chapter we have seen that national sign languages often carry the name of the country where they are used (e.g. Irish Sign Language is used in Ireland). The name of a language does not, however, always match the name of the country where it is spoken. While German is spoken in Germany and Norwegian is spoken in Norway, Canadians speak English and/or French (not "Canadian") and Israelis speak Hebrew (not "Israeli"). Think of 10 more languages where the name of the language does not match the name of the country.

4. While signed languages are used by Deaf communities, hearing people sometimes use signs with some sort of limited linguistic meaning. Describe briefly other signed languages or sign systems used by hearing people. Who uses these systems, in what context or for what reason? (For example, sports teams may use prearranged signals to communicate among themselves in a way that the opposing team does not understand.)

5. How similar are sign languages? Using dictionaries of two different sign languages that you believe to be basically unrelated compare 30 entries ("headwords") with similar meanings, for example "child" or "horse". How many of the signs are the same or similar (e.g. only differ slightly in handshape or movement)? Would you expect a similar percentage of similarities in two spoken languages?

6. In this chapter we have mentioned that sign language dictionaries do not contain the same information as spoken language dictionaries. Look up 10 similar "headwords" in a sign language dictionary and a spoken language dictionary and describe and comment on the way that the entries differ.

7. The research by the European Union of the Deaf (EUD) found that many deaf people believed that they could not understand signers who lived in a town 100 kilometers away. Ask 20 people in your town if they believe they can understand speakers who live in a town 100 kilometers away. What do your findings tell you about regional differences between some spoken languages and some sign languages? What do they tell you about attitudes to regional differences?

3   Bilingualism and language contact*

Jean Ann

> ...People say our signs [in Singapore] come from Australia, China and America. So I am worried that [this means that] we do not have our own sign language...Also, why are there so many signs for the same thing? Which is the right sign?...Why can't everyone just sign the right way?
>
> Excerpted from a fax to the author from a Singaporean deaf person, 1994

> It is probably true that no language group has ever existed in isolation from other language groups, and the history of languages is replete with examples of language contact leading to some form of bilingualism.
>
> François Grosjean, Life with Two Languages (1982: 1)

Spoken languages have always been in contact with each other, and there have always been linguistic and sociolinguistic consequences of this phenomenon. Languages come into contact through their speakers, who are brought together under different sorts of conditions, including political turmoil, immigration, education and geography. Indeed, languages are sometimes said to be "in contact" within bilingual individuals (Grosjean, 1992: 309). The immense and engaging field of the study of language contact points up interesting linguistic situations. For example, examination of the current position of English in the world confirms that English is an extremely prestigious language that is learned as a second language with great frequency. It is the world's lingua franca; that is, it is the language chosen by speakers of diverse languages in the hearing world for many sorts of needs, from science and technology to business and scholarship. In multilingual areas of the world, pidgins based on English have sprung up. Given this, it is almost impossible to imagine that English-speaking scholars once lamented the fact that English was barely spoken outside of a very local area, and had neither a dictionary nor a written grammar.

The study of language contact in the Deaf world, given the sustained, even overwhelming contact between sign languages and spoken languages, for one example, might have been seized upon first by researchers. However, despite its

---

* I am indebted to Ceil Lucas and Bruce Peng for a great number of helpful comments on earlier drafts of this chapter. Yang Hao, Chen Li and Chen Chun assisted me with the Mandarin data.

rich possibilities, it has been taken up rather slowly. Explanations for this involve an understanding of political considerations. Sign languages are often oppressed by speakers of spoken languages. For example, sign languages may be kept from developing in the first place because deaf signers are prevented from establishing a community. Even when sign languages exist, their status as real languages can be questioned, or they might not be encouraged or even permitted in schools for the Deaf. Sign languages and spoken languages then are rarely at parity in the larger hearing community: hearing people prefer spoken languages. But among members of some Deaf communities such as in the USA, sign languages like American Sign Language (ASL) are deeply embraced, while spoken languages like English do not enjoy this status. It is understandable then that many people find the idea that English would influence ASL disquieting in a political sense, although, in a linguistic sense, it is natural and expected that this should be the case. (For much more discussion of these and related issues, see Fischer, 1978: 309–310; Lucas, 1989; Padden, 1990; 1991; Johnston, 1991; Lucas and Valli, 1992: 112.) In any case, researchers have begun examining language contact issues in Deaf communities, producing very interesting research.

The world's contact situations which involve sign languages provide a seemingly endless source of challenging linguistic and sociolinguistic data. This cannot all be discussed in great detail; my goal will be to introduce as many as possible. In this chapter, I discuss the phenomena in language contact and bilingualism in spoken languages that find in the study of sign languages some parallel, or presumed parallel. In this way, the claims about sign languages will be contextualized and can be considered more clearly. We focus first on outcomes of bilingualism which are not unique to sign language situations. We begin with a discussion of societal and individual bilingualism and proceed to the phenomenon of diglossia (a kind of bilingualism in which two language – or varieties of one language – occupy different social positions in certain societies). The notion of linguistic interference – that is, when a speaker speaks a second language with features from the first language – is discussed. Next, we consider language shift, i.e. speakers ceasing to use one language in favor of another. In the remainder of the chapter, we examine some of the outcomes of language contact which are unique to sign language situations, namely the creation of loan vocabulary and how that terminology and thinking has been used to understand sign language situations. We touch briefly on the subject of mouthing. Finally, we discuss pidgin and creole languages, the phenomena of code switching and code mixing and their relevance to sign languages and Deaf communities.

Societal and individual bilingualism in the hearing world

Researchers have described two possibilities for the distribution of bilingualism in hearing societies: societal bilingualism and individual bilingualism.

If a society declared itself "bilingual", this would not necessarily mean that every person in the society is bilingual. In fact it is often the case that such a society has a bilingual language policy although many or most of its speakers are monolingual. The cases we present to demonstrate this are Canada and Belgium. Individual bilingualism – in which an individual speaks more than one language – occurs in many societies as well. We take Singapore as a case in point.

Canada

Canada is considered a "bilingual" country, although most Canadians are monolinguals. Although many languages are spoken in Canada besides English, the renowned situation in Canada of interest to sociolinguists is that between the English speakers and the French speakers. Some French speakers live in virtually every province, but they are concentrated in New Brunswick, where they constitute about one-third of the population, and Québec, where they constitute about 90 percent of the population. Canadian French speakers are almost uniformly associated with Québec. A look at the history of Canada reveals that, for about 200 years, English-speaking Canadian lawmakers passed laws which had the effect of oppressing French-speaking Canadians. For example, monolingual English speakers even in Québec could obtain jobs much more easily than monolingual French speakers and, therefore, much of the Francophone community was bilingual. Until the 1960s, the French speakers were poor and did not have access to many of society's benefits. Something remarkable happened in the 1960s that brought abiding changes to the lives of the French-speaking people of Canada and their English-speaking counterparts. Francophones began to be "increasingly critical of English domination in all aspects of their lives" (Grosjean, 1982: 16), and thus began a "quiet revolution". The "quiet revolution" refers to a bloodless rethinking of all aspects of life, and the taking of positive action on the part of Québecois, such as obtaining education and demanding equal rights in their own province. Most Québecois want to see Québec as a truly French-speaking province in which French speakers are advantaged. Indeed, there is a significant number of people who want Québec to be a separate political entity from the rest of Canada. All of these efforts have been successful, and although Québec is still part of Canada, it is clear that the effects of the quiet revolution will be long-lasting.

The situation in Québec points up several facts of great importance. First, French and English have never been at parity in Canada; that is, despite the status of French as a world language, in Canada English has been dominant and French has been a minority language. English speakers and French speakers have always been in conflict. Second, in general, bilinguals are the linguistic minority. In such situations, a language policy which ensures societal

bilingualism sounds workable, even desirable, as a philosophy and a way to re-
duce conflict. Since each group continues to use its own language, bilingualism
seems to suggest that no one compromises. However, when members of the linguistic minority group are the ones who are bilingual in a given society, and the
members of the linguistic majority group are monolingual (as is the situation in
Canada), to become bilingual is tantamount to giving up one's language. Thus,
in fact, in the Canadian situation and many others like it, bilingualism begets
a conundrum explained in Grosjean (1982: 17) in a citation from a Québecois
writing in 1961:

The more bilingual our children become, the more they use English; the more they use
English, the less they find French useful; the less they find French useful, the more they
use English. The paradox of French–Canadian life is the following: the more we become
bilingual, the less it is necessary to be bilingual.

Belgium

In Belgium, another "bilingual" country, the social relations between the two
major groups – the French speakers (the Walloons) and the Flemish speakers
(the Flemings) – are a matter of great concern. At present, the French speakers in
Belgium, less than half the population, live in Wallonia. The Flemish speakers –
Flemish is a dialect of Dutch – are the majority and live in Flanders. Brussels, the
capital of Belgium, is bilingual. There has been conflict between these groups
for nearly two centuries. Attempting to solve their problems at various stages,
three series of language laws were passed in Belgium. In the late-nineteenth
century the laws that were passed ensured that Flanders was bilingual (that
is, the Flemings spoke Flemish and French), and the rest of the country was
monolingual French speaking. Unrest followed. In the 1930s, Belgium began
to practice a policy of "territorial unilingualism" (Grosjean, 1982: 14; Hooghe,
1991) in Flanders and Wallonia, and bilingual institutions in Brussels, which
is in a Flemish-speaking area. The laws passed in the 1960s kept territorial
unilingualism in place, and now the country remains essentially divided in half,
with the Flemish speakers in Flanders and the French speakers in Wallonia, and
bilingual Brussels (Hooghe, 1991). During the nineteenth century the fact that
French was a world language and Flemish was only useful in the Netherlands
and Belgium added to the conflict: the French-speaking minority was advantaged because they had access to the world. At the same time, the Flemings were
disadvantaged, although they were a numerical majority. Now the situation is
reversed (Grosjean, 1982). Although attempts are still being made to "give the
two languages involved an equal place in the life of the state", resentments run
deep and conflicts between Walloons and Flemings are intense (Calvet, 1998:
37). In fact, all of Belgium's major political parties have split into Flemish- and
French-speaking versions (Hooghe, 1991: 5).

Singapore

Singapore is a tiny Southeast Asian island nation situated at the southern tip of Malaysia among the islands of Indonesia. It is a case of a multilingual country which does not attempt to solve its language conflicts by dividing the country and enforcing regional boundaries along linguistic lines. Its ethnic situation is complex – four major ethnic groups live in an area of 226 square miles – and its linguistic situation is even more so. As Pakir (1994: 158–159) explains:

Officially Singapore's population of 2.6 million has the following ethnic components: 77% Chinese, 15% Malay, 6% Indian, 2% others, which includes Eurasians, Europeans, and Arabs . . . Such heterogeneity does not reflect the actual complexities of the linguistic situation in Singapore, since each of the three major ethnic groups (Chinese, Malay, Indian) also employs a variety of languages and/or dialects. Traditionally, the ethnic Chinese speak one or more of the following: Hokkien, Teochew, Cantonese, Hainanese, Hakka, Foochow, Mandarin and other, less known, Chinese dialects. The ethnic group labelled Malay speak Malay generally but Javanese and Boyanese are also spoken. The ethnic Indians speak a variety of languages: Tamil, Malayalam, Telugu (which are Dravidian in origin) and Punjabi, Hindi, Bengali, Gujerati (which are Indo-Aryan languages).

The government of Singapore has imposed order upon this situation by practicing a policy labeled as "pragmatic multilingualism" (Kuo and Jernudd, 1994: 72). Four official languages – Mandarin, Malay, Tamil and English – are, in principle, treated equally. In actuality, the languages are not equal in historical, social or political senses, and each is used toward a particular end in Singapore. Malay was selected as the national language since it is the major language in the region (Indonesian and Malay are essentially the same language) and "proficiency in Malay is believed to help build rapport with Indonesia and Malaysia" (Kuo and Jernudd, 1994: 83). Malay, once used as a lingua franca in Singapore, now serves a ceremonial role, and virtually no one of non-Malay descent learns it. Mandarin is the native language of very few of the Chinese ethnic majority in Singapore. However, it is the official language of the People's Republic of China, Hong Kong and Taiwan. Owing to these considerations, the Singapore government periodically pushes the highly successful "Speak Mandarin" campaign. Posters which can be seen everywhere urge, "For Chinese Singaporeans, [Mandarin is] more than a language." Government attempts to unify the Chinese community through language have been successful in many senses: many Chinese have acquired Mandarin as a second language. Tamil, on the other hand, is the language which the government would like to use to unify the Indian community in Singapore. However, attempts have not been very successful since "at best, half of all individuals classified as Indians appear to use Tamil to any extent . . . Thus the position of Tamil as an official language has by and large been ignored, but tolerated, by the non-Tamil Indians ..." (Kuo and Jernudd, 1994: 73). This leaves English, the only non-Asian language, and as such a "neutral" language, which is used as a lingua franca between speakers of all the rest of the languages. The utility of English for Singaporeans in science, technology and business is obvious, and its position goes unchallenged. Indeed, Singaporeans are generally at least bilingual: they speak English and the language of their ethnic group. Although there are a few parts of Singapore where ethnic businesses thrive (such as Little India), Singaporeans of all ethnic and linguistic groups live together in government housing, a deliberate move on the part of the government. Civil strife, language or ethnic conflicts in Singapore are rare according to government statistics.

This examination points up a few revealing generalizations; among them, that various bilingual/multilingual countries are quite different in character from each other, and some have a great number of monolinguals. The outcomes of bilingualism for linguistic majorities and bilingualism for linguistic minorities are very different. Language policies are adopted to unify people, sometimes successfully.

Societal and individual bilingualism in the Deaf world

As far as we know, no society has ever existed whose inhabitants were all deaf. Consequently we would not expect to find a case of territorial unilingualism, in which deaf people who are signers of a natural sign language live in regionally separate areas from hearing people who are speakers of some other language. Perhaps the closest phenomenon we can find which would resemble a case of territorial unilingualism (at least in some senses) are cases in which, in a given society, everyone signs a natural sign language. Three such cases have emerged in the literature, and we review these below. In these cases, as we will see, both the Deaf and the hearing are signers, and, in some sense, they form a community separate from the larger hearing world around them in which virtually no one signs.

Martha's Vineyard in the USA

In an absorbing book, Groce (1985) details the story of a community that once thrived on Martha's Vineyard, an island off the coast of Massachusetts. This community, for a period of 250 years, had an incidence of deafness above the national norm. "In the nineteenth century, and presumably earlier, one American in every 5,728 was born deaf, but on the Vineyard, the figure was one in every 155" (Groce, 1985: 3). Because the last surviving deaf person died in the early 1950s, Groce's data sources only included the written records she could locate and interviews with those people she could find who were old enough to remember the generally forgotten way of life on the island.

Groce's (1985) engaging account points up some facts of great interest. First, it seems clear that informants recall the high incidence of deafness and the fact that everyone used sign language, including the hearing people, as something of an afterthought. Groce's hearing informants show no evidence of having paid much attention to the fact that some people on the island were deaf. Deafness was accepted as part of life and was regarded as "something that occasionally happened, not as something to be ashamed of" (Groce, 1985: 10). In fact, one of Groce's informants, in answer to Groce's question about those who were "handicapped by deafness", remarked, "Oh, those people weren't handicapped. They were just deaf" (Groce, 1985: 106). Deaf people were remembered as individuals, not as part of a Deaf ethnic group. They were, by all reports, integrated fully into society (Groce, 1985: 106). In most societies today, this state of affairs is unfamiliar, and perhaps unbelievable.

The second of Groce's most powerful points goes a long way toward explaining how this society could have existed. Of particular interest to sociolinguists are the facts related to the way the hearing people on Martha's Vineyard learned the sign language of the island deaf people. They learned it as a matter of course (p. 53). They learned it in childhood and therefore might be presumed to have been fairly fluent in the language (p. 58). They were aware of but unconcerned by the fact that the grammar of the sign language was not like that of English (p. 58). Informants describe their fluency and the quickness of rendering a message in the sign language by saying "one word might mean a whole sentence" (p. 59). People talked of social occasions when deaf and hearing intermingled would be relaxing together in town. The community apparently attend to this code: "if there were more deaf than hearing there, everyone would speak sign language – just to be polite you know" (p. 60). And although there were occasionally people who served as interpreters, overall there was no appreciable need for interpreters because everyone knew the sign language "well enough to get by" (p. 63). Hearing people were in the habit of signing to such an extent that they often communicated with signs even when there were no deaf people present (p. 65). Groce's account and conclusions are a cautionary tale: she points out that the notion that deafness necessarily results in a "handicap" is socially constructed, not inherent.

A Yucatec Mayan village, Mexico

A second case that resembles that of Martha's Vineyard is described in Johnson (1994a). Among the world's communities in which a high incidence of deafness occurs is a traditional Mayan village located in the state of Yucatan, Mexico. Johnson and his colleagues visited the village twice in as many years and report that the village had approximately 400 inhabitants, 13 of whom were deaf. The village is traditionally structured such that it stands out from the other "towns and cities of the region, which have fully adopted the urban, industrial lifestyle of central Mexico" (p. 105). The men are mostly farmers and the women have "relatively narrowly defined economic roles, involving primarily food preparation, the maintenance of domestic animals, and child rearing" (p. 105). The values of the society are traditional and the villagers "do not strongly identify with life outside the village" (p. 105).

As expected, "the thirteen deaf villagers interact and communicate exclusively in sign language" but, surprisingly, "all hearing adults we met could sign, and some could sign very well. It appears that all people in the village, both hearing and deaf, have acquired sign language naturally, through interaction" (p. 106). Johnson explains that in industrial societies, politicization of deafness occurs when deaf people perceive themselves as not having access to the advantages of the hearing world. It is under these circumstances that they have risen up and fought for their rights. But the fact that all the hearing people sign, and the Deaf are nearly fully integrated into the culture "creates a condition in which both social and economic benefits are more readily accessible to deaf people and in which the formation of a strong ethnic group and politicization of deafness are unnecessary" (p. 106). Johnson reports that the deaf villagers have nearly full access to the entire culture, except in two areas. These are, first, that deaf people have a "lower marriage rate than the general population, among whom almost everyone gets married" (p. 108) and, second, that although everyone can sign, "deaf people do not have access to the majority of discourse, which is conducted in Mayan" (p. 108).

Desa Kolok in Bali, Indonesia

A third case of a similar phenomenon exists in Indonesia, a Southeast Asian archipelago. On one of its most famous islands, Bali, is a village known as Desa Kolok ("Deaf Village") in which the incidence of deafness is very high. Here too the Deaf and the hearing communicate with each other using a sign language and enjoy harmonious relations. As Branson *et al.* (1996: 39–57) explain:

Although there are only 43 kolok [deaf] in a village of more than 2,000 people, they have been part of village life far beyond living memory and have a rightful and taken-for-granted role in village life. The kolok children play happily and naturally with the hearing children, all signing. Adult men and women, Deaf and hearing, go about the business of village life together, aware of the sensory difference but unperturbed by it and unhampered in their communication with each other, given the ready access to the village sign language. (p. 41)

The authors explain that the deaf villagers are fully integrated in society and that there is no stigma attached to being deaf or marrying a deaf person. This, they point out, differs from the Yucatec Mayan society described in Johnson (1994a: 47).

Despite the apparently comfortable relation between hearing and deaf members of society, the authors are quick to point out that "this does not mean that the island is a deaf paradise". They explain that the fact that everyone can sign and that the Deaf are full members of society

does not imply that it is not necessarily the case that life is unproblematic. It does not mean that all hearing villagers are competent signers. It does not mean that the children and adults do not make fun of each other and that aspects of deafness may not be seized upon as the basis for teasing . . . (p. 41)

In a real sense, then, the Deaf in Desa Kolok seem to "have the same rights and village obligations" as the hearing and "participate with them in the performance of economic, political and ritual tasks" (p. 54).

In all three cases – Martha's Vineyard, the Yucatec Mayan village and Desa Kolok – deaf people and hearing people lived together, which, by itself, is an unstartling fact. But presumably the high incidence of deafness in each of these societies resulted in an interesting phenomenon: everyone signed, including the hearing. We have no evidence that any of these societies forced a sense of majority group and minority group based on hearing status and, thus, no Deaf ethnic groups developed. The hearing, who spoke their respective spoken languages and who signed perhaps with varying degrees of fluency, simply became bilingual presumably because it was useful. Although these societies might not be said to have an overt language policy of bilingualism, it seems obvious that each has a commitment to bilingualism because each has a necessity for it.

Bilingualism in most of the Deaf world

The sign language situation which is attested most often does not resemble this sort of bilingualism. In fact, most deaf people live in societies that are dominated in every aspect by hearing people and their values. This fact ensures (assuming that deaf people in such societies are not isolated from each other and that sign languages can be established and flourish) that sign languages will certainly come in contact with spoken languages, for example, through children who go to schools and are faced with the need to learn to read and write the spoken language. The fact that there is such highly sustained contact with spoken languages ensures that most deaf people are bilingual to some extent in a spoken language in some form. It has not meant that the hearing people in these societies learn the sign language.

Grosjean (1982) defines bilingualism as the "regular use of more than one language". The idea that Deaf communities (or individuals) could be said to be bilingual has been controversial in at least two ways. First, in order for bilingualism to exist, there must be two languages. It is not unheard of that a spoken language is doubted to be a language. For example, Creoles (a type of language we discuss below) are often thought to be incomplete, incorrect versions of established languages. However, throughout history, it has more commonly been the case that the status of natural sign languages as real languages has been disputed. Although the research conducted over the last 40 years has shown that sign languages are full-fledged languages, and this is no longer seriously challenged by researchers, in many parts of the world the reality for deaf individuals has not caught up with research. Thus, many deaf people who sign a natural sign language and know a spoken language as well might not be considered bilingual by the hearing people around them. Second, it is sometimes thought that a person who is a bilingual feels equally comfortable in both languages. Such a person is referred to as a "balanced" bilingual, but this sort of bilingualism is not the usual case, in either the hearing or the Deaf worlds. Most bilinguals have a dominant language and a non-dominant language. They function variously in both during their lives. Just as a hearing person fluent in Mandarin Chinese who knew enough English to work at a job, but could not read academic articles or discuss esoteric subjects in English, would be considered bilingual, so would a deaf person fluent in a natural sign language who also knew how to read and write a spoken language but did not speak it.

When we looked at bilingualism above, we considered it from a societal perspective. Here we change course and consider it as an individual phenomenon. In individual bilingualism, the knowledge of the non-native language is very unpredictable among hearing people. That is, while native speakers of the same language reach roughly the same place – that is, the same level of proficiency in that language – when we look at individuals who learn second languages, things become much less predictable. An individual's second language can end up at all levels for many different reasons. These include age, reasons for learning the second language, type of training in the second language, motivation to learn the second language, function that the second language will play in one's life, and sociolinguistic reasons for preserving bits of the first language in the production of the second. Thus, bilingualism produces extremely diverse kinds of language in the hearing world, and in the Deaf world things are, perhaps, even more unpredictable.

So what exactly is a deaf bilingual? Davis (1989: 87), Lucas and Valli (1992) and Grosjean (1992) discuss this extensively. They show that there is a great range of diversity in experience and behavior among the Deaf community. Some of the kinds of bilingualism are listed here. In what follows, I use x in the names of sign languages as a variable to stand for any sign language:

- native signers of *x*SL who are fluent in a spoken language (reading, writing and speaking);
- native signers of *x*SL who read and write a spoken language fluently but do not speak it;
- native signers of *x*SL who are fluent to varying degrees in reading and writing a spoken language;
- deaf signers of *x*SL as a second language who read and write a spoken language fluently but do not speak it;
- second language *x*SL signers who first learned a signed version of a spoken language;
- native signers of *x*SL who learned another sign language as a second language;
- first/second language *x*SL signers who speak a spoken language.

Clearly, there is great diversity of linguistic experience and behavior in bilinguals in the hearing and the Deaf worlds. But what seems clear from our discussion is that bilingualism is a very common and natural phenomenon in most places in the world. For bilinguals, being bilingual is part of life (Grosjean, 1982). Of this diversity of possible kinds of deaf bilinguals, there has been little written on deaf people who are bilingual in two sign languages, except for a few studies that attempted to understand the notion of foreign accent as it relates to learners of second sign languages. Most of the research about deaf bilinguals take as a source of data language produced by deaf people who know a sign language and a spoken language.

One final note: some people who are signers or who communicate with some kind of manual system are not bilinguals. For example, signers of a manual code for a spoken language exclusively, who perhaps read and write in that spoken language, are monolinguals. This might include people who are late deafened after acquiring a spoken language, and who then use a signed code for that spoken language. Some deaf people use a system of communication known as cued speech, more accurately cued English or cued French, for example. Cued speech is a response to the problem that only a small percentage of the sounds of spoken languages are able to be distinguished through lip reading. Cued speech replaces the auditory signal by using handshape–mouthshape pairs to represent consonant phonemes and hand placement–mouthshape pairs to represent vowel phonemes. Cued English is not a natural language but a way of making a spoken language clear to a deaf person. Some deaf cuers of English are not signers of ASL. In this case, they would not be bilinguals, since there are not two languages being used (Fleetwood and Metzger, 1998). Last, there are still many cases of deaf people who remain misdiagnosed with other conditions, when they are merely deaf, who have never been exposed to a sign language. Such a case was recorded in Schaller (1991). People who learn a natural sign language as a first language later in life and who know no other language in any form are not bilinguals.

Diglossia

We turn our attention now to the phenomenon of diglossia, first described in Ferguson (1959). According to Ferguson, diglossia occurs when two varieties of one language – one labeled high (H) and one labeled low (L), corresponding to attitudes about each variety – coexist in the same community. H is used for a distinct set of purposes and L is used for a different distinct set of purposes; that is, these varieties occur in complementary distribution. Both Fishman (1971) and Ferguson (1973) reworked the definition of diglossia to include situations in which two different languages (not varieties of one language) were used.

A diglossia, then, is a sort of "linguistic division of labor" (Holmes, 1992: 32). Ferguson (1959) laid out nine criteria to which situations of diglossia must conform. The nine criteria – widely regarded as including six which are sociolinguistic and three which are linguistic – are as follows.

1. Function: There are specialized functions for H and L.
2. Prestige: Speakers regard H as superior to L in some respects.
3. Literary heritage: There is a large, respected body of written literature in H.
4. Acquisition: Adults use L in speaking to children. Children use it in speaking to one another. L is acquired naturally and H is learned, usually in school.
5. Standardization: There is a strong tradition of grammatical study of H.
6. Stability: The situation in which H and L occur persists for several centuries.
7. Grammar: H has grammatical categories not present in L.
8. Lexicon: The bulk of vocabulary in H and L is shared.
9. Phonology: There is a single phonological system of which L is basic. H has phonological distinctions that L does not have (e.g. French vs. Haitian Creole).

An example of a diglossia in multilingual Switzerland follows. Switzerland has four official languages (Swiss German, French, Italian and Romansh). Each of these official languages is spoken in different areas.

In Eggenwil, a town in the Aargau canton of Switzerland, Silvia, a bank teller, knows two very distinct varieties of German. One is the local Swiss German dialect of her canton which she uses in her everyday interactions with other Swiss Germans. The other is standard German which she learnt at school, and though she understands it very well indeed, she rarely uses it in speech. Newspapers are written in standard German, and when she occasionally goes to hear a lecture at the university it may be in standard German. The sermons her mother listens to in church are generally in standard German too, though more radical clerics use Swiss German dialect. The novels Silvia reads also use standard German. (Holmes, 1992: 32)

With this background in mind, we turn our attention to the situation in which deaf people find themselves in many societies. Stokoe (1969) claimed that deaf individuals in the USA were living with a diglossia. ASL was L and spoken English was H, the high variety. Much of Stokoe's evidence for diglossia made use of the fact that people had a very low regard for ASL, considering it broken English. The claim of an ASL–English diglossia in the USA was later re-examined. Lee (1982) found that none of the nine characteristics that Stokoe cited as evidence of diglossia seemed to fit the situation when she was writing. For example, she pointed out that where the lexicon was concerned, most of the vocabulary of Signed English is actually from ASL, not the other way around. Further, with respect to literary heritage, Lee pointed out, rather prophetically, that ASL poetry was beginning to be composed. Now there is a proliferation of ASL poetry, and a great deal of interest in it among researchers and the general public alike. Indeed, the criticism that sign languages cannot have literatures is being challenged with the increased use of videotape as a means to collect and record stories and poems composed in sign languages. The question of whether diglossia is a reasonable way to describe the situation in several countries has been posed and, it seems, abandoned. However, the idea that diglossias exist in sign language situations captured the idea that societies by and large have hearing values. This means that sign languages are still not as prestigious as spoken languages in general, and that deaf individuals are still prevented from doing many things in their sign languages in their societies. Rather, they must learn a spoken (or a written) language or hire an interpreter to accomplish certain things.

The transfer hypothesis: The influence of a first language upon the second

Here we examine the notion of "foreign accent": where it comes from, what it refers to and what it has to do with sign languages. When a person learns a second language, it is frequently obvious that the learner produces second language utterances that are decidedly different from those of native speakers of the second language. In such cases, the learner might be said to have a "foreign accent". What this lay terminology is attempting to express is that the first language of the learner influences his or her production of the second language. This can occur in any area of language (phonology, morphology, syntax, semantics or pragmatics) although it is generally regarded as having to do with phonology.

The notion that the first language of a learner interferes with full acquisition of a second language is known as the "transfer hypothesis" (Ellis, 1986). Despite the fact that the transfer hypothesis is enormously appealing, and has received a great deal of attention from researchers, it is not uncontroversial. It was initially advanced during an era in linguistics when the speakers' production in the second language that deviated from native speaker utterances was thought of as consisting of "errors". In order to explain these errors, researchers hypothesized that the structure of the first language was transferred to the production of the second language. In other words, the structure of the first language caused "interference" (commonly known as "foreign accent") in the second language. A great deal has been written by linguists on the subject of "foreign accent" for spoken language bilinguals. Among various threads of research on transfer are identifying the structure in the first language that is transferred to the second language and investigating attitudes toward speakers with various "foreign accents": some accents are associated with positive attitudes, and other accents are associated with negative attitudes (Lippi-Green, 1997).

In the spoken language literature, "foreign accent" has been characterized contradictorily. It has been said that "foreign accent" results from incomplete acquisition of the phonology of the new language. It has also been claimed that what might sound like a "foreign accent" is a thoroughly legitimate, integral part of a new variety of a language, as Indian English is a variety of English, for example (Kachru, 1992).

In the sign language literature, one source that deals with "interference" arises from the teaching of spoken/written languages to deaf school children. Much of this literature claims that interference from ASL, for example, is carried into the learning of English. More rare are sources that examine "foreign accent" in learners of one sign language who are signers of another sign language. We will examine the few sources available.

Budding *et al.* (1995) showed that native signers of Langue des Signes Québécoise (LSQ) who signed ASL as a second language exhibited interference when they produced ASL. Accent was evident on the syntactic, morphological, lexical and discourse levels. Based on the native intuitions of a Japanese Sign Language (JSL) signer, Mori (1996) pointed out some possible sources of "accent" in the signing of the ASL native signers learning JSL. Hess (1997) attempted to find out whether there was an identifiable "accent" in the signing of native signers of Irish Sign Language (ISL) who were also fluent in ASL. In her study, two Deaf informants were asked to do three tasks. First, they produced a list of signs and short phrases in isolation. Second, they were asked to watch a videotape of native signers producing ASL sentences and then to reproduce the sentences. Third, they were asked to converse freely with the researcher for 10–15 minutes. Videotaped data were reviewed by the researcher and by two native signers of ASL. Hand configuration and orientation were analyzed. The results were that hand configuration presented the greatest number of phonological variations, and it was in this domain that accent seemed to be more prevalent. Orientation revealed much less phonological variation. The two native signers who reviewed the videotapes identified two further areas where phonological variation occurred: during the free conversations both noticed "accent" in fingerspelling, and the "general flow". Hess (1997) did not analyze this further. The study of foreign accent in signers who use one sign language natively and learn a second is of necessity in its infancy (Lucas and Valli, 1992: 35); it is not completely clear what elements of a sign language might correspond to accented pronunciations.

Language shift

Language shift occurs when speakers in a community give up speaking their language and take up the use of another in its place. Language shift has clear (and often devastating) implications for many minority communities, such as Native Americans, many of whose languages are slowly dying as the number of speakers diminishes and those speakers grow old and die. Language shift has been documented in the hearing world with great frequency. It occurs in both immigrant and non-immigrant communities. Immigrants arrive in a new country speaking their language. They may find that the number of reasons to speak their language grows fewer and fewer, and the number of reasons to speak the dominant language grows greater. In non-immigrant communities, language shift may happen very slowly over hundreds of years, but results in the eventual cessation of using a particular language and the replacement with another. Language shift has been characterized as the return of a bilingual state of affairs to a monolingual one (Grosjean, 1982: 38).

In this section, we discuss some perplexing questions raised in Turner (1995) about the phenomenon of language attrition and shift, which, for Turner, occurs when people begin to stop speaking one language and switch to another language, or when the language changes drastically. To be sure, Turner does not expect that deaf people will begin to speak spoken languages and abandon their sign languages, because it is obvious that there is a physiological restriction on this possibility. However, Turner notes that there is reason to suppose that natural sign languages are changing rather drastically as a result of being in close contact with spoken languages. In the case of BSL there are changes as a result of being in close contact with English, a spoken language which is widely used and very powerful indeed.

Couching his observations in the model of "reversing language shift" of Fishman (1991), Turner cites the great proliferation of "contact varieties" being signed (about which more will be said later in this chapter), but also of contact varieties being preferred to natural sign languages. Second, he cites the changes in sign languages that contact varieties are causing. He suggests, from examination of a rather large body of research, that BSL (and, he predicts, other sign languages) is undergoing huge changes, and that perhaps these changes are detrimental to the long term survival of natural sign languages.

Loan vocabulary in spoken languages

For the remainder of this chapter, we focus on outcomes of language contact in sign language situations that produce unique results, unlike what is found in spoken language situations.

In spoken language literature, a very full and captivating research program involves the study of the linguistic results of language contact; that is, what kinds of things happen to languages themselves when they come into persistent contact with other languages. We examine here a few examples and focus mostly on phonology, although it is important to keep in mind that these sorts of phenomena can also take place at the morphological, syntactic, semantic and pragmatic levels.

Generally, languages deal with the words they borrow in two ways. First, a borrowing might obey the phonological constraints of the new language and might therefore change considerably from its original form. Second, a borrowing might not be required to conform to the constraints of the new language and might retain some or all of its original form, with the possible consequence that the loan would remain somewhat outside the phonological system of the new language. A few cases (Japanese, Mandarin, Hausa and Spanish loanwords from English) illustrate how languages require that the new word be restructured to fit the new language.

Japanese and Mandarin have very restricted syllable structures in comparison with English. In fact, each language has as its phonological base a finite set of syllables (113 in Japanese and 398 in Mandarin; De Francis, 1984: 111) which combine with each other, and other phonological material (such as tone in Mandarin) to produce the words of the language. Simplifying details, neither Japanese nor Mandarin can tolerate consonant clusters in the same syllable. English, on the other hand, is a very different sort of language. It has some 8,000 syllables, far more than either Japanese or Mandarin, and its possible syllable structures include some with up to three consonants in the onset of a syllable.

When English words of certain sorts are borrowed into Japanese, one of the classic phonological restructurings that occur is that consonant clusters are broken up with vowels to conform to Japanese syllable structure. Thus, English words like *strike* and *Christmas* are rendered as Japanese loanwords as *sutoraiku* and *kurisimasu*, respectively. And in Mandarin loanwords, the closest Mandarin syllables are chosen to represent the sound of the foreign word faithfully. The Mandarin rendering of the trisyllabic Romanian surname,

Ceausesçu, is represented in pinyin (the Chinese romanization system, and almost a phonetic representation) as *qi ao sai si ku*. Similarly, *Seattle* is *xi ya tu* and *Arizona* is *ya li sang na*. Among the world's languages are some which make use of "tones" to construct words and some which make use of "stress" to construct words. Between languages of these sorts, interesting borrowings occur. Hausa, a language spoken in Nigeria, is a tone language. English is a stress language. Simplifying details, when some English words are borrowed into Hausa, the English syllable with primary stress receives a high tone in Hausa. For example, the following data, with syllable boundaries marked by slashes, all have primary stress in English on the first syllable: *sol/dier*, *par/king*, *chi/sel*, *o/ffice* and *ra/cket*. The Hausa loanword for each receives a high tone for the first syllable in each case, and a low tone for the second syllable in each case: *soo/ja*, *faa/kin*, *cii/zal*, *oo/ffis*, *raa/ket* (Leben, 1996: 142). Latin American varieties of Spanish are in contact with English. In the new Spanish verbs *parquear* ("to park") and *lonchar* ("to eat lunch"), English root words are embedded into Spanish phonology, morphology and orthography.

Cases such as these are plentiful across the world's contact situations. But there are also other possibilities. For example, instead of restructuring a word to some extent to meet the constraints of the new language, in some cases foreign material is borrowed. Two cases – one from Malayalee English and one from English – provide examples.

Malayalee English is one of a number of varieties of Indian English. It is a contact variety between Malayalam, spoken in the state of Kerala, India and English. English possesses the phoneme [f], and Malayalam has neither [f] nor a close equivalent to render English loanwords which contain [f]. Therefore, Malayalee English imports the new phoneme [f] in the loanword for "office" (Mohanan and Mohanan, 1987: 17–19).

English borrowed the phoneme [ʒ] from French. It occurs as the final sound in some pronunciations of words such as *garage* and *beige*. There are a great number of examples of borrowing from many languages besides English. Borrowing is an extremely common and natural occurrence in language contact situations.

"Loan" phenomena in sign language situations

Turning our attention now to sign language situations, it is clear there is a great deal to discuss. First of all, what kinds of language contact can occur? Two sign languages might be in contact or a sign language and a spoken/written language might be in contact. Researchers' attention seems to be concentrated largely in this second area, specifically concerned with the area of how the structure of the sign language is affected by the spoken or written language. Second, we must realize that outcomes of contact situations between sign and spoken languages are not precisely analogous to cases of contact between two spoken languages. It seems reasonably uncontroversial to assert, for example, that *parquear* and *lonchar* are English loanwords in Spanish. However, the sign language cases that seem to parallel these spoken language examples must be dealt with cautiously, as was briefly mentioned in Tervoort (1978: 170–171), Davis (1989) and Lucas and Valli (1989). Lucas and Valli (1992), however, take a closer look at the complexity of the issue. Lucas and Valli argue that the term "borrowing" and the concept of "borrowing" between two spoken languages as compared to between a sign language and a spoken language are not necessarily parallel. They argue that while some possible outcomes of contact between sign and spoken languages are analogous to spoken language situations, some outcomes clearly occur exclusively in sign language situations as described in Lucas and Valli (1992: 26). For example, following an idea originally presented in Lucas and Valli (1989; 1992, especially 25–29), they argue that when signers of one sign language adopt signs from another sign language – for example, place names – this is not necessarily "borrowing". This is because the two sign languages might have exactly the same phonological devices, and the borrowed sign does not therefore have to be restructured (Lucas and Valli, 1992: 28–30). Similarly, following an idea originally proposed by Liddell (personal communication, 1989), Lucas and Valli (1992: 43) argue that "fingerspelled loan signs", so coined in Battison (1978), are not loans at all, because they are not from English, but rather from "the orthographic system used to represent English".

Keeping these cautions in mind, we will discuss several cases of "loan" phenomena. Other phenomena might be studied as well, such as CODA-speak and tty conversations (for other sorts of contact outcomes, see Lucas and Valli, 1992: 26), but for lack of space we leave the reader to explore these for himself or herself.

ASL "fingerspelled loan signs".   Battison (1978) is a rich source of many generalizations about ASL structure, many of which are still being discussed and debated today. This book also makes a significant contribution to the sociolinguistic study of contact situations, describing and analyzing in detail ASL's "fingerspelled loan signs". Battison's work is based on the premise that fingerspelled events were English events. Battison reasoned, then, that a borrowing occurred when these fingerspelled English events took on path movements or other indications that they were being made into signs, that is, borrowed into ASL. He analyzed the structures of 93 "fingerspelled loan signs" such as ASL #EARLY, #NO and #BUS (following the convention in the sign language linguistics literature, fingerspelled loan signs are written in upper case letters preceded by hash). Davis (1989: 97, again, following Liddell, 1989) refuted the notion that a fingerspelled event is essentially an English event. Neither spoken nor written English has any manual handshapes or morphemes to lend, and so, Davis reasoned, fingerspelling was simply a representation of an English event, but not the event itself. He likened it to the English phonological event of pronouncing the letters that are used to spell a Spanish word such as *junta* [jei yu ɛ n ti ei]. Lucas and Valli (1992) also argue against the idea that "fingerspelled loan signs" are borrowings from English to ASL, although it is undeniably the case that there is contact between the English and ASL. Lucas and Valli (1992) point out that loans are generally restructured to fit the new language to some extent, since there could be missing phonemes, differing syllable structures or different intonational structures. But in sign languages, sometimes the borrowing language and the lending language appear to have the same phonological tools at their disposal, such as in the case of signs which have recently been adopted by ASL signers for place names. If Lucas and Valli (1992) are on the right track, then the sign is not restructured at all, but even so, apparently fits seamlessly into the new language. This would be a curious situation indeed if it occurred in a spoken language contact situation.

Fingerspelling in the acquisition of ASL. Acquisition issues have also been examined with respect to contact phenomena in sign languages. For example, Kelly (1995) discusses the acquisition of fingerspelling in a young deaf child of deaf parents. The parents used ASL to communicate with the child who had been exposed to fingerspelling since shortly after her birth. Kelly analyzed videotaped interactions of the parents with the child. Her research turned up some interesting findings. First, the child fingerspelled to herself at age two. This finding accords with others in the literature. Second, the child invented a fingerspelled name for her doll at 30 months (#SILA) which was a name unknown to her or her family, but phonologically consistent with English. The child showed signs of recognizing lexicalized forms which were fingerspelled but she did not necessarily understand the same words when they were just fingerspelled. Examples are RICE (not recognized by the child) and #RICE (easily recognized by the child).

Acceptability and structure of initialized signs in Langue Des Signes Québécoise (LSQ). An interesting line of research (Machabée, 1995; Machabée and Dubuisson, 1995) examines both linguistic and sociolinguistic aspects of a sort of sign which occurs in many sign languages that make use of fingerspelling systems. This is known as initialized signs. Initialized signs are signs which are created partly by using the handshapes which correspond to the first letter of the translation of the sign into a spoken language, in this case, French. These two studies established linguistic criteria on which to decide whether or not a sign in question was indeed an initialized sign. They then tried to ascertain whether deaf Québécois accepted the signs or not. Class 1 signs are "fingerspelling reductions" and Class 2 signs are produced in the LSQ signing space. The researchers found that initialized signs in Class 2 space were less easily accepted, while initialized signs in Class 1 space were more easily accepted. Although they did not carry out a formal study on acceptability of all the possible contact phenomena – such as mouthing and fingerspelling – they did pick up indications that mouthing and fingerspelling (unless it occurs too frequently) seem to be much more acceptable to deaf people than initialized signs.

Syntactic restrictions on BSL fingerspelled loans.   In an interesting paper, Sutton-Spence (1998) reveals a puzzle: in a corpus of 19,450 BSL fingerspellings, a paucity were verbs and a great number were nouns. She notes that this state of affairs obtains in many contact situations. She advances some possible reasons for this. First, she considers class size; namely, that in English nouns constitute 60 percent of the vocabulary, while verbs constitute 14 percent. Naturally then, there are fewer English verbs to borrow. She rejects class size as an explanation because the number of verb loans in BSL is far smaller than 14 percent. Second, length of contact between the two languages is considered: nouns are borrowed before verbs, so perhaps the great number of nouns and the paucity of verbs is due to the fact that the two languages, BSL and English, have not been in contact long enough to have verb borrowings. But Sutton-Spence also rejects this idea, because BSL and English have been in contact for at least 200 years. Finally, she focuses on what she considers a syntactic explanation for the paucity of fingerspelled loan verbs: they have to move through space to add inflection while they are changing handshapes, and this violates BSL phonology.

"Loan" vocabulary from sign languages with "character signs".   Not every sign language makes use of a fingerspelling system. In Taiwan Sign Language (TSL) for example, fingerspelling does not exist. However, another method capable of representing parts of Chinese written language exists in TSL. This system makes use of signs known as "character signs". Essentially, character signs are signs that represent all or part of a Chinese character. They are not plentiful – it is estimated that there are 30–40 character signs in TSL, for example (Smith and Ting, 1979: 29; 1984; Smith, 1989) – but they have very interesting properties. To understand character signs, a little information about Chinese spoken language is needed. A written Chinese character which means "introduce" and is pronounced *jie* (suppressing information about tone which is irrelevant here), has a corresponding character sign as in Figure 3.1. And another character which is pronounced *gong* (again, suppressing irrelevant

Fig. 3.1 Taiwan Sign Language, JIE.

tonal information) has a corresponding character sign as in Figure 3.2. Some characters have character signs in different sign languages, and different sign languages might render the same character in different ways. For example, the sign REN ("person") is signed one way in TSL in southern Taiwan and another way in JSL and northern Taiwan.

Just as we saw that English words must be restructured to become Japanese or Chinese, it seems clear that a character written on paper must be restructured in order to become a sign. This was an insight mentioned in Fok *et al.* (1988). They claim that in Hong Kong Sign Language "as forms are borrowed . . .

Fig. 3.2 Taiwan Sign Language, GONG.

from Chinese script . . . to Chinese Sign Language they undergo radical change to conform to the linguistic constraints that have developed in Chinese Sign Language" (1988: 194). This implies that character signs fit so well into Hong Kong Sign Language that they would be indistinguishable from other signs. However, since character signs are iconic (in the sense that they imitate characters), one might expect their structural properties to differ from those of non-iconic signs. Ann (1998a, 1998b) demonstrates that a close examination of TSL character signs reveals that they conform to some linguistic constraints of TSL and violate others. Violations occur in the phonology of the signs. Character signs, as a group, possess some curious properties. For example, a handshape that does not appear in native TSL signs appears in some character signs. Second, certain handshape combinations that are attested in character signs are never attested in signs in the native lexicon. Third, in two-handed character signs, the point of contact where the two hands touch is unattested in native TSL signs. Finally, in the native lexicon, handedness is not contrastive. This means that a two-handed sign in which the hands have different handshapes and/or movements could be signed by left-handed signers with the left hand dominant, and right-handed signers would produce the sign with the right hand dominant. But both versions would mean the same thing. Character signs do not share all of these properties; rather, each character sign has one and only one property.

Mouthing

Researchers talk in terms of a typology of mouthing behaviors in natural sign languages. First, some mouth configurations have never been thought to have anything to do with the spoken language with which the sign language is almost inevitably in contact. For example, even early descriptions of ASL contained explanations of the mouthing of the adverbials CHA, MM, TH, PAH (Davis, 1989: 93). None of these are English or associated with an English word. But there are other cases in which the mouthing that accompanies the ASL signs LATE, HAVE and FINISH seem to have been borrowed and subsequently lexicalized into ASL by way of mouthing (Davis, 1989: 95–96).

There is, however, another sort of mouthing of concern here: mouthing which, although fully integrated into a sign language, seems to result from the contact between a sign language and a spoken language (Lucas and Valli, 1992: 78–79). For example, Davis (1989) notes that there is such a thing as English mouthing, and that there is also reduced English mouthing for signers of ASL. His data show examples of full mouthing, such as for MOST HOUSEHOLDS (while the interpreter signed MOST #US HOME) (Davis, 1989: 94). Reduced English mouthing occurred in the case of the interpreter signing MANY PEOPLE KNOW NAME, while what was mouthed was MA, PE, KNO, NM (Davis, 1989: 94). Mouthing behavior is not rare. It has been observed in many European sign languages, including Italian Sign Language (Padden, 1991), Sign Language of the Netherlands (Schermer, 1990), British Sign Language (Turner *et al.*, 1998) and German Sign Language (Ebbinghaus and Hessman, 1996).

Pidgins and creoles

One of the most compelling areas of sociolinguistics is the study of pidgins and creoles. Pidgins are languages which result "from colonial expansion ... which have evolved from master–servant type of contact between speakers of European tongues and speakers of so-called 'exotic' languages" (Todd, 1984: 12). The conditions under which a pidgin could arise are very special. Among them are that the groups of speakers among whom the pidgin develops do not share the same language, and the speakers need to communicate for a restricted set of reasons. The native languages of each group are regarded as widely disparate in status and there is little access to native speakers of the European language. Not all pidgins are based on English, but some 60 English-based pidgins currently exist in the world. Given the description of the circumstances under which pidgins develop, it should not be too surprising that a pidgin characteristically has some vocabulary and some syntactic structures from the language of the socially dominant group, and some from the languages of the non-dominant groups. Pidgins are typically restricted in form and in function. They, and their speakers, are often looked down upon.

If contact between the groups among whom the pidgin develops remains superficial – that is, if no demands are put on the pidgin to be able to be used for additional purposes – then the pidgin never expands grammatically, and it remains a limited and restricted communication system. When the groups of people who speak the pidgin are no longer in contact, it falls out of use and dies. Pidgins are often short lived: they tend to die when the need for them dies (Todd, 1984: 3). Such was the case with the American soldiers and the Vietnamese who created a pidgin that ceased to be spoken with the end of the Vietnam war. But in certain spoken language situations in which there is sustained contact between multilingual communities, it is sometimes the case that a pidgin becomes useful to its speakers and continues to expand to fit all the communication needs of its speakers. When this happens, a pidgin is said to be stabilized. Sometimes a stabilized pidgin becomes the native language of speakers who find it useful; in this case it becomes a creole. The native speakers of a creole are children, and they play a crucial role in its development, expanding the creole along both linguistic and sociolinguistic dimensions. That is, a creole's linguistic properties and sociolinguistic uses change; it begins to expand its grammar and lexicon, as its speakers use it for ever-increasing social purposes. The end product of the process of creolization is a full-fledged language. Todd (1984: 16) explains that Creole Englishes usually develop in countries in which Standard English is an official language. Such situations are usually not described as having two completely separate languages: Standard English and a creole in which the standard English sentence *the boy shouted* would be *di man pikin dEm bin hala*. Rather, in such societies, the proposition *the boy shouted* can be made in any of varied ways, such as the following:

di bɔi dEm bin hala, di bɔi dEm bin shaut, di bɔiz dEm bin hala, di bɔiz dEm hala, di bɔiz hala, di bɔiz halad (from Todd, 1984)

Sociolinguists have made puzzling observations about pidgins and creoles. For example, although pidgins have features (such as vocabulary, syntactic structures, etc.) of the languages in contact, they also have features that belong to none of the languages in contact. Furthermore, sociolinguists have pointed out that the world's pidgins and creoles look more like each other than they look like the languages that were in contact to create them.

Armed with the knowledge of spoken language situations, early sign language researchers began to believe that a pidgin was being created between ASL and English in the USA. Its features were described in work such as Woodward (1973c) and Reilly and McIntire (1980), and it was referred to as Pidgin Sign English (PSE). Woodward (1973c) pointed out linguistic features of PSE in four areas: articles, plurality, copula and aspect. PSE was said to have "variable use of articles" (Woodward, 1973c: 41), while ASL does not have articles and English does have articles. Plurality in PSE was acknowledged to have some of ASL's noun reduplication, and does not generally use a marker to represent English 's'. The PSE copula was said to be the ASL sign TRUE. Although Woodward's (1973c) research led him to believe that there were many parallels between the "pidgin" he was seeing and other pidgins, Reilly and McIntire (1980: 152) were more circumspect: they claimed that despite the label "Pidgin Signed English" this variety of sign language "differs from most pidgins in important ways". For example, they pointed out that the linguistic features of PSE were too complex to be those of a pidgin. And Cokely (1983: 11, 20, cited in Lucas and Valli 1992: 19) points out that the conditions for development of a pidgin are not met in the case of PSE. Eventually, the notion that a pidgin between ASL and English existed in the USA was seriously challenged in Lucas and Valli (1992). Among their criticisms of this idea is that neither the social conditions for a pidgin nor the linguistic features of pidgins exist in the American Deaf community. Lucas and Valli (1992) do not claim that there is not language contact between ASL and English, rather that the outcome of this contact is not a pidgin. They refer to this outcome as "contact signing" – neither English nor ASL, but the creation of a third system. Lucas and Valli (1992) shed light on a behavior that was assumed unequivocally to exist in the Deaf community in the USA, namely that deaf Americans sign ASL with other deaf Americans and that they switch to contact signing with hearing people. That claim was seriously challenged by Lucas and Valli's work; among other things, they found that some signers use ASL with both deaf and hearing interlocutors, and that sometimes deaf people switched from ASL to contact signing in the presence of deaf researchers. Lucas and Valli (1992: 38) also noted that natural sign languages have structural similarities; that is, that they are, indeed, structured more like each other than unlike each other.

Another relevant line of questioning should also be discussed here. It has been argued that ASL was originally a creole about 200 years ago. It has been argued that it was created when the signers of the American mainland and the signers of French methodical signs met (J. Woodward, 1978). But Fischer (1978), citing many examples of ASL grammatical features, claims that ASL still looks like a creole. She claims that in every generation deaf children recreolize ASL due to the fact that most of them don't learn ASL from deaf parents but, rather, from other sources. Among these are hearing parents who may sign a sort of "pidgin sign English" (and not ASL) with their children, which the children creolize. Fischer (1996) supports her view of creolization by citing evidence from the number systems of ASL and French Sign Language (LSF).

Code switching and code mixing

While borrowing is generally regarded as the integration of an item from one language into a new language, code switching and code mixing are quite different. Both refer to a complete switch from one language to another without integration into the first language. Although these definitions are somewhat controversial, generally, code switching is defined as occurring across the borders of a sentence. Code mixing is defined as occurring within a sentence (Lucas and Valli, 1992: 34). An example of code switching follows. In this conversation, a group of Mandarin speakers are discussing finishing a basement. A free translation of Mandarin appears in parentheses:

> *Speaker A*: Zhèi gè cái jǐ qīan yúan jiù kéyǐ wán chén le.
> ("It's only several thousand dollars to finish.")
> *Speaker B*: Hěn guì a!
> ("Very expensive!")
> *Speaker A*: Bù, zhèi ge bú gùi-jiaò ní zhàng fū, "if you want to finish it, take a summer job!"
> ("No, it's not expensive – tell your husband), 'if you want to finish it, take a summer job!' "

Notice that the switch from Mandarin to English occurs at a sentence boundary. Examples of code mixing of Mandarin–English bilinguals follow. In (1) through (7) the speakers introduce English nouns into Mandarin sentences, while in (8) an English verb is introduced and in (9) an adjective is introduced:

1. Huàn yí gè muffler.   ("Change the muffler/Get a new muffler.")
2. Ní yǒu bù yǒu cellular phone?   ("Do you have a cellular phone?")
3. Níde phone number shì shenme?   ("What's your phone number?")
4. Ní mǎile house méiyǒu?   ("Did you buy your house?")
5. Ní gěi wǒ yí gè call.   ("Give me a call.")
6. Wǒ zhūle yí taò apartment.   ("I rented an apartment.")
7. Zhèi gè yǒu shenme difference?   ("How is this different?")
8. Ní call wǒ!   ("Call me!")
9. Ní shì Chinese ma?   ("Are you Chinese?")

Spoken language situations of this sort have been well documented. Code switching and code mixing behavior is well attested among hearing bilinguals. Interested readers might begin with Kachru (1992) and references cited there.

Turning our attention now to sign language situations, we note that the only ones described so far are those that involve a sign and a spoken language. This fact confounds matters since, as Lucas and Valli (1992) mention, if we were to follow the criteria for code switching and code mixing for spoken languages exactly, what code switching would mean is that a bilingual stops signing and starts speaking at a sentence boundary. Code mixing would mean that, within a sentence, a bilingual stops signing and starts speaking a word or phrase. But this does not describe what occurs in the contact situation between, say, ASL and English. This is because what is described for spoken languages is clearly sequential. That is, in code mixing a bilingual is speaking a sentence of one language and adds a word or phrase from another, but the switch to the other language and back to English necessarily occurs in a sequential order. So, for example, the sentence uttered by a Mandarin–English bilingual, "Is it 'convenience' – ma?" is basically English. The bilingual is trying to find out if one synonym for a particular English word is "convenience" and adds the Mandarin *yes–no* question marker *ma* to the end of her English sentence. Crucially, the elements of both English and Mandarin are sequentially ordered. In the sign language contact situation they studied, however, Lucas and Valli (1992) note that the situation was very different. Although the term "code mixing" (rather than code switching) more accurately describes sign language contact cases, even code mixing is misleading because it implies sequentiality. They found that the

phonological, morphological, syntactic, lexical and pragmatic features of two different languages are most often produced *simultaneously*, [so] assigning stretches of discourse to ASL or to English seems like a fruitless exercise and also misses the point. The point *is* [the creation of] a third system which combines elements of both languages and may also have some idiosyncratic data. Lucas and Valli (1992: 108)

One thing that remains clear is that contact signing is abundant in sign language contact situations, just as code mixing and code switching are abundant in spoken language contact situations. And although cases of code mixing and code switching between two sign languages have not yet been examined by researchers, it certainly takes place.

Conclusions

In this chapter, we have discussed a variety of language contact phenomena in both spoken language and sign language communities. The typology and distribution of bilingualism in both worlds was discussed, and we saw that in this area in general, outcomes are largely parallel in spoken language and sign language situations. The remainder of the chapter described outcomes which are unique to sign language situations. The creation of "loan" vocabulary was examined in two sorts of languages: those with fingerspelling, and those without fingerspelling but with a form of representing written language called "character signs". The mouthing that occurs in sign languages which is connected to speech was discussed, as was the mouthing that has never been claimed to have anything to do with speech. Finally, pidgins and creoles, and their relevance to sign language research, were discussed as were the phenomena of code switching and code mixing.

Suggested readings

Readers are invited to examine all the references included throughout this chapter. On the general issue of bilingualism and biculturalism in Deaf communities, readers should consult Grosjean (1992; 1996) and references cited there. Anyone interested in language contact with the outcome of creation of "loan" words should certainly include Battison (1978) since the position put forward there was influential and went without question for a number of years. For more recent ideas about language contact, Davis (1989), Lucas and Valli (1989) and especially Lucas and Valli (1992) are essential reading. Lucas and Valli (1992) should be regarded as a basic text in the area of language contact. In it are contained seeds for future research in many areas. On the issue of language shift, Turner's work (1995) would be of great use.

Exercises

1. (a) For each example, explain what is happening in terms of the contact phenomena described in this chapter. Say as much as you can about each example.

English	Mandarin
microphone	maì kè fēng
taxi	dē sì
internet	yīn tè wǎng
That's the connection I have.	*That's my guānxī.*
There's no discrimination.	Méiyoǔ zhèi gè *discrimination.*

(b) Observe deaf bilinguals signing together. What is their signing like? Are there "borrowed" items? If so, what exactly is "borrowed"? Make a list (or a videotape) of all the signs you suspect to be "loans". Are there any examples in your data which are better explained as code switching or code mixing?

2. Examine the following children's poem from Todd (1984: 275). It is an example of Tok Pisin, a creole currently spoken in Papua New Guinea. Translate it:

> dis smɔl swain i bin go fɔ maket
> dis smɔl swain i bin stei fɔhaus
> dis smɔl swain i bin chop sup witi fufu
> dis smɔl swain i bin chɔp no nɔting
> an dis smɔl swain i bin go wi, wi stei fɔhaus

3. How would you characterize the sign language situation in your country, if there is one, in terms of its bilingualism? Explain as much as you can. Does it resemble Canada, Belgium, Singapore or Switzerland, or does it have features of each of these countries? Are there features of Martha's Vineyard, Desa Kolok or the Yucatec Mayan village? Would you say there is a diglossia? What are the features of the Deaf community's bilingualism?

4. The Singaporean deaf person who wrote the fax quoted at the beginning of this chapter had several serious questions about language contact in her country. Based on what you have learned in this chapter, write a sample answer to her fax.

4   Sociolinguistic variation

Ceil Lucas, Robert Bayley, Clayton Valli, Mary Rose and Alyssa Wulf

[George Trager and Henry Lee Smith] insisted that language could not be studied by itself, in isolation, but must be looked at in direct connection to the people who used it, the things they used it to talk about, and the view of the world that using it imposed on them.

Stokoe (1994: 333)

Language varies both in space and in time, as well as according to the linguistic environment in which a form is used. For example, the American Sign Language (ASL) sign DEAF[1] has three possible forms. It can be produced with a movement from ear to chin (the citation or dictionary form), with a movement from chin to ear, or simply by contacting the cheek once (both non-citation forms). Even though the form of DEAF varies from signer to signer and even within the signing of the same signer, the variation we observe is far from random. Rather, signers' choices among the three forms of DEAF are systematically constrained by a range of factors at both the linguistic and the social levels. Thus, compared to signers in other parts of the USA, signers in Boston, Massachusetts tend to be quite conservative in the choice of a form of DEAF. In contrast, signers in Kansas, Missouri and Virginia tend to prefer non-citation forms. Indeed, a recent study conducted by three of the authors of this chapter showed that signers in these states used non-citation forms of DEAF 85 percent of the time, more than twice the rate of signers in Boston (Bayley *et al.*, 2000; Lucas *et al.*, 2001).

The region of the country where a signer lives is not the only factor that affects the choice of a form of DEAF. For example, although ASL signers in Boston generally used more citation forms of DEAF than signers in other areas of the USA, Boston signers aged 55 and over were far less likely to choose a non-citation form of DEAF than were younger signers. Bayley *et al.* (2000) reported that Boston signers aged 55 and over used the citation form of DEAF 76 percent of the time. In contrast, signers aged between 26 and 54 used the citation form only 54 percent of the time, and signers aged between 15 and 25 used the citation form only 46 percent of the time. In addition, variation can be affected by linguistic factors. To continue with the example of DEAF, Lucas (1995) and

61

Bayley *et al.* (2000) found that signers were very likely to use a non-citation form of DEAF when it was part of a compound, as in DEAF∧CULTURE or DEAF∧WORLD. However, when DEAF was a predicate adjective, as in PRO.1 DEAF ("I am deaf"), signers were likely to choose the citation form.

As the example of variation in the form of DEAF shows, choices among variable linguistic forms are affected both by *social* (e.g. region, age) and by *linguistic* (e.g. grammatical class) factors or constraints. In this chapter, we review the study of language variation, with particular emphasis on the insights that such study can provide into language structure and social relations. We pay special attention to the many intersecting social factors that can influence variation and to the kinds of linguistic units and processes that vary in sign and spoken languages. We conclude with a detailed examination of three studies that represent some of the different types of research on variation in sign languages.

The study of linguistic variation

We begin our discussion of linguistic variation by examining the concept of the "sociolinguistic variable". This leads to an examination of the kinds of units that can be variable in spoken languages and the processes that govern variation. Although our interest in this chapter is primarily sign languages, research on spoken language has provided much of the framework within which research on variation in sign languages has been conducted.

The sociolinguistic variable

Several researchers have offered useful explanations of the concept of a *sociolinguistic variable*. Drawing upon the work of Labov (1972a; 1972b), Fasold characterized the sociolinguistic variable as "a set of alternative ways of saying the same thing, although the alternatives will have social significance" (1990: 223–224). Lesley Milroy referred to the "bits of language" that "are associated with sex, area and age subgroups in an extremely complicated way" (1987b: 131), the "bits of language" being sociolinguistic variables. She defined a sociolinguistic variable as "a linguistic element (phonological usually, in practice) which co-varies not only with other linguistic elements, but also with a number of extra-linguistic independent social variables such as social class, age, sex, ethnic group or contextual style" (1987b: 10). Wolfram defined a linguistic variable as a "convenient construct employed to unite a class of fluctuating variants within some specified language set" (1991: 23). He drew the distinction between a linguistic variable, which has to do with variation within a language, and a sociolinguistic variable, a construct which unifies the correlation of internal variables and external constraints. Internal variables are the features of a linguistic nature – a sound, a handshape, a syntactic structure – that vary.

External constraints are the factors of a social nature that may correlate with the behavior of the linguistic variable.

Variable units in spoken languages

Linguists generally accept that spoken languages are composed of segments of sound produced by the vocal apparatus and that these segments are themselves composed of a variety of features. In spoken languages, whole segments or features of segments may be variable. For example, a word-final voiced consonant may be devoiced, a non-nasal vowel may acquire the feature of nasalization, and vowels may vary from their canonical position and be raised or lowered within the vowel space.

A new segment may also be created from the features of other segments, as often happens in palatalization. Individual segments may be variably added or deleted, and syllables (that is, groups of segments) can be added or deleted. Parts of segments, whole segments, or groups of segments can also be variably re-arranged, as we see with metathesis in English, in the variable pronunciations *hundred* and *hunderd*.

Variation may also be seen in word-sized combinations of segments or in combinations of words. In lexical variation, we find separate morphemes for the same concept, and use of these separate morphemes correlates with non-linguistic categories such as region, ethnicity and gender. But we may also see syntactic variation characterized by the deletion of whole morphemes or by the variable position of whole morphemes.

Variation is also present in units of discourse (i.e. units consisting of many words), as in variation in text type or in lists used in narratives (Schiffrin, 1994). What varies in spoken languages, then, may range from the features of a segment to a discourse unit that consists of many segments, from the very smallest unit we can identify to the largest.

It is evident even to a casual observer that people vary in their use of linguistic forms. At the level of phonology, speakers of English sometimes pronounce the progressive morpheme ING with the apical variant /n/, as in *workin'*, and sometimes with the velar nasal /ŋ/ (Fischer, 1958; Trudgill, 1974; Houston, 1991). Speakers of all dialects of English also sometimes delete the final /t/ in words such as *mist* in *mist by the lake* and sometimes pronounce it *mis*, as in *mis/t/ my bus* (Shuy *et al.*, 1968; Labov *et al.*, 1968; Guy, 1980; Labov, 1997; Roberts, 1997). It is important to note here that what is being deleted may be a morpheme, i.e. a segment with independent meaning, as in *mis/t/*. Numerous studies have shown that language varies at the level of morphology. For example, speakers of many English dialects variably use third person singular verbal -*s*, as in *he want/he wants* (Poplack and Tagliamonte, 1989; Godfrey and Tagliamonte, 1999), while learners of English as a second language exhibit great variability in the extent to which they mark past-reference verbs for tense (Bayley, 1994b).

Language also varies at the level of syntax. Speakers of Spanish and many other languages as well as ASL signers, for example, sometimes use an overt subject pronoun and sometimes omit it (Poplack, 1979; Cameron, 1993; Wulf *et al.*, 1999), as shown in (1), from Spanish, and (2), from ASL:

1. Yo/Ø quiero ir a la playa.
   "I want to go to the beach."
2. PRO.1/Ø WANT MEET PRO.3
   "I want to meet him/her."

In addition, in English, the alternation between pied-piped relative pronouns and stranded prepositions provides a convenient example of syntactic variation (Guy and Bayley, 1995), for example:

3. (a) To whom did you give the money?
   (b) Who(m) did you give the money to?

Furthermore, as Poplack (1980), Lucas and Valli (1992), Zentella (1997) and others have shown, language users vary in their choice of code. Thus, ASL signers sometimes alternate between ASL and Signed English and many bilingual speakers alternate between two (or more) languages in the same discourse and often even within the same sentence; for example:

4. (a) *La* security *viene pa' chequear el* building.
   "Security comes to check the building."
   (b) PRO.1 NOT SAY-ING 100 PERCENT SUPPORT, NO . . .
   "I'm not saying 100% support, no . . .", with a sign produced for the suffix -ing and continuous English mouthing.

Variable processes in spoken languages

These examples lead us to ask what kinds of *processes* are involved in spoken language variation. Our discussion here takes its departure from Wolfram's (1991; 1993) work on variation in spoken languages. One set of processes involved in variation has to do with the phonological component of a language. For example, variation may be the result of the process of assimilation, such as vowel nasalization or consonant gemination. Variation may result from weakening, as in vowel or consonant deletion. We may see variation resulting from the processes of substitution or addition of elements, as with coalescence (the creation of a new segment from two other segments), metathesis (the re-arranging of the order of segments or features of segments) or epenthesis (the addition of a segment). Variation may result from analogy, as in the generalization of third person singular -*s* to other present tense forms of a verb in English or, conversely, the deletion of third person singular -*s* by analogy with all other verb forms in a given paradigm.

As we see from the examples, other processes involved with variation may have to do with the morphosyntactic structure of a language. For example, variation may have to do with the process of the co-occurrence of items in syntactic structure. We examine negative concord in English more closely below, whereby some varieties allow the co-occurrence of more than one negative element while other varieties disallow such co-occurrence. Another process involved in variation at the syntactic level concerns permutation of items within sentences. The variable placement of adverbs in English provides a convenient example:

5. (a) *Quickly*, John ran to the door.
   (b) John *quickly* ran to the door.
   (c) John ran *quickly* to the door.
   (d) John ran to the door *quickly*.

Internal constraints. This brings us to what the internal constraints on variation might be in spoken languages. Recall that internal constraints on variation are features within the immediate linguistic environment that may play some role in the occurrence of variation. Wolfram (personal communication, 1994) has stated that the internal constraints on variables may be compositional, sequential, functional, or having to do with structural incorporation. Compositional constraints are those that have to do with the linguistic nature of the variable itself. For example, Wolfram (1989) studied final nasal absence in the speech of three-year-old African American children. He found that final alveolar nasals were much more likely to be absent than either velar or bilabial nasals. A sequential constraint has to do with the role of an element occurring in the same sequence as the variable, either preceding or following it. For example, the final consonant in a word-final consonant cluster is more likely to be deleted if the following segment is another consonant than if it is a vowel. Functional constraints relate to the function of the variable. For example, as explained above, the final consonant in a word-final consonant cluster may function as a past tense morpheme, and that function may influence the frequency of deletion of this consonant. Finally, the constraint of structural incorporation concerns the syntactic environment in which a variable finds itself. For example, copula deletion in African American Vernacular English (AAVE) is more likely in a construction with *gonna* (e.g. *He is gonna do it* / *He gonna do it*) than in one in which the copula is followed by a noun phrase (e.g. *He is my brother* / *He my brother*).

External constraints. External constraints on variation include demographic factors such as region, age, race, gender and socioeconomic level, all factors that have been shown to co-vary with linguistic factors. Co-variance here means that a correlation can be seen between the behavior of a linguistic variable and social factors, so that working-class speakers use more of a variable than middle-class speakers, or African American speakers use a particular variable less than white speakers, and so forth. These correlations make the variation sociolinguistic. Earlier studies of both spoken and sign languages focused on a fairly limited inventory of demographic factors such as those listed above but, as Wolfram (1997) points out, more recent studies have focused on the nature of communication networks (L. Milroy, 1987a), the dynamics of situational context (Biber and Finegan, 1993) and the projection of social identity (LePage and Tabouret-Keller, 1985), "in an effort to describe more authentically the social reality of dialect in society" (Wolfram, 1997: 116). That is, researchers have realized that the external constraints on variation are more complex than they thought. They may certainly include the more discrete factors such as region and socioeconomic level, but other factors such as who a person interacts with on a daily basis and a person's desire to project a particular identity to others may also play a central role in constraining variation.

For students of language variation, the examples given above, as well as the many other examples that could be given, raise important questions. Is the variation that we observe in all human languages systematic? If the observed variation is, indeed, systematic, what are the linguistic and social factors that condition a signer's or a speaker's choice among variable linguistic forms? What does the patterning of linguistic and social factors reveal about the underlying grammar of the language under investigation? Are the patterns that we observe stable or are they the result of ongoing linguistic change? What does linguistic variation reveal about the social structure of the community to which users of the language belong? Finally, what can the study of linguistic variation reveal about the similarities and differences between sign and spoken languages? Is variation in sign languages subject to the same kinds of processes as variation in spoken languages? Are there processes that are unique to sign languages? Are there processes that operate only in spoken languages? Although many outstanding questions remain, particularly with respect to sign languages, after nearly four decades of research on linguistic variation we are in a position to answer the questions posed in this paragraph with considerable confidence, as we show in the following sections.

Linguistic variation in spoken languages

Early studies of variation in spoken languages

A number of studies of linguistic variation were undertaken before the full development of sociolinguistics as a field in the 1960s. One of the earliest studies was conducted by Gauchat (1905), who correlated changing linguistic features in the French of Charmey, Switzerland with the age and gender of the speakers. Somewhat later, Fischer (1958) studied the variable use of *-in'* and *-ing* in the speech of New England children. He found that *-ing* was associated with formal situations such as testing and *-in'* with informal interviews. In addition, he found that girls tended to use a greater percentage of the standard form than boys, who typically preferred the *-in'* form. Finally, Fischer noted differences between the speech of "model boys", children who excelled in school and were favored by their teachers, and "typical boys", who were physically strong and domineering. As we might expect, the *-ing* form predominated in the speech of the "model boys", while the *-in'* form predominated in the speech of the "typical boys".

Labov's (1972a) study of language change on the island community of Martha's Vineyard, Massachusetts marks the transition between early studies of linguistic variation and the development of modern variationist sociolinguistics. Labov studied changes in the pronunciation of the diphthongs (ay) and (aw)[2] in words such as *spider, pie, fry, mow* and *outhouse*. These variables were selected because they met the three criteria that Labov had established for a variable to be a useful focus of investigation:

First, we want an item that is frequent, which occurs so often in the course of undirected natural conversation that its behavior can be charted from unstructured contexts and brief interviews. Secondly, it should be structural: the more the item is integrated into a larger system of functioning units, the greater will be the intrinsic linguistic interest of our study. Third, the distribution of the features should be highly stratified: that is, preliminary explorations should suggest an asymmetric distribution over a wide range of age levels or other ordered strata of society. (1972b: 8)

On the basis of interviews with slightly more than one percent of the permanent population, stratified by age, ethnicity, occupation and area of residence, Labov found that islanders with the most positive attitudes toward Martha's Vineyard centralized the onsets of these diphthongs most frequently. Speakers with neutral or negative attitudes centralized them much less frequently, preferring instead the pronunciation common among the mainlanders who vacation on the island every summer. The correlation between centralization and attitude towards life on the island can be seen clearly in Table 4.1. Labov concluded that "when a man says [rəɪt] or [həʊs], he is unconsciously establishing the fact that he belongs to the island, that he is one of the natives to whom the island belongs" (1972b: 36).

Large-scale urban studies

Later in the 1960s, Labov in New York (1966b) and Shuy *et al.* (1968) and Wolfram (1969) in Detroit carried out studies of sociolinguistic variation on a much larger scale than Labov's original study on Martha's Vineyard. These

Table 4.1 *Centralization and orientation toward Martha's Vineyard*

Persons	Attitude	(ay)	(aw)
40	Positive	63	62
19	Neutral	32	42
6	Negative	9	8

Source: Labov, 1972b: 39.

large-scale urban studies established the systematic nature of a great deal of linguistic variation that had previously been thought to be random, or "free". To illustrate the types of factors that have been shown to influence variation, we will briefly examine three variables: /r/ in New York City, and multiple negation and final consonant cluster reduction in Detroit African American English.

Labov (1966b) studied variation in New York City English in a representative sample of residents of the city's Lower East Side. Among the variables he investigated was the presence or absence of post-vocalic (r) in words such as "guard". Although "(r)-lessness" is characteristic of some prestige dialects of English, including upper-class British English, in New York the (r)-less variant is associated with socially stigmatized lower-class speech.

Labov's investigation showed that variation in the pronunciation of post-vocalic (r) was strongly correlated with speech style and social class. The data included samples of five speech styles, designed to represent a continuum from a style in which speakers paid the greatest amount of attention to form to a style in which speakers attended only minimally if at all to form: minimal pairs, for example, "god" [gɔːd] and "guard" [gɔɹd], a word list, a reading passage, interview speech and casual speech. The analysis of this extensive corpus of data showed that the more speakers attended to their speech, the more likely they were to pronounce post-vocalic (r). Conversely, the more speakers attended to the content of their speech rather than the form, the less likely they were to pronounce (r). Moreover, in each speech style, middle-class speakers were more likely to pronounce (r) than working-class speakers, who in turn were more likely to pronounce (r) than lower-class speakers. That is, the pronunciation of post-vocalic (r) showed clear social stratification. Table 4.2 shows the results for three social classes and five speech styles. These same results are displayed graphically in Figure 4.1.

These data show that lower-class, working-class and middle-class speakers pronounce post-vocalic (r) at different rates. However, speakers of all three social classes may be regarded as members of the same speech community because they are all affected in the same way by an increase in the level of

Table 4.2 *(r) indices for three social classes in five styles in New York City*

| | Class | | |
Style	Lower class	Working class	Middle class
Minimal pairs	50.5	45.0	30.0
Word list	76.5	65.0	44.5
Reading passage	85.5	79.0	71.0
Interview style	89.5	87.5	75.0
Casual speech	97.5	96.0	87.5

Source: Labov, 1966a, cited in Chambers, 1995.

formality and hence in the amount of attention paid to speech. That is, the more careful the style, the more likely they are to use the more prestigious form. Conversely, the less careful the style, the less likely they are to use the prestige form. Thus, New Yorkers, regardless of social class, can be said to subscribe to

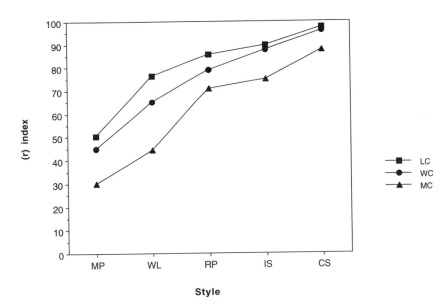

Fig. 4.1   *(r) indices for three social classes in five styles in New York City*
Source: Labov, 1966a, cited in Chambers, 1995.
Notes: (r)-index measures (r)-less variants. MP - minimal pairs; WL - word list; RP - reading passage; IS - interview style; CS - careful speech. LC- lower class; WC - working class; MC - middle class.

a common set of linguistic norms, and it is precisely these common linguistic norms that define a speech community in Labov's terms:

The speech community is not defined by any marked agreement in the use of language elements, so much as by participation in a set of shared norms: these norms may be observed in overt types of evaluative behavior, and by the uniformity of abstract patterns of variation which are invariant in respect to particular levels of usage. (1972b: 120–121)

Numerous studies conducted in cities around the world might serve to illustrate the relationship between use of variable linguistic forms and social structure. These studies range from Harlem in New York City, USA (Labov, 1969b; 1972a), Norwich, UK (Trudgill, 1974) and Rio de Janeiro, Brazil (Guy, 1981) to Appalachia, USA (Wolfram and Christian, 1976) and Compton, California, USA (Baugh, 1983). Recent work includes studies of communities ranging from Kingston, Jamaica (Patrick, 1999) and San Juan, Puerto Rico (Cameron, 1998) to Canterbury, New Zealand (Maclagan *et al.*, 1999) and Xining, China (Dede, 1999). Thus, we might have chosen a large number of examples from a wide variety of languages to further illustrate the relationship between use of variable linguistic forms and social structure and the effects of linguistic factors on patterns of variation. However, we shall confine ourselves to two examples, both from African American speakers in Detroit.

Multiple negation in Detroit.   In English, double, or multiple, negation (*He don't want none* vs. *He doesn't want any*) is a well established and stable sociolinguistic variable. Although every child who has attended school in the English-speaking world is presumably told at some point (or at many points) that use of more than one negative in a clause is ungrammatical, and, by false analogy to mathematics, that two negatives make a positive, people persist in saying things like *He don't got none*. Wolfram's (1969) pioneering study of African American English provides a convenient example of the social distribution of this widespread variable. His results, by social class and gender, taken from a large and representative sample, are shown in Table 4.3.

As in the case of (r) in New York City, use of multiple negation by Detroit African Americans is stratified by social class. Thus, upper middle-class men

Table 4.3 *Percentage of multiple negation in Detroit African American English by gender and social class*

	Upper middle	Lower middle	Upper working	Lower working
Male	10.4	22.3	68.2	81.3
Female	6.0	2.4	41.2	74.3

Source: Wolfram, 1969: 162.

use multiple negation only 10.4 percent of the time that they could use multiple negation. In sharp contrast, lower working-class men use multiple negation more than 80 percent of the time. The situation with women is similar. In Wolfram's data, multiple negation is rare in the speech of middle-class women. Lower working-class women, however, use multiple negatives 74.3 percent of the time.

Wolfram's study of African American speech in Detroit confirms Labov's (1966b) work in New York with respect to showing that use of variable linguistic forms is correlated with social class. Table 4.3 also shows a clear gender difference. Not only is use of double and multiple negatives associated with social class, but it is also associated with gender. Although men and some women of all social classes sometimes use multiple negatives, women use fewer multiple negatives than men of the same class.

Like the pattern for social stratification shown for (r)-lessness in New York and multiple negation in Detroit, the gender difference revealed by Wolfram's study has been replicated (see, for example, Trudgill, 1974; Milroy and Milroy, 1978).

The case of -t,d *deletion.*   Final consonant cluster reduction, usually restricted to -*t,d* deletion (the pronunciation of words such as *kind, mist* and *west*, as *kin'*, *mis'* and *wes'*) is among the best-documented variable processes in English. In fact, Patrick refers to -*t,d* deletion as a "showcase variable" (1999: 122). Among the varieties in which -*t,d* deletion has been studied are AAVE (Labov *et al.*, 1968; Wolfram and Fasold, 1974; Baugh, 1983), Chicano and Tejano English (Santa Ana, 1992; Bayley, 1994a; 1997), Jamaican Creole (Patrick, 1999), Philadelphia and New York white English (Guy, 1980; Labov 1989) and Lumbee English (the dialect spoken by the Lumbee Indians of North Carolina) (Wolfram *et al.*, 2000), to name just a few. Final cluster reduction has been of enduring interest to linguists because it occurs at the intersection of phonological and grammatical processes and thus provides a convenient testing ground for linguistic theories (for a review see Labov, 1997: 148–151).

Research has shown that -*t,d* deletion is affected by multiple aspects of the linguistic environment, including syllable stress, the features of the segments that precede and follow -*t,d*, and the grammatical function of the word in which -*t,d* appears. Moreover, although speakers of different dialects delete -*t,d* at very different rates, speakers of most English dialects exhibit remarkable cross-dialectical consistency in the effects of particular factors (for a summary of pan-English constraints, see Labov, 1989: 92). For example, as we have seen above, speakers of most English dialects are more likely to delete -*t,d* when it is part of a word stem, for example *the band played on*, than when it is a past tense morpheme, for example, *they bann/d/ publication of the results*. Speakers are also more likely to delete -*t,d* when it is followed by another consonant,

Table 4.4 *Percentages of* -t,d *deletion in Detroit African American English by linguistic environment and social class*

	Social class			
Environments	Upper middle	Lower middle	Upper working	Lower working
Following vowel				
-*t,d* is past morpheme (e.g. "missed in")	7	13	24	34
-*t,d* is not past morpheme (e.g. "mist in")	28	43	65	72
Following consonant				
-*t,d* is past morpheme (e.g. "missed by")	49	62	73	76
-*t,d* is not past morpheme (e.g. "mist by")	79	87	94	97

Source: Wolfram and Fasold 1974: 132.

for example *mist by the lake*, than when it is followed by a vowel, for example *mist in the morning*. That is, -*t,d* deletion is conditioned by both grammatical and phonological factors. An example, from Wolfram's early work in Detroit, is shown in Table 4.4 and Figure 4.2.

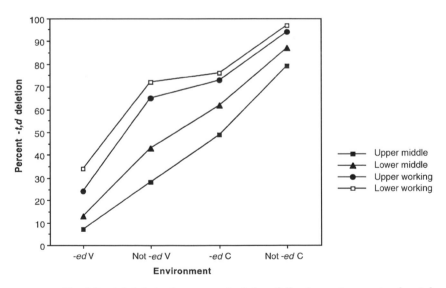

Fig. 4.2   -t,d *deletion by grammatical class, following environment and social class in Detroit African American English*
Source: Wolfram and Fasold, 1974.

As Wolfram's data show, not only does the range of -*t,d* deletion in the speech of Detroit African Americans vary as a function of social class, but it is also affected by the linguistic environment. For speakers of all social classes, -*t,d* is most likely to be retained when it functions as a past tense marker and is followed by a vowel. In this linguistic environment, rates of -*t,d* deletion range from a low of seven percent among upper middle-class speakers to a high of 34 percent among lower working-class speakers. Similarly, for all social classes, -*t,d* is most likely to be deleted when it is not a past tense marker and when it is followed by another consonant, with rates of deletion ranging from 79 percent among upper middle-class speakers to 97 percent among lower working-class speakers.

Recent research on sociolinguistic variation in spoken languages

Studies such as those summarized here have served to confirm Weinreich *et al.*'s (1968) hypothesis that language is characterized by "structured heterogeneity". That is, although all human languages are variable, for the most part variation is not random. Rather, it is systematically constrained by a wide range of social and linguistic factors. More recent work in language variation has not only expanded the number of language varieties investigated, but researchers have also analyzed social categories in more sophisticated ways and related empirical studies of variation in language communities to developments in contemporary linguistic theory. For example, in most contemporary sociolinguistic studies, gender is no longer viewed as a fixed dichotomous variable. Rather, as in other disciplines, gender is viewed as a social construct that interacts with other aspects of personal identity in particular situations (see, for example, Milroy, 1987b; Bucholtz, 1999; Eckert and McConnell-Ginet, 1999; Eckert, 2000). Similarly, ethnicity is no longer viewed as a fixed category. Rather, recent work has explored the ways in which people construct ethnic identities in fluid situations. Rampton (1997), for example, studied the dynamic and shifting perspectives on language and ethnicity of members of multi-ethnic peer groups in Britain. Schecter and Bayley (1997) examined the diverse ways in which members of Mexican-descent families in California and Texas interpreted, created and recreated identities as they attempted to reconcile the sometimes conflicting demands of school success for their children and cultural and linguistic continuity. Zentella (1997), in a longitudinal study of the Puerto Rican residents of a single block in East Harlem, New York City shows in detail how the young women she studied chose among language varieties (e.g. popular Puerto Rican Spanish, standard New York English, AAVE) to express different aspects of their identities, to fulfill expected roles in the community and to accommodate to the linguistic preferences of their interlocutors.

In addition to incorporating more finely-nuanced concepts of gender and ethnicity and to drawing upon ethnographic as well as interview data, recent work in sociolinguistic variation has sought to relate the results of empirical studies conducted in the language community to work in formal linguistics. Guy (1991), for example, developed an exponential model, based on lexical phonology (Kiparsky, 1982) in order to account for the different rates of retention of final consonant clusters (i.e. -t,d) in past tense, semiweak and monomorphemic clusters. He predicted that final -t,d would be retained in the ratio of $x : x^2 : x^3$ as a consequence of a deletion rule operating one, two and three times for words of different morphological classes. The results of empirical study, later replicated by Santa Ana (1992) and Bayley (1997), confirmed the prediction.

More recently, Wilson and Henry (1998) explored the relationship between Chomsky's (1986; 1995) principles and parameters framework and sociolinguistic studies of variation. They suggest that dialects are "constrained and partly defined at the level of grammar by internal operations of the language faculty" (Wilson and Henry, 1998: 13) and that understanding parameter settings can enable sociolinguists to understand which structures are liable to change. Finally, the development of optimality theory, which attempts to provide a formal account of variation, has given rise to renewed dialogue between variationist sociolinguists and formal linguists (see, for example, Antilla, 1997; Guy, 1997; Nagy and Reynolds, 1997).

Sociolinguistic variation and language change

Up to this point, we have been concerned with sociolinguistic variation at the synchronic level. However, studies of sociolinguistic variation have also proven important in explaining language change (Labov, 1984). It is evident that all living languages undergo change. It is also evident that change does not take place immediately. Rather, new forms are gradually introduced into a language and, for a considerable period, sometimes lasting for many generations, both old and new forms are in variation. As we would expect, innovative forms are more common in the language of young people than in the language of their elders. This fact has enabled sociolinguists to employ the construct of "apparent time" to model ongoing linguistic change in communities around the world. That is, students of language variation have examined the distribution of older and innovative linguistic forms by age group (as well as other social factors) in order to predict the course of linguistic change.

The work of Bailey and his associates on Texas and Oklahoma dialects of English (Bailey et al., 1991; 1993) offers a convenient example of how studies of synchronic variation may be used to model linguistic change. Bailey and his colleagues drew on random samples of the populations of both states in order to assess the general direction of linguistic change; then they compared their results with data collected 15 years earlier for the Texas portion of the *Linguistics Atlas of the Gulf States* (LAGS) (Pedersen *et al.*, 1981). The comparison of results for a number of phonological variables validated the apparent time construct. Changes that LAGS indicated were gaining strength, for example, loss of /j/ after alveolars as in Tuesday ([tju] vs. [tu]) were even stronger among younger speakers in the later studies. Conversely, changes that LAGS had indicated were receding, for example, intrusive /r/ in the word *Washington*, were even rarer in the speech of the youngest participants in the later studies. Comparison of non-phonological variables provided additional confirmation of the utility of the apparent time construct. To take just one example, in the studies conducted by Bailey *et al.*, *fixin' to* had gained strength among younger Texans, as predicted by the LAGS results.

Summary

To summarize, we now know that much of the linguistic variation that was previously thought to be random is highly systematic. That is, although we cannot predict whether any particular instance of a variable form will be realized as one variant or another, we can predict that users of a language who belong to particular social groups generally use more of one variant than users who belong to other social groups, and that some variants appear more frequently in certain linguistic environments than in others. Variation is constrained by both social and linguistic factors. Among the social factors are class, age, gender, ethnicity, educational level and region of origin. Particularly with respect to factors such as class, gender and ethnicity, in recent years researchers have sought to incorporate ethnographic perspectives rather than simply to impose preexisting social categories. In this regard, recent research has incorporated many of the original insights of Labov's (1963) pioneering study on Martha's Vineyard, which sought explanations for language change in the local meanings ascribed to linguistic variables. With respect to linguistic factors, research has shown that variation operates at all linguistic levels and that variation may be conditioned by constraints operating at more than one linguistic level, as in the case of *-t,d* deletion in English. Finally, studies of linguistic variation have contributed greatly to our understanding of language change. The apparent time construct, in particular, has enabled us to model ongoing change by examining the language of people of different ages. Some of the characteristics we observe in teenage language use, particularly in the lexicon, for example, will doubtless be discarded as people move into adulthood. However, some differences between adult and teenage (or younger) language use, especially in phonology, do reflect ongoing changes rather than cohort effects. Since people do not generally alter their basic phonological systems after they have fully acquired their first language, we can predict the course of language change with reasonable confidence.

Linguistic variation in sign languages

Since William C. Stokoe's pioneering work in the 1960s, linguists have recognized that natural sign languages are autonomous linguistic systems, structurally independent of the spoken languages with which they may coexist in any given community. This recognition has been followed by extensive research into different aspects of sign language structure and accompanied by the recognition that, as natural sign languages are full-fledged autonomous linguistic systems shared by communities of users, the sociolinguistics of sign languages can be described in ways that parallel the description of spoken languages. It follows that sign languages must exhibit sociolinguistic variation similar to the variation seen in spoken languages. In the following sections, we review a broadly representative sample of research on variation in ASL and other sign languages.

Variation in ASL

A number of scholars have investigated sociolinguistic variation in ASL, but for the most part their investigations have been limited to small numbers of signers, based on data collected with a wide variety of methods and focused on a disparate collection of linguistic features. Patrick and Metzger (1996), for example, reviewed 50 sociolinguistic studies of sign languages conducted between 1971 and 1994. They found that more than half of the studies involved 10 or fewer signers, and that one third included only one or two signers. Only nine studies involved 50 or more signers, and a number of these drew on the same data set. Patrick and Metzger found that although the number of sociolinguistic studies increased during the period they surveyed, the proportion of quantitative studies declined from approximately half during the period 1972 to 1982 to between one third and one quarter during the period 1983 to 1993. The percentage of studies involving large samples (more then 50 signers) also declined from 33 percent during the first period to just six percent during the latter period. The result is that we have yet to have a complete picture of what kinds of units may be variable in ASL and of what kinds of internal and external constraints might be operating on these variable units, although, as Padden and Humphries (1988) observed, deaf people in the USA are aware of variation in ASL, even though it has not been fully described from a linguistic perspective.

Padden and Humphries describe:

a particular group of deaf people who share a language – American Sign Language (ASL) – and a culture. The members of this group reside in the United States and Canada, have inherited their sign language, use it as a primary means of communication among themselves, and hold a set of beliefs about themselves and their connection to the larger society. [They continue that] this . . . is not simply a camaraderie with others who have a similar physical condition, but is, like many other cultures in the traditional sense of the term, historically created and actively transmitted across generations. (1988: 2)

Certainly there is an ever-growing awareness among its users of the existence and use of a language that is independent and different from the majority language, English. ASL users are also aware of sociolinguistic variation in ASL. However, there are many aspects of that variation that have yet to be explored. In terms of linguistic structure, many of the studies to date focus on lexical variation, with some studies of phonological variation, and very few of morphological or syntactic variation. In terms of social factors, the major focus has been on regional variation, with some attention paid to ethnicity, age, gender and factors that may play a particular role in the Deaf community, such as audiological status of parents, age at which ASL was acquired and educational background, for example residential schooling as opposed to mainstreaming.

Until very recently, no studies have examined the relationship between socioeconomic status and variation in a systematic way. So, for example, there is a widespread perception among ASL users that there are "grassroots" deaf people (Jacobs, 1980) whose educational backgrounds, employment patterns and life experiences differ from middle-class deaf professionals, and that both groups use ASL. Accompanying this perception is the belief that there are differences in the variation exhibited in each group. However, the sociolinguistic reality of these perceptions has yet to be explored. In this regard, Padden and Humphries state that "even within the population of deaf people in Boston, Chicago, Los Angeles, and Edmonton, Alberta [smaller groups] have their own distinct identities. Within these local communities, there are smaller groups organized by class, profession, ethnicity, or race, each of which has yet another set of distinct characteristics" (1988: 4).

Early observations and research on variation in ASL.   Users and observers of ASL have clearly been aware of the existence of variation in the language for a long time, and evidence of this awareness can be seen in writings about deaf people's language use. For example, in 1875, Warring Wilkinson, principal of the California School for the Deaf in Berkeley, wrote about how "the sign language" comes about. He stated:

The deaf mute child has mental pictures. He wants to convey similar pictures to his friends. Has speech a genesis in any other fact or need? In the natural order of thought the concrete always precedes the abstract, the subject its attribute, the actor the act. So the deaf mute, like the primitive man, deals primarily with things. He points to an object, and seizing upon some characteristic or dominant feature makes a sign for it. When he has occasion to refer to that object in its absence, he will reproduce the gesture, which will be readily understood, because the symbol has been tacitly agreed upon. Another deaf mute, seeing the same thing, is struck by another peculiarity, and makes another and different sign. Thus half a dozen or more symbols may be devised to represent one and the same thing, and then the principle of the "survival of the fittest" comes in, and the best sign becomes established in usage. (1875: 37)

Wilkinson's statement provides some evidence of early awareness of lexical variation, at least among educators of the Deaf, although systematic research did not begin until the 1960s, with Carl Croneberg's two appendices to the 1965 *Dictionary of American Sign Language (DASL)* (Stokoe *et al.*, 1965). "The linguistic community" (Appendix C) describes the cultural and social aspects of the Deaf community, and discusses the issues of economic status, patterns of social contact and the factors that contribute to group cohesion. These factors include the extensive networks of both a personal and organizational nature that ensure frequent contact even among people who live on opposite sides of the country. Croneberg wrote:

There are close ties also between deaf individuals or groups of individuals as far apart as California and New York. Deaf people from New York on vacation in California stop and visit deaf friends there or at least make it a practice to visit the club for the deaf in San Francisco or Los Angeles ... The deaf as a group have social ties with each other that extend farther across the nation than similar ties of perhaps any other American minority group. (1965: 310)

Croneberg pointed out that these personal ties are reinforced by membership in national organizations such as the National Association of the Deaf (NAD), the National Fraternal Society of the Deaf (NFSD) and the National Congress of Jewish Deaf (NCJD). These personal and organizational patterns of interaction, of course, are central to understanding patterns of language use and variation in ASL.

In "Sign language dialects" (Appendix D), Croneberg dealt with sociolinguistic variation, specifically as it pertains to the preparation of a dictionary. As he stated:

One of the problems that early confronts the lexicographers of a language is dialect, and this problem is particularly acute when the language has never before been written. They must try to determine whether an item in the language is *standard*, that is, used by the majority of a given population, or *dialect*, that is, used by a particular section of the population. (1965: 313)

He outlined the difference between what he termed horizontal variation (regional variation) and vertical variation (variation that occurs in the language of groups separated by social stratification) and stated that ASL exhibits both. He then described the results of a study of lexical variation undertaken in the USA in North Carolina and Virginia, and in Maine, New Hampshire and Vermont using a 134-item sign vocabulary list. He found that for ASL, the state boundary between North Carolina and Virginia also constituted a dialect boundary. North Carolina signs were not found in Virginia and vice versa. He found the three New England states to be less internally standardized (i.e. people within each of the three states exhibited a wide range of variants for each item) and the state boundaries in New England to be much less important, with considerable overlap in lexical choice observed among the three states. He pointed out the key role of the residential schools in the dissemination of dialects, stating, "At such a school, the young deaf learn ASL in the particular variety characteristic of the local region. The school is also a source of local innovations, for each school generation comes up with some new signs or modifications of old ones" (1965: 314).

In his discussion of vertical variation, Croneberg mentioned the influence of age, ethnicity, gender, religion and status. His definition of status encompassed economic level, occupation, relative leadership within the Deaf community, and educational background. He further noted that professionally-employed individuals who were financially prosperous graduates of Gallaudet University

tend to seek each other out and form a group. Frequently they use certain signs that are considered superior to the signs used locally for the same thing. Examples of such signs are Gallaudet signs, transmitted by one or more graduates of Gallaudet who are now teaching at a school for the deaf, and who are members of the local elite. The sign may or may not later be incorporated in the sign language of the local or regional community. (1965: 318)

Finally, Croneberg commented on what a standard sign language might be and stated that "few have paid any attention to the term *standard* in the sense of 'statistically most frequent.' The tendency has been to divide sign language into good and bad" (1965: 318), with older signers and educators of the Deaf maintaining the superiority of their respective signs for various reasons. He neatly captured the essence of the difference between prescriptive and descriptive perspectives on language when he wrote, "What signs the deaf population actually uses and what certain individuals consider good signs are thus very often two completely different things" (1965: 319).

As we saw in the quotation that opens this chapter, Stokoe (1994) cited the thinking of George Trager and Henry Lee Smith, who emphasized the connection between a language and its users. The importance of including information about variation in the *DASL* was two-fold. First, the recognition that ASL exhibits variation like other systems that we recognize as languages reinforced the status of ASL as a real language. As a corollary, since variation is often the precursor to change (Milroy, 1992), the study of variation in ASL, as in other languages, leads us to an understanding of how the language changes. Second, the inclusion of information about variation in the *DASL* – that is, in a volume that by definition aimed to represent the structure of the language and that was accepted by the community as a reliable representation – reinforces the position that, rather than being just a curiosity or an anomaly, variation is an integral part of the structure of a language. That is, if we are to truly understand the nature of a language, we must account for variation. In this regard, Weinreich *et al.* (1968), in their work on the role of variation in language change, introduced the idea of orderly or "structured heterogeneity" as the most useful metaphor for understanding the nature of language:

If a language has to be structured in order to function efficiently, how do people continue to talk while the language changes, that is, while it passes through periods of lessened systematicity? Alternatively, if overriding pressures do force a language to change, and communication is less efficient in the interim . . . why have such inefficiencies not been observed in practice?

   This, it seems to us, is the fundamental question with which a theory of language change must cope. The solution, we will argue, lies in the direction of breaking down the identification of structuredness and homogeneity. The key to a rational conception of language change – indeed, of language itself – is the possibility of describing orderly differentiation in a language serving a community. We will argue that nativelike command of heterogeneous structures is not a matter of multidialectalism or "mere" performance, but is part of unilingual linguistic competence. One of the corollaries of our approach is that in a language serving a complex (i.e. real) community, it is the *absence* of structured heterogeneity that would be dysfunctional. (1968: 99–100)

The inclusion of information about variation in the *DASL*, published in the same era as the early studies of Labov and the pioneering work of Weinreich *et al.*, thus provided a much wider perspective on the fundamental nature of ASL structure and laid the foundation for future investigations.

   Lexical variation.   The years following the publication of the *DASL* witnessed a number of studies of lexical variation in ASL. For example, Woodward (1976) examined differences between African American and white signing. His data, based on a small number of signers, included both direct elicitation and spontaneous language production. He suggested that African Americans tended to use the older forms of signs.

   In 1984, Shroyer and Shroyer published their influential work on lexical variation, which drew on signers across the USA. They collected data on 130 words (the criterion for inclusion of a word being the existence of three signs for the same word) from 38 white signers in 25 states. Their findings also included instances of phonological variation, but they did not discuss them as such. They collected a total of 1,200 sign forms for the 130 words. The 130 words included nouns, verbs and some adverbs.

   Phonological variation.   In the mid-1970s, Battison *et al.* (1975) examined variation in thumb extension in signs such as FUNNY, BLACK, BORING and CUTE. All of these signs may be produced with the thumb closed or extended to the side. Thirty-nine signers participated in the study. The social factors determining participant selection were gender, parental audiological status, and the age at which the signer learned to sign (before or after age six). Signers provided intuitive responses as to whether they would extend their thumb in certain signs, in addition to being asked to sign 10 sentences under three conditions: "as if" to a deaf friend, "as if" to a hearing teacher, and in a practice situation. In the third condition, signers were asked to practice the sentences and were videotaped doing so without their knowledge. Six internal constraints on thumb extension were reported to distinguish the signs being investigated:

1. indexicality: i.e. is the sign produced contiguous to its referent, as in a pronoun or determiner?;
2. bending of fingers: i.e. do the other fingers involved in the sign bend, as in FUNNY?;
3. mid-finger extension: i.e. is the mid finger extended as part of the sign?;
4. twisting movement: i.e. does the hand twist during the production of the sign, as in BORING?;
5. whether the sign is produced on the face, as in BLACK or FUNNY;
6. whether the sign is made in the center of one of four major areas of the body.

All of these features are what Wolfram (personal communication, 1994) would call compositional, that is, features of the signs themselves that may be playing a role in the variation. The analysis found that signs that were indexic, such as the second person pronoun PRO.2 ("you"), had the most thumb extension, followed by signs with bending such as FUNNY. Signs produced in the center of the signing space such as PRO.1 ("I") had less thumb extension. The analysis found no correlation between the linguistic variation and the social factors used to select participants.

Another study of phonological variation, conducted by Woodward *et al.* (1976), focused on face-to-hand variation, that is, certain signs that are produced on the face in some regions are produced on the hands in other regions. Such signs include MOVIE, RABBIT, LEMON, COLOR, SILLY, PEACH and PEANUT. Signers from New Orleans were compared with signers from Atlanta. Data were collected by means of a questionnaire. Results from 45 respondents suggested that New Orleans signers produced signs on the face that Atlanta signers produced on the hands.

Phonological variation can also be seen in the one-handed and two-handed form of the same sign. Woodward and DeSantis (1977b), for example, examined a subset of such signs produced on the face, including CAT, CHINESE, COW and FAMOUS. They proposed that the features conditioning the variation included outward movement of the sign, high facial location as opposed to low facial location and complex movement, again all compositional features. On the basis of questionnaire data, they claimed that the signs that tended to become one-handed were those with no outward movement, made in a salient facial area, produced lower on the face and characterized by complex movement. They also reported that Southerners used two-handed forms more than non-Southerners, that older signers used two-handed signs more than younger signers, and that African American signers tended to use the older two-handed signs more often than white signers of the same age.

Finally, DeSantis (1977) examined variation in signs that can be produced on the hands or at the elbow, such as HELP or PUNISH. The analysis was based on videotapes of free conversation and on responses to a questionnaire. Data for the study were collected in France in the summer of 1975 and in the USA in the spring of 1976. Ninety-nine signers participated, including 60 from France and 39 from Atlanta, Georgia. The results were similar for both French and American signers. Men used the hand versions of the signs more frequently, and women used the elbow versions more frequently.

Morphological and syntactic variation.   Woodward (1973a; 1973b; 1974) and Woodward and DeSantis (1977a) explored the variable use of three morphosyntactic rules: negative incorporation, agent–beneficiary directionality and verb reduplication. Negative incorporation is a rule in ASL whereby negation is indicated in a verb by outward movement, as in DON'T-KNOW, DON'T-WANT and DON'T-LIKE, as opposed to KNOW, WANT and LIKE. Agent–beneficiary directionality is the term used by Woodward and DeSantis for verb agreement. For example, in the verb "1st-person-GIVE-to-2nd-person", the hand moves from the signer to a space in front of the signer; in "2nd-person-GIVE- to-1st-person", the hand moves from a space in front of the signer to the signer. What Woodward and DeSantis refer to as verb reduplication entails the repetition of the movement of the verb as a function of aspect, as in STUDY-CONTINUALLY or STUDY-REGULARLY. For the study of these three rules, data were gathered from 141 signers (132 white and nine African American signers). Other social variables included whether or not the signer was deaf (i.e. some signers were hearing, non-native signers), whether or not the signer's parents were deaf, the age at which sign language was learned, whether or not the signer attended college, and gender. Signers were shown examples of the linguistic variables in question and asked to indicate on a questionnaire whether or not they used the forms presented. The overall results showed that deaf signers who had learned to sign before age six and who had deaf parents used the form of the rules being investigated that was closer to ASL. Internal linguistic constraints were reported only for agent–beneficiary directionality: a continuum of semantic features ranging from "extremely beneficial" to "extremely harmful" was proposed to account for the variation, so that signs like GIVE (beneficial) tend to show directionality, while signs like HATE (harmful) do not.

Diachronic variation.   Any review of research on variation in ASL must also include Frishberg's study (1975) of historical development in ASL signs. Frishberg compared signs from earlier stages of ASL and from French Sign Language with present day usage in ASL to demonstrate that changes have occurred in sign formation. While Frishberg's study is usually viewed as an historical study, it pertains directly to the study of variation in ASL for two related reasons, one general and one specific. The general reason is that historical change manifests itself first in the form of variation. That is, historical change does not occur from one day to the next. Rather, it normally begins as variation, that is, with "different ways of saying the same thing", whether those ways are sounds, parts of signs or grammatical structures, coexisting within the language of an individual or community. As mentioned earlier, the focus of variation studies is what Weinreich *et al.* called "structured heterogeneity", i.e. heterogeneity that is not random but rather governed by internal and external constraints. Moreover, as James Milroy remarked, "In the study of linguistic change, this heterogeneity of language is of crucial importance, as change in progress can be detected in the study of variation" (1992: 1). In some cases, the variation may become stabilized and continue indefinitely, while in other cases, it eventually gives way to the use of one form to the exclusion of the other (or others). Viewed across the broad landscape of history, it may be difficult to see the variation that gives rise to large-scale historical changes, such as the change from Old English to Middle English to Modern English or the changes in Romance languages as they developed from Latin. However, a closer look reveals that change does not happen suddenly and that the transition from one period to the next is characterized by considerable synchronic variation. We may infer that this is the case for sign languages as well. In addition, we suspect that the historical changes that Frishberg described first manifested themselves as synchronic variation.

The second reason for the pertinence of Frishberg's study (1975) to the study of variation is that the processes resulting in historical change that she described are still operative in the language today. She stated:

Signs which were previously made in contact with the face using two hands now use one, whereas those which have changed from one-handed articulation to two-handed are made without contact on the face or head. Signs which use two hands tend to become symmetrical with respect to the shape and movement of the two hands ... As part of a general trend away from more "gross" movement and handshapes toward finer articulation, we find the introduction of new movement distinctions in particular signs, the reduction of compound forms to single sign units, a decreased reliance on the face, eyes, mouth, and body as articulators, and a new context-dependent definition of "neutral" orientation. (1975: xvii)

Frishberg also found:

1. the signs that change from two hands to one are also typically displaced, i.e. change their location from the center of the face and/or from contact with the sense organs, to the periphery of the face;
2. the signs that change from one hand to two hands tend to centralize by moving toward what Frishberg called the line of bilateral symmetry (an imaginary line that runs vertically down the center of the signer's head and torso) and up toward the hollow of the neck.

These findings are important because they are described as examples of historical change in ASL. However, some aspects of what Frishberg characterized as historical change, implying perhaps that the change was complete, may be better characterized as change in progress.

Recent research on variation in ASL.   In recent years, the amount of research on variation in ASL and other sign languages has increased substantially. This body of work includes studies of variation at all linguistic levels, from features of individual segments to discourse units.

Lexical variation.   The work on lexical variation in ASL is quite extensive. In addition to general studies of lexical variation, such as Shroyer and Shroyer discussed in the previous section, the literature contains small-scale studies of various social and occupational categories, most undertaken in the 1990s. Researchers have looked at gender differences (Mansfield, 1993), differences in the use of signs for sexual behavior and drug use (Bridges, 1993), variation related to socioeconomic status (Shapiro, 1993) and lexical variation in the signing produced by interpreters for Deaf-Blind people (Collins and Petronio, 1998).

Phonological variation.   Variation in ASL phonology has also received considerable attention in recent years. Metzger (1993), for example, looked at variation in the handshape of second and third person pronouns, which can be produced either with the index finger or with an S handshape with the thumb extended. Metzger's data yielded one example of the thumb variant, and one unexpected variant, the fingerspelled pronoun S-H-E. There is some indication that the sign that precedes the thumb variant, AGO, with its closed handshape, may play a role in the occurrence of the thumb variant.

Lucas (1995) studied variation in location in the sign DEAF. In its citation form (the form of the sign that appears in dictionaries and is most commonly taught to second language learners), the one-handshape moves from a location just below the ear to a location on the lower cheek near the mouth. However, this sign is commonly produced with movement from the chin location to the ear location or simply with one contact on the lower cheek. Observation might suggest that the final location of the sign (chin or ear) would be governed by the location of the preceding or following sign, so that the sign DEAF in the phrase DEAF FATHER might be signed from chin to ear, since the location of the following sign is the forehead, higher than the ear. Similarly, in the phrase DEAF PRIDE, one might expect that DEAF would be signed from ear to chin, as the sign that follows DEAF begins below the chin.

Contrary to expectations, Lucas' results (based on 486 examples produced by native signers in both formal and informal settings) using the VARBRUL statistical program[3] indicated that the location of the following and preceding signs did not have a significant effect on the choice of a variant of DEAF. Rather, the key factor turned out to be the syntactic function of the sign itself, with adjectives being most commonly signed from chin to ear or as a simple contact on the cheek, and predicates and nouns being signed from ear to chin.

Pinky (fourth finger) extension formed the subject of a recent investigation by Hoopes (1998) who studied in detail the signing of one native signer. Some signs that in citation form have a handshape in which the pinky finger is closed and not extended variably allow the extension of the pinky. Examples include the signs THINK, LAZY and CONTINUE. Hoopes' findings, discussed in detail below, parallel Lucas' finding about the relative lack of importance of the location of the preceding or following sign. In both cases, the phonological factors that might seem to be most important – location in the case of DEAF and handshape in the case of pinky extension – in fact did not appear to condition the variation.

Recently, Kleinfeld and Warner (1996) examined ASL signs used to denote gay, lesbian and bisexual persons. Thirteen hearing interpreters and 12 deaf ASL users participated in the study. Kleinfeld and Warner focused on 11 lexical items and provided detailed analysis of phonological variation in two signs, LESBIAN and GAY. The analysis showed that the variation can be correlated to some extent with external constraints such as the signer's sexual identity (straight or gay/lesbian).

Variation in fingerspelling.   Turning to the area of fingerspelling, Blattberg *et al.* (1995) examined a subset of the data from Lucas' project on sociolinguistic variation in ASL (Lucas *et al.*, 2001). They compared two groups of middle-class signers – aged 15–25 and 55 and over – from Frederick,

Maryland and Boston, Massachusetts. They found that both groups of young people used fingerspelling in either full or lexicalized forms, and that finger-spelling was produced in the area below the shoulder generally used for fingerspelling. The young people used fingerspelling primarily for proper nouns and for English terms that have no ASL equivalents. The adults also used fingerspelling for these purposes, but their use of fingerspelling also resembled the use of locative signs. In addition, Maryland adults and adolescents used fingerspelling much more frequently than their counterparts in Massachusetts. Finally, Mulrooney (2001) found clear evidence of a gender effect in fin-gerspelling, whereby men were more likely to produce non-citation forms (e.g. produced outside of the usual fingerspelling area) than women.

Discourse.   Recently, scholars have begun to investigate variation in ASL discourse. Haas *et al.* (1995), for example, examined backchanneling, turntaking strategies and question forms in a conversation between Deaf-Blind individuals, comparing them to the same features in sighted ASL signing. They found that "in the tactile mode, Deaf-Blind signers use remarkably similar turn-taking and turn-yielding shift regulators as Deaf-sighted signers" (1995: 130). Touch is often substituted for eye-gaze and

turn-yielding often uses a combination of dominant and non-dominant hands in yield-ing to the addressee. The dominant hand rests, and the non-dominant hand moves to "read" the signer's dominant hand. Turn-claiming occurs with the dominant hand of the addressee repeatedly touching or tapping the non-dominant hand of the signer until the signer yields and moves their non-dominant hand to the "reading" position.

As for question forms, in this particular study, none of the question forms found seemed unique to Tactile ASL. Collins and Petronio (1998), however, found that for *yes–no* questions, non-manual signals that in sighted ASL include the raising of the eyebrows are conveyed manually in Deaf-Blind signing, as either an outward movement of the signs or the drawn question mark.

Malloy and Doner (1995) looked at variation in cohesive devices in ASL dis-course and explored gender differences in the use of these devices. Specifically, they looked at reiteration and expectancy chains. Reiteration is one type of lex-ical cohesion that "involves the repetition of a lexical item, at one end of the scale; and a number of things in between – the use of a synonym, near-synonym, or superordinate" (Halliday and Hasan, 1976: 278). Expectancy chains have to do with the fact that, in discourse, certain words or phrases are expected to follow certain others. The predictability of their order makes for cohesion. In their analysis of the use of reiteration and expectancy chains in the re-telling of a story by two native signers (one male and one female), Malloy and Doner found that the male signer used reiteration more frequently than the female signer, but that the signers were similar in their use of expectancy chains.

Research on African American signing

African American signing has been the object of several recent investigations. Studies include Aramburo (1989), Guggenheim (1992), Lewis *et al.* (1995) and Lewis (1996). Aramburo and Guggenheim observed lexical variation during the course of structured but informal interviews. Lewis *et al.* (1995) studied the existence of and attitudes toward African American varieties. Specifically, they described the differences in body movement, mouth movement, and the use of space in the signing of one African American signer who code-switched during the course of a monologue. In addition, they explored how interpreters handled the code-switching in spoken language from Standard English to African American Vernacular English (AAVE). Lewis (1996) continued the examination of African American signing styles in his paper on the parallels between communication styles of hearing and deaf African Americans. His investigation took its departure from two observations: first, ASL users recognize the existence of what is often referred to as "Black signing" but have difficulty in explaining what it is that makes it Black; second, uniquely Black or "ebonic" (Asante, 1990) kinesic and non-verbal features exist, and these features occur in the communication of both hearing and deaf African Americans. His investigation described some of these kinesic and non-verbal features – specifically, body postures and rhythmic patterns accompanying the production of signs – in the language used by a deaf adult African American woman. The frequently articulated perspective that African American signing differs markedly from White signing in all areas of structure – and not just lexically – is thus beginning to be explored.

An international perspective on variation in sign languages

Sutton-Spence and Woll (1999), in their volume on the linguistics of British Sign Language, report on several studies of variation in that language. For example, Woll (1991) found that there were many features that differentiated older and younger signers. Older signers used more fingerspelling and had less clear mouthing patterns than the younger signers. Younger signers showed more influence from English in their signing. These differences are attributed to:

1. the small number of deaf families, making for a discontinuity between generations;
2. changes in the educational system for deaf people; and
3. changing technology.

Woll also found lexical differences between older and younger signers and across regions.

In terms of family backgrounds, Day (1995) compared British signers from deaf and hearing families and found that their signing differed significantly.

Le Master and Dwyer (1991) report on the lexical differences between male signing and female signing found in Dublin, a direct result of segregated schooling for deaf children in Ireland. Sutton-Spence and Woll also describe differences between Roman Catholic and Protestant signers in Britain:

> The signing of British Catholics is strongly influenced by Irish Sign Language (ISL) because Irish monks and nuns have provided education for Catholic deaf children that is suitable for Catholic beliefs, and Irish-trained priests serve the Catholic Deaf communities in Britain. The Catholic signing uses many initialized signs that are based on the Irish manual alphabet. (1999: 28)

Variation due to religious background extends to the Jewish Deaf in Britain, reported on by Weinberg (1992). There was at one time a school for Jewish deaf children in London that was oral but permitted the use of signing after the arrival of deaf German refugee children in the 1930s. The variety of signing that emerged at this school continued as long as graduates of the school remained in the community and did not associate much with other deaf people. However, it has been little used since the school closed in the early 1960s. More recently, it has been noted that Israeli Sign Language is influencing the signing of British Jewish deaf people, as many Jewish deaf people visit Israel and are increasingly adopting Israeli signs (Sutton-Spence and Woll, 1999: 28). In addition, Sutton-Spence and Woll mention that there may be variation correlated with social group identity, i.e. Nigerian, Pakistani or Greek, to name several.

In Italian Sign Language (LIS), Radutzky (1990), while focusing on historical change, described phonological variation. Furthermore, in her 1992 dictionary of LIS, Radutzky makes mention of lexical variation at the regional and inter- and intra-urban levels. Lexical variation is also discussed in Brien and Brennan's work (1995) on the preparation of sign language dictionaries, and has been explored by Collins-Ahlgren (1990) in New Zealand Sign Language, by Schermer (1990) in Dutch Sign Language, by Boyes-Braem (1985) in Swiss German Sign Language and Swiss French Sign Language, by Yau and He (1990) in Chinese Sign Language and by Campos (1994) in Brazilian Sign Language.

Perspectives on the structure of sign languages

Up to now, we have concentrated on the results of individual studies. However, the varying perspectives on the basic structure of ASL and of sign languages in general also need to be considered. Current thinking about the linguistic structure of sign languages sheds new light on some of the earlier studies of sign language variation, while at the same time raising important issues for data analysis. For example, the perspective on the fundamental structure of signs has changed dramatically since the earliest studies of variation. Stokoe's perspective, which shaped sign language studies from 1960 until fairly recently, held that signs are composed of three basic parts or parameters (the location at which the sign is produced, the handshape and the movement of the sign) and that, unlike the sequentially-produced segments of spoken languages, these parts are produced simultaneously. In a more recent perspective developed by Liddell (1984) and Liddell and Johnson (1989), signs are viewed as composed of movement and hold segments, sequentially produced, somewhat analogous to the consonants and vowels of spoken languages. We recognize that there is considerable ongoing debate as to the nature of the segments in question (see, for example, Coulter, 1992; Perlmutter, 1992; and Sandler, 1992). However, the Liddell-Johnson framework, as Liddell (1992) amply demonstrates, allows not only for an accurate account of the description of any individual sign, but also for an accurate account of phonological processes such as assimilation, metathesis, epenthesis and segment deletion, processes that play central roles in variation.

A central concern of any variation study is to define clearly the linguistic variables being examined and to make sure that they are indeed variable. Current thinking about the linguistic structure of sign languages and about data collection methodology also has implications for the identification of variables in the earlier studies of sign language variation. It is not clear, for example, that the rules of negative incorporation, agent–beneficiary directionality and verb reduplication in Woodward's (1973a; 1973b; 1974) studies are, in fact, variable in native ASL. The apparent variability of these rules merits re-examination, as it simply may have been an artifact of combining data from native and non-native signers. For example, in terms of the semantic continuum proposed for agent–beneficiary directionality (from "beneficial" to "harmful"), it may be that directionality is obligatory in most of the verbs in question, and is unrelated to semantic considerations. It is basically the way in which agreement is shown with the subject and the object of the verb, and is not optional. Failure to use space properly in these verbs would seem to result not in a variable form, but in an ungrammatical one. While the semantic categorization does seem to work for some verbs (e.g. "beneficial" for GIVE and "harmful" for HATE), it does not work at all for others. For example, it is not clear at all why FINGERSPELL would be labeled as "harmful". It may be that at the time of the study, FINGER-SPELL as an agreement verb was an innovation and hence not widely attested, placing it at the "less frequent use of directionality" end of the continuum. But FINGERSPELL cannot therefore be said to have a semantic characteristic of "harmful", the researcher's account of this end of the continuum that he set up.

Table 4.5 *Variability in spoken and sign languages*

	Examples	
Variable unit	Spoken languages	Sign languages
Features of individual segments	final consonant devoicing, vowel nasalization, vowel raising and lowering	change in location, movement, orientation, handshape in one or more segments of a sign
Individual segments deleted or added	-*t,d* deletion, -*s* deletion, epenthetic vowels and consonants	hold deletion, movement epenthesis, hold epenthesis
Syllables (i.e. groups of segments) added or deleted	aphesis, apocope, syncope	first or second element of a compound deleted
Part of segment, segments or syllables re-arranged	metathesis	metathesis
Variation in word-sized morphemes or combinations of word-sized morphemes (i.e. syntactic variation)	copula deletion, negative concord, *avoir/être* alternation, lexical variation	null pronoun variation, lexical variation
Variation in discourse units	text types, lists	repetition, expectancy chains, Deaf-Blind discourse, turntaking, backchanneling, questions

Sign languages vs. spoken languages

Based on the review of research on linguistic variation in sign and spoken language communities, as well as our understanding of the changes in perspective on the nature of sign languages, we are now in a position to compare variation across modalities. In this section, we compare variable units, variable processes and internal constraints in both sign and spoken languages. We then focus on the social constraints that are particular to Deaf communities, as well as on the specific circumstances that need to be taken into account even when evaluating the effect of social constraints that are common to all communities, such as age and gender.

Variable units in sign and spoken languages

Table 4.5 compares variability in spoken and sign languages. From this table we can see the same kinds of variability in sign languages as have been described for spoken languages. Specifically, the features of the individual segments of signs can vary. In spoken languages, a consonant may become nasalized or may be devoiced, for example. In sign languages, the handshape, the location and the palm orientation may vary. Pinky extension or thumb extension in one-handshape signs (PRO.1 "I", BLACK, FUNNY) are examples of handshape variation, while signs like KNOW and SUPPOSE provide examples of location variation, as they can be produced at points below the forehead. Individual segments may be deleted or added. This is seen in spoken English with -*t,d* deletion. In sign languages, movement segments may be added between holds (as in the phrase MOTHER STUDY) or hold segments may be deleted between movements (as in the phrase GOOD IDEA). Groups of segments (i.e. syllables) can be deleted. The English words *because* and *supposed (to)* are sometimes pronounced as *'cause* and *'posed to*. The first element of a sign compound, such as the sign WHITE in the compound sign WHITE^FALL ("snow") is often deleted, and many signers are not even aware of its existence. Parts of segments, segments or syllables can be re-arranged. As mentioned earlier, English speakers sometimes pronounce the word *hundred* as *hunderd*. In sign languages, this can be seen in the location feature of the sign DEAF. That is, the sign may begin at the ear and end at the chin or vice versa. Everything else about the sign is the same, but the location feature is re-arranged. And there can also be variation in word-sized morphemes, otherwise known as lexical variation, and in combinations of word-sized morphemes, i.e. syntactic variation. Variation has also been described in bigger units, that is, in the units of discourse. In spoken languages, for example, researchers have described variation in the way speakers use lists in discourse (Schiffrin, 1994) and variation in sign language discourse has also been explored (see discussion above of Haas *et al.*, 1995; Malloy and Doner, 1995). The one kind of variation that we have not seen in sign languages yet is coalescence, whereby a new segment is created from the features of other segments. We see this in English, for example, when the sound *sh* (/ʃ/) is created by the interaction between *t* and *i* in the word *demonstration*. *sh* is created and the original segments disappear.

In addition, while we assume that syntactic variation exists, there is very little research in this area. Although Woodward (described earlier) claimed that there was variation in three syntactic rules, the data upon which the claim is based combine the signing of native and non-native signers. However, one kind of syntactic variation in sign language involves variable subjects with plain verbs. That is, in addition to the many verbs in sign languages in which the pronominal information is incorporated into the structure of the verb (e.g. GIVE or FLATTER in ASL), there are many so-called "plain verbs" (Padden, 1988) (e.g. LIKE or KNOW in ASL) that would seem to require the production of separate signs for subject and object. However, ASL is a "pro-drop" language. That is, the subject and object pronouns that accompany plain verbs are variably deleted (Lucas *et al.*, 2001).

Table 4.6 *Variable processes in spoken and sign languages*

	Examples	
Process	Spoken languages	Signed languages
Concerning the phonological component of language		
Assimilation	vowel harmony, consonant harmony, gemination, nasalization	assimilation in handshape, location, orientation
Weakening	deletion, CC reduction, haplology, aphesis, syncope, apocope, vowel reduction	hold deletion, deletion of one articulator, first or second element of a compound deleted
Substitution, Addition	coalescence, metathesis, epenthesis	metathesis, epenthetic movement, substitute hand base
Analogy	3rd person singular -*s*	add second hand to one-handed sign
Concerning morphosyntactic structures		
Co-occurrence relations	negative concord	possibly non-manual signals
Item permutation	adverb placement	possibly placement of interrogative words

Finally, in terms of what kinds of units can be variable, we have noticed one kind of variability that seems to be an artifact of a language produced with two identical articulators, i.e. two hands as opposed to one tongue. That is, sign languages allow the deletion, addition or substitution of one of the two articulators. Two-handed signs become one-handed (ASL CAT, COW), one-handed signs become two-handed (ASL DIE), and a table, chair arm or the signer's thigh may be substituted for the base hand in a two-handed sign with identical handshapes (ASL RIGHT, SCHOOL). Variation is also allowed in the relationship between articulators, as in the ASL sign HELP, produced with an A handshape placed in the upward-turned palm of the base hand. Both hands can move forward as a unit or the base hand can lightly tap the bottom of the A handshape hand.

Variable processes in spoken and sign languages

Variable processes are summarized for both spoken and sign languages in Table 4.6. Here, we see that the same kinds of processes that pertain to spoken language variation also pertain to sign language variation: processes of assimilation, weakening, substitution and addition, and analogy. We see assimilation, for example, when a one-handshape in the sign PRO.1 ("I") becomes an open eight-handshape in the phrase PRO.1 PREFER ("I prefer"). We also see it in the compound sign THINK∧MARRY ("believe"), in which the palm orientation of the sign THINK assimilates to the palm orientation of the sign MARRY. We see weakening when holds are deleted or when a two-handed sign becomes one-handed, as in CAT or COW. Substitution can be seen when a table top or the signer's knee is substituted for the base hand of a two-handed sign or in the version of the sign DEAF that begins at the chin and moves to the ear, as opposed to beginning at the ear and moving to the chin. Addition is seen when movements are added between holds. Finally, the process of analogy is seen when a one-handed sign becomes two-handed.

In terms of morphosyntactic variation, we may expect to find variation in co-occurrence relations, as found in spoken languages. Recall the example of the co-occurrence of negative items in spoken English, so that a sentence such as *Ain't nobody seen nothing like that before*, with three negative items co-occurring, is acceptable in AAVE, while the sentence *No one has seen anything like that before*, with only one negative element is preferable in middle class standard English. We are not exactly sure what variable co-occurrence relations might look like in ASL, but a possible candidate for investigation is the co-occurrence of non-manual signals with lexical signs or with morphological or syntactic units. For example, must a given non-manual signal (such as the mouth configuration in the sign NOT-YET) co-occur with the manual sign? Is there any variation in the morphological and syntactic non-manual signals that occur with manual adverbs and sentences? Another kind of morphosyntactic variation concerns the fact that certain items – for example, adverb placement in spoken English – can occur in different positions in a sentence. Again, item permutation is an area that has yet to be explored in sign languages. One possible candidate in ASL is the placement of interrogative signs (WHO, WHERE, WHAT, WHEN, WHY, FOR-FOR) in sentences and also their repetition.

Internal constraints on spoken and sign languages

Table 4.7 summarizes the internal constraints on variable units. Earlier studies of variation in ASL focused on compositional constraints. That is, variation was seen to be conditioned by some feature of the variable sign itself. For example, Battison *et al.* (1975) hypothesized that thumb extension in signs such as FUNNY or BLACK was conditioned by the number of other fingers extended, the secondary movement of the sign and other features of the sign itself. Sequential constraints are those that have to do with the immediate linguistic environment surrounding the variable, such as the handshape or palm orientation of the sign immediately preceding or following the variable sign, as we see with one-handshape signs. Functional constraints have to do with the role that the function of the sign has in the variation, as we will see in our discussion of the ASL sign DEAF. The constraint of structural incorporation

Table 4.7 *Internal constraints on variable units in spoken and sign languages*

	Examples	
Constraint	Spoken languages	Signed languages
Compositional	phonetic features in nasal absence in child language	other parts of sign in question, e.g. handshape, location, orientation
Sequential	following consonant, vowel, or feature thereof	preceding or following sign or feature thereof
Functional	morphological status of -*s* in Spanish -*s* deletion	function of sign as noun, predicate or adjective
Structural incorporation	preceding or following syntactic environment for copula deletion	?syntactic environment for pronoun variation
Pragmatic	emphasis	emphasis (e.g. pinky extension)

has to do with the preceding or following syntactic environment surrounding the variable. One would consider structural incorporation as a constraint when trying to understand what conditions the variable subjects in plain verbs, for example PRO.1 LIKE vs. (PRO.1) LIKE. Finally, pragmatic features may act as constraints. As we will see below, Hoopes (1998), for example, found that the lengthening of a sign for emphasis played a role in the occurrence of pinky extension. Emphasis is a pragmatic factor, a feature chosen by the signer in a particular context to convey a particular meaning. It is not an inherent feature of the sign.

Furthermore, a fundamental difference between sign language variation and spoken language variation may be emerging from the analysis of internal constraints. This difference relates to the fact that variation in spoken languages is for the most part a sequential phenomenon; that is, it is a phenomenon that affects linguistic segments which occur in sequence, segments occurring at the boundaries of larger units, i.e. words. The examples of -*t,d* deletion and the (ING) variable discussed above are representative of this phenomenon.

It is beginning to be clear that sign languages make considerably less use of affixation, such that deletable final segments may not be morphemes in the same way that they are in spoken languages. The past tense marking accomplished by the -*t* or -*d* in English or the plural marking accomplished by -*s* is accomplished in different ways in ASL. Similarly, verb agreement is not accomplished by affixation as in many spoken languages, but rather by a change in the location and/or palm orientation feature of one segment of a sign. There are many agreement verbs in ASL, and there are also plain verbs, i.e. verbs that do not allow agreement to be incorporated into the location or orientation feature of the verb and that require separate lexical signs for subject and object. There is some anecdotal evidence for plain and agreement variants of the same verb, for example CALL-ON-TELEPHONE. But since verb agreement is not accomplished by the sequential affixation of morphemes, the internal constraints on such variation will have nothing to do with the sequential occurrence of morphemes, as it does in Caribbean Spanish, for example, with final -s aspiration and deletion in verbs. Clearly, we will most likely have to search elsewhere in the linguistic environment for some of the internal constraints on variation.

Social constraints particular to Deaf communities

Social constraints like gender, age and ethnicity have been examined in numerous studies of sociolinguistic variation. However, many of these constraints need to be articulated more fully when they are put into research practice in a particular community. This is especially true for studies of linguistic variation in Deaf communities. Notions like socioeconomic status or even age cannot simply be borrowed whole from studies of variation in spoken language communities. The differences in social constraints when applied to Deaf communities are of two types. First, there are constraints like age whose labels have a common application, but which might have a different meaning considering the history of Deaf communities around the world. Second, there are constraints like language background, which are unique to Deaf communities.

Considering constraints of the first type, definitions of gender, age, regional background and ethnicity need to be reevaluated in studies of Deaf communities. For deaf people, regional background, or where they grew up, may be less significant than where their language models acquired a natural sign language or where they attended school, i.e. if this was a residential school, or if it was oral or used a sign language as a medium of instruction. Age as a sociolinguistic variable may have different effects on linguistic variation, because of the differences in language policies in Deaf schools in the twentieth century. Thus, while differences in the signing of older and younger people may appear to be due either to age group differences or to natural language change (such as occurs in all languages), these differences may also be the result of changes in educational policies, like the shift from oralism to "total communication" (i.e. manualism) that occurred in the USA, or from total communication to a bilingual–bicultural approach. These language policies affected not only what language was used in the classroom, but also teacher hiring practices (deaf signers of ASL, or hearing teachers who knew no ASL). These language policies affected deaf children's access to appropriate language models, and this access may have varied across time to such an extent as to affect the kind of variation we see in sign languages today.

With respect to ethnicity, demographics and oppression may work doubly against our understanding of language use in minority deaf communities. The linguistic and social diversity in the Deaf community is just beginning to be explored by researchers (Lucas, 1996; Parasnis, 1998), and many questions remain about how ethnic minority deaf people self-identify and how they use language. Are the boundaries of these groups such that they form coherent groups whose ethnic identity is stronger than their Deaf identity? Or do the members of these groups construct a separate minority Deaf identity? Is it reasonable to acknowledge multiple potential language influences? Is the use of a particular variant related to a person's identity as a deaf person, or as an African American deaf person, for example? Through the social network technique of contacting potential informants, Lucas *et al.* (2001), described in more detail below, uncovered one way in which ethnicity and age have intersected to create a situation of oppression multiplied. Lucas *et al.* were unable to find any African American deaf people over age 55 who were members of the middle class, that is, who had a college education and were working in professional occupations. This finding suggests political, social and economic factors intersect with race and ethnicity in ways that have profound effects on minority language communities like the Deaf community.

With respect to gender, several questions emerge that are also related to the minority language community status of Deaf people. Those yet to be answered include: Is there a solidarity in language use between men and women in a language minority group because of oppression from the outside and shared experiences rooted in being deaf? Or are usage differences as pronounced as in other communities?

Other differences in social constraints arise from the unique characteristics of Deaf communities. The question of the language background of signers who participate in studies is one such characteristic. Most participants in variation studies acquired the language under study as a native language from native-speaking parents, as well as from exposure in their everyday environment. In Deaf communities, some participants had neither of these kinds of exposure to the language at the earliest stages of their development. Even deaf parents may not be native signers. It may seem that this problem conflicts with the goal of describing use of a particular language. However, if all signers who learned a natural sign language from people other than their parents were excluded from sociolinguistic studies, such studies would be invalidated, because they would not be representative of the community. Researchers should simply take account of the language background of their participants while drawing conclusions from the data. If the analysis is qualitative, the language background of the participants should be expressly stated in the report, and taken account of in the analysis. If the analysis is quantitative, the influence of language background differences on the variables being investigated may be included as a factor in the statistical model.

A related constraint is the school background of informants. Whether the signers attended a residential or mainstream school may influence their signing. Some questions related to this issue are: Did the signers acquire a natural sign language at a very early age from signing adults, or did they learn it at a later age, having entered the community later? At what age did they acquire the sign language in use in their community? Did their language models use an artificial system such as Signed Exact English (SEE) or the natural sign language of the community?

Three recent studies of variation in ASL

A number of recent studies of linguistic variation in sign languages reflect the changing perspective on the nature of sign languages. In this section, we describe three of these studies: Hoopes' study of pinky extension, Collins and Petronio's (1998) study of variation in Tactile ASL, the language of the US Deaf-Blind community, and Lucas et al.'s study (2001) of variation in the form of the sign DEAF. The three studies all adopted theoretical frameworks that incorporate recent insights into the nature of ASL. They also illustrate the range of contemporary investigations into variation in ASL and other sign languages. Hoopes (1998) is an exploratory case study based on data from a single signer. Collins and Petronio's (1998) study is also exploratory. The authors aimed to understand the parameters of variation in the language variety of a group that had not previously been studied systematically. Lucas et al. (2001) is a large-scale study based on a representative sample of the US Deaf population.

An exploratory case study of a phonological variable

Signing with one's pinky extended on some signs has been anecdotally discussed as a possible phonological variable. Signs like THINK, WONDER and TOLERATE (the latter two illustrated in Figure 4.3a and 4.3b) can be signed either with the pinky (the fourth finger) closed or fully extended. Hoopes (1998) sought to determine whether pinky extension showed patterned variation that correlated with phonological, syntactic or discourse constraints, and to consider functional explanations for these correlations. He set out to describe this potential variable as part of one individual's signing style, and to discuss possible constraints on the use of pinky extension (PE). In this study, Hoopes decided to focus on the signing of a single individual because, as numerous studies have shown, individuals normally use all of the variants that are common to their community, even within the same conversation (Guy, 1980).

The signer for this study was a 55-year-old Euro-American deaf woman, who was deafened in infancy; she was the only deaf member of her immediate

(a)   Wonder, +cf   Wonder, −cf

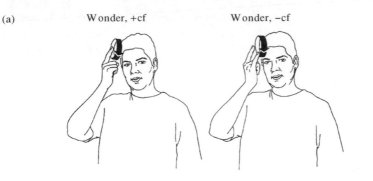

(b)   Tolerate, +cf   Tolerate, −cf

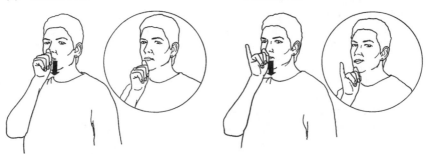

Fig. 4.3a, b   *WONDER, TOLERATE, citation and non-citation forms*

family. She attended a residential school and Gallaudet University. She was videotaped in conversation in four separate sessions, each lasting one to two hours, creating a total of seven hours of conversational data. Her conversational partners included a close friend and deaf and hearing interlocutors.

For the analysis, Hoopes extracted 100 occurrences of pinky extension from the videotaped data. Each of these occurrences was coded for the following linguistic and social factor groups:

1. preceding handshape;
2. following handshape;
3. sign in which PE occurs;
4. discourse topic;
5. handshape of the PE sign;
6. syntactic category of the PE sign;
7. level of intimacy between informant and conversational partner.

A subset of these occurrences was also coded for prosodic features. This coding involved timing the duration of the tokens by the number of frames each lasted.

These durations were averaged and then compared with the duration of tokens of the same lexemes (i.e. signs) without pinky extension. The following possible constraints were investigated for this subset of tokens:

1. duration of the sign;
2. preceding or following pause;
3. repetition of the sign.

Some potential occurrences were excluded from the pool of tokens. Occurrences in fingerspelling were excluded because it was assumed that in these cases PE resulted from processes other than those that could cause pinky extension in lexical signs. Also excluded were instances of "lexicalized" pinky extension, in which case the non-PE variant and the PE variant would not co-occur in the signing of one individual. Lastly, signs in which pinky extension did not occur over the full production of the sign were excluded.

The analysis of the full 100 tokens, not including the prosodic analysis, consisted of comparing percentages of tokens in each of the sub-groupings of the constraints. In the prosodic analysis, Hoopes compared the average duration of the signs with and without pinky extension.

The findings indicated that the frequency of occurrence of pinky extension did in fact vary and did correlate with linguistic factors (handshape and syntactic category) and the one social factor analyzed (degree of social distance). The most intriguing finding, however, was that pinky extension tended to co-occur with prosodic features of emphatic stress. Specifically, it tended to occur:

1. with lexemes used repeatedly within a discourse topic;
2. before pauses; and
3. with lexemes lengthened to almost twice their usual duration.

This suggests that pinky extension is itself a prosodic feature of ASL that adds emphatic stress or focus to the sign with which it co-occurs. It is quite analogous to stress in spoken language as indicated by a stronger signal as a result of greater articulatory effort.

It should be noted that sociolinguistic methodology was crucial to this last finding, i.e. that pinky extension played a prosodic function in the variety used by the subject. Prosody has largely been ignored by linguists working within either the Chomskian or the earlier structuralist framework due to the tendency of these frameworks toward categoricity. Prosody tends not to be subject to categorical rules. But, as Hoopes' study shows, when one searches for factors that constrain, but do not absolutely determine, the occurrence of a linguistic form, the patterning of prosodic features emerges.

Exploring the Dimensions of Variation: A Study of Tactile ASL

A second recent study looked at the signing of Deaf-Blind people, known as Tactile ASL. While the ASL of sighted deaf people has been studied for 40 years, the signing of Deaf-Blind people is a new subject of linguistic research. Collins and Petronio (1998) set out to describe changes in signing that occur when ASL is used in a tactile, rather than a visual, mode. The goal was to describe the particular variety of ASL used in the Deaf-Blind community, when Deaf-Blind people converse with other Deaf-Blind people. The authors considered that variation between sighted ASL and Tactile ASL could occur at any level of linguistic structure.

To collect representative samples of Deaf-Blind conversation, Collins and Petronio used two sets of conversational data, one relatively informal and one relatively formal. Informal data were collected at a party attended by 11 Deaf-Blind people. The more formal data came from another set of conversations between three pairs of Deaf-Blind people, all using Tactile ASL to tell stories to each other. The 17 signers had all been born deaf, knew and used ASL prior to becoming legally blind, became blind as a result of Usher's Syndrome I, and regularly socialized with Deaf-Blind adults who use Tactile ASL. Tactile ASL can be received with one or both hands. In order to limit the possible variation that could occur even within Tactile ASL, only one-handed conversations were included in the data set.

Collins and Petronio focused on the differences and similarities of the phonological form of signs used in visual and Tactile ASL. (Space does not permit a discussion of the findings pertaining to morphology, syntax and discourse, but a full account can be found in Collins and Petronio, 1998.) Signs were examined in terms of their handshape, location, movement and orientation.

Early studies on visual ASL sought minimal pairs to determine the distinctive parts of signs. Minimal pairs were interpreted as providing evidence for three parameters: handshape, location and movement. For instance:

- handshape: the signs DONKEY and HORSE use the same location and movement but differ in handshape;
- location: MOTHER and FATHER use the same handshape and movement but differ in location; and
- movement: SICK and TO-BECOME-SICK use the same handshape and location but differ in movement.

Battison (1978) later identified a fourth parameter, orientation, based on pairs such as CHILDREN and THINGS. These two signs have identical handshape, location and movement. However, they differ in the palm orientation: the palm of the hand faces upward for THINGS, but toward the floor for CHILDREN. Using these four parameters, Collins and Petronio examined signs in the Tactile

ASL data to see if there were any phonological differences between the same sign when it was used in visual ASL.

Collins and Petronio found no variation or changes in the handshape parameter. The other three parameters (movement, orientation and location) displayed the same type of variation due to phonological assimilation that occurs in visual ASL. However, although the same forms of variation occurred in Tactile ASL, this variation was sometimes due to the receiver's hand being on the signer's hand and the close physical proximity of the signer and the receiver. For example, because of the physical closeness, the signing space used in Tactile ASL was generally smaller than that used in visual ASL. This smaller space usually results in smaller movement paths in signs. In addition, because the signer's and receiver's hands were in contact, the signing space shifted to the area where the hands were in contact; correspondingly, the location of signs articulated in neutral space also shifted to this area. The orientation parameter showed some variation that resulted from modifications the signer made to better accommodate the receiver. One change, unique to Tactile ASL, occurred with signs that included body contact. In addition to the signer's hand moving toward the body part, the body part often moved toward the hand in Tactile ASL. This adaptation allowed the receiver to maintain more comfortable tactile contact with the signer.

The variation, adaptations and changes that Collins and Petronio described are examples of linguistic change that has occurred and is continuing in the US Deaf-Blind community. In the past several years, in addition to an expansion of the American Association of the Deaf-Blind, there has been growth in chapters of this organization based in various US States. Deaf-Blind people are increasing their contact with other Deaf-Blind people. The opportunity for Deaf-Blind people to get together and form communities has resulted in sociolinguistic changes in ASL as Deaf-Blind people modify it to meet their needs. From a linguistic viewpoint, Tactile ASL provides us with a unique opportunity to witness the linguistic changes ASL is experiencing as the Deaf-Blind community adapts the language to a tactile mode.

A large scale quantitative study: Lucas et al. (2001) on DEAF

We began this chapter with observations about variation in the ASL sign DEAF. These observations are based on the results of a large-scale study of variation in ASL (Lucas *et al.*, 2001) that analyzed phonological, syntactic and lexical variation. Conversational ASL was videotaped in seven sites around the USA (Massachusetts, Virginia, Maryland, Louisiana, Kansas/Missouri, California and Washington State). Participants were from three age groups (15–25, 26–54, 55+) and included male and female, Caucasian and African American, and working-class and middle-class signers. The analysis of the sign DEAF is based on 1,618 examples taken from the data. Although the sign DEAF has many possible forms, only three of these forms were extracted from the video-tapes. In citation form (+cf), the sign begins just below the ear, and ends near the corner of the mouth. A second variant begins at the corner of the mouth and moves upward to the ear. This variant was labeled the "chin to ear" vari-ant. In the third variant, the "contact-cheek" variant, the index finger contacts the lower cheek but does not move up. The three variants are illustrated in Figures 4.4a, 4.4b and 4.4c.

These variants were compared using a multivariate statistical program that requires many examples as input, but which allows the researcher to investigate the effects of many potential constraints at the same time. Results of the analysis of the 1,618 examples indicated that variation in the form of DEAF is systematic and conditioned by multiple linguistic and social factors, including grammatical function, the location of the following segment, discourse genre, age and region. The results confirmed the earlier finding of Lucas (1995), which showed that the grammatical function of DEAF, rather than the features of the preceding or following sign, is the main linguistic constraint on variation.

The analysis was divided into two stages. In the first stage, the citation form was compared with the two non-citation forms. In the second stage, the two non-citation forms were compared with one another. For the choice between citation and non-citation forms, among the linguistic factors, only grammati-cal function and discourse genre proved to be statistically significant. For the choice between the two non-citation forms, both the grammatical function of DEAF and the location of the following segment proved significant. Among the social factors, only age and region contributed significantly to the observed variation. The other non-linguistic factors for which the researchers coded – ethnicity, gender, language background and social class – failed to reach statis-tical significance.

Specifically, while the youngest and oldest signers in four of the seven sites (Virginia, Louisiana, California, Washington) preferred non-citation forms, in these sites signers aged 26 to 54 were more likely to use citation forms. In one site (Kansas/Missouri) the non-citation form was favored by signers in all age groups, while in another (Massachusetts) non-citation forms were disfavored by signers in all age groups. Finally, in one site (Maryland) older signers preferred the non-citation forms, while the middle age and younger ones preferred the citation form. The results clearly show that DEAF is a classic sociolinguistic variable, and the challenge for researchers is to explain the correlation between the linguistic factors and the social ones. One explanation directly concerns the history of Deaf education in the USA.

The history of Deaf education had a direct impact on the recognition of ASL as a language, independent in structure from English. Before 1880, while opponents questioned its status, ASL was accepted widely as the medium of

(a)

(b)

(c)

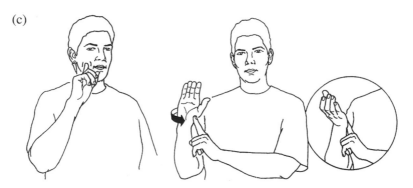

Fig. 4.4a, b, c   *DEAF ear to chin, chin to ear, contact cheek* (DEAF CULTURE)

instruction. Between 1880 and 1960, however, the status of ASL was very fragile, even among its users. Recall that in 1960 William Stokoe published the first linguistic description of ASL (Stokoe, 1960), and the recognition of ASL as a viable natural language slowly began to grow. The history of Deaf education and the recognition of ASL appear to be reflected in the patterns of variation in this study. Specifically, in the majority of sites studied, older signers use more non-citation forms. Many of them were attending residential schools at a time when ASL was actively suppressed and forbidden. While they were certainly fluent users of the language, there was very little metalinguistic awareness or prescriptivism accompanying that use. Indeed, many of the older signers in the study could not provide a name for their language – ASL – as the two younger groups could. Rather, many of the older signers still referred to their fluent language production simply as "sign". In contrast, the 26- to 54-year-old signers in the sample were in school at the time when ASL was beginning to be recognized and valued as a language separate from English. ASL was still not accepted in classrooms, but there was a rapidly growing awareness in the Deaf community of the need for recognition. In the late 1960s and early 1970s, formal instruction in sign language began, along with the preparation of teaching materials. This new awareness of the status of ASL helps explain the preference among the 26- to 54-year-old signers in the majority of sites examined for the citation forms of DEAF. The prescriptivism seen here in the use of citation forms may be regarded as a tool in maintaining the hard-won recognition of ASL. Finally, the youngest signers in the sample all attended school at a time when, for the most part, the status of ASL was no longer in question. The change in the status of ASL may explain the more frequent use of non-citation forms by younger signers. The status of the language is not threatened by the use of non-citation forms. This would seem to account for the general patterns that we see. Deviations from this pattern, such as the preference in the older Massachusetts signers and the youngest Maryland signers for citation forms, may be explained by the specific history of those communities, which is now being explored.

Other policy changes in Deaf education may also play a role in the patterns exhibited in the data. For example, in recent years, educational policies in many US States have favored placing deaf children in mainstream public school classes (Ramsey, 1997). As a result of such policies, children have fewer opportunities to interact on a daily basis with communities of ASL users. In addition, the Deaf community in the USA has long been characterized by its own social institutions and by dense social networks (Baynton, 1996).

Summary of the studies

The three studies reviewed here are examples of current work being carried out on variation in sign languages. This is work that reflects changing perspectives on sign language structure and use. The studies of DEAF and of pinky extension, in particular, show us that the analysis of internal constraints on variation in ASL needs to proceed with caution, as the identification of such constraints may not always be completely straightforward. While casual observation might suggest the presence of phonological constraints, further examination reveals functional constraints (as in the case of DEAF) or pragmatic ones (as in the case of pinky extension). The analysis of DEAF highlights the importance of considering the social factors particular to Deaf communities.

Methodological issues for the studies

The three recent studies discussed also illustrate the methodological issues that need to be considered when studying linguistic variation. Three of the main issues are:

1. defining and sampling a community;
2. describing natural language; and
3. defining variables and constraints.

We will discuss each one in turn, with particular attention to the implications for the study of sign languages.

Defining and sampling a community. The first issue common to studies of variation in both sign and spoken languages concerns sampling. The goal of all variation studies is to describe the patterns of variable linguistic structure within and across language communities. Whether the study is qualitative or quantitative, participants in the study must be members of the communities whose language use is being described. Further, quantitative sociolinguistic work that seeks to reach conclusions about language use in a community as a whole must take steps to ensure that its participant group is as representative as possible of the entire community. A study of variable sign language use in the Deaf community, for example, must study the language use of deaf people who use the particular sign language being studied. The language community may be defined in both linguistic and social terms. If the study finds that a group of ASL users have some aspect of their language in common – for example, if the constraints on a particular variable affect all members of the community in the same way – then this is evidence that that group is a linguistic community (Labov, 1972b). When defining the language community in social terms, variation studies have taken two main approaches. One approach is to use broad social categories, like socioeconomic status and gender, to draw boundaries around sub-groups within a community (Labov, 1966b; 1972b). Another is to use community-based social networks. This latter approach looks at a community in terms of the number and nature of connections among individuals, in order to correlate these connections with patterns of language use (Labov, 1972a; Milroy, 1987a; 1987b; Eckert, 1989). A researcher who employs either approach, however, has an explicit definition of the language community in terms of common social factors.

The three recent studies described above examine variation in language structure and use in the US Deaf community. The researchers in each case took steps to ensure that all participants were deaf users of ASL, and that they were all connected socially to their local Deaf communities. In Hoopes' (1998) study of pinky extension and Collins and Petronio's (1998) study of Tactile ASL, the participants were known by the researchers to be members of local Deaf communities. They had grown up as users of ASL, attended residential schools and participated in social relationships with other deaf people, and in Deaf organizations like Deaf clubs. In Collins and Petronio's study, it was also important that participants be members of a community of Deaf-Blind people. The researchers defined this membership both in terms of physical blindness and in terms of language use and socialization. All 17 participants were legally blind as a result of Usher's Syndrome I, all regularly socialized with other Deaf-Blind adult users of Tactile ASL, and all were comfortable and experienced users of Tactile ASL. In Lucas *et al.*'s (2001) study, not all participants in the seven communities were personally known to the researchers. Rather, the project relied on contact people in each area to recruit a sample that was as representative of the community as possible. This strategy was informed by the social network approach of Milroy (1987b). Potential participants were approached by a contact person; this was a deaf individual who lived in the area, who possessed a good knowledge of the local community and who was a respected member of the community. A major concern of this study was representativeness. Therefore, the researchers and contact people tried to recruit a group of participants diverse enough to match the diversity of the US Deaf community.

Describing natural language.   The second issue concerns the type of data analyzed. Studies of sociolinguistic variation differ in a fundamental way from formal studies of abstract linguistic competence; studies of variation are committed to studying language in context (Labov, 1966b; 1972b; Milroy, 1987a; 1987b; Lucas, 1995). Directly eliciting different variants of a sociolinguistic variable would defeat the purpose of studying how the social and linguistic environments of language use condition variation. The sociolinguistic interview, although it has been used in many studies as a way in which linguists could record conversational language use, has been criticized as not being conducive to "natural speech" (Milroy, 1987b; Schilling-Estes, 1999). The ideal would be to record and study the full range of the community's styles of language use, from formal lectures given to an audience of strangers, to casual daily encounters with friends and acquaintances. In reality, this is impossible. First of all, few people, if any, whether they are deaf or hearing, sit around waiting for linguists to come and record their conversations. Also, as we discuss further below, the camcorder would be distracting.

Despite these fundamental limitations on linguists' access to "natural language use", each of the three recent studies reported on here made methodological accommodations toward gathering conversations that were as natural as possible. The conversation types that were recorded differed on many dimensions: how well the conversational participants knew one another, the degree to which the conversations were about language itself, the length of the conversations, and the presence or absence of the researchers during the videotaping. Each of these dimensions might have provided an environment that would affect variation. For this reason, the conclusions take into account these aspects of the recorded conversations.

Hoopes, for example, recorded the signer during four different one- to two-hour conversations with other ASL users. The first and third conversations were with a close friend of hers, also deaf, from her residential school. The second recording was made during a conversation with a deaf graduate student from Gallaudet University, someone with whom the signer was casually acquainted. During these conversations, the deaf signer and her conversational partner were asked to "just chat". The final conversation was with a hearing interpreter, a good friend of the signer. Before this conversation, the researcher suggested some topics they might discuss. During all of these conversations, the researcher was not a participant; in fact, he was absent from the room.

In their study of Tactile ASL, Collins and Petronio relied on conversational data videotaped under two different circumstances. The first recording was made during an informal party, which lasted about four hours. Eleven Deaf-Blind adults who regularly socialized together attended the party. The researchers videotaped their Tactile ASL conversations with one another. The second situation was one which one of the researchers had set up for an earlier study. In this situation, three pairs of Deaf-Blind adults were recorded telling stories to one another using Tactile ASL. The researcher viewed this second set of data as coming from more formally situated language use.

In Lucas et al.'s study, groups of signers were videotaped during one- to two-hour data collection sessions. These sessions were divided into three parts. The first consisted of approximately one hour of free conversation among groups of participants, without the researchers present. In the second part, at least two participants were selected from each group and interviewed in depth by deaf researchers about their educational and linguistic backgrounds, social networks and patterns of language use. The final part involved eliciting lexical variants from the participants who had been interviewed. All participants in this part of the data collection were shown the same set of 33 pictures and asked to supply signs for the objects or actions represented in the pictures.

Defining variables and constraints.   The third issue that the studies described here share with all studies of sociolinguistic variation is a concern that what is being investigated is, in fact, a sociolinguistic variable. The three studies are on a frontier, as they are some of the first studies of variation in ASL in about 20 years. The hope is that we now know enough about the structure of ASL in order (1) to identify what varies, (2) to describe this variation and (3) to quantify it. The first steps in variation analysis are to define the variable and the envelope of variation. That is, what forms count as instances of the variable? Are the forms that vary indeed two ways of saying the same thing?

The three studies required, first, a consideration of what features were noticeably variable. These variables might be found at any level of linguistic structure, from phonology to discourse. For a quantitative study like Lucas *et al.*, the hope was that these variables would also correlate with both linguistic and social factors. For qualitative studies like Collins and Petronio, in which a language variety is being described in detail for the first time, the goal is that the variables that are described will uniquely identify the community being studied and will be amenable to further quantitative or applied work.

An additional issue that arises early in a variation study concerns specifying the factors that may potentially influence a signer's choice of a variant. Lucas (1995), for example, investigated the potential effects of eight separate linguistic factors on the choice of a variant of DEAF. As it turned out, most of these constraints proved not to be statistically significant. However, the labor of coding for many factors was not in vain. The study demonstrated that Liddell and Johnson's (1989) hypothesis that variation in the form of DEAF is influenced primarily by the location of the preceding sign is, at best, incomplete. The studies discussed in detail here are at different stages in the process of identifying constraints. Collins and Petronio's study, because its purpose was simply to describe the differences between visual and Tactile ASL, set out to note features that were known to be unique to tactile signing. The researchers knew that being Deaf-Blind is a conditioning factor for some changes in language use, but the question was "what linguistic changes take place?" Hoopes and Lucas *et al.*, on the other hand, needed to propose constraints, both linguistic and social, on the variables to be quantified. A central theoretical issue for variation studies is the identification of internal constraints on the variables. As Labov states, the issue "is to discover whatever constraints may exist on the form, direction or structural character of linguistic change" (1994: 115). Phonological constraints on the variables considered by Hoopes and Lucas *et al.* could include the segmental phonological environment or suprasegmental, or prosodic, environment. Other linguistic constraints could be morphological, syntactic or related to discourse topic or type of discourse.

As for social constraints, the researcher's knowledge of the community should inform what factors are considered in the model of variation. Hoopes did not design his study of pinky extension to take into account social constraints other than the level of intimacy between conversational partners, as it was expressly limited to investigating the variable signing of a single individual. Collins and Petronio's study suggests that if Deaf-Blind and sighted individuals are included in the same study of variation in ASL, then this should be taken into account, as the sighted or blind status of a deaf person could affect how they use the language. Owing to the much larger sample size, Lucas *et al.* were able to include several social factors in the statistical analysis of variants of DEAF.

Finally, data collection itself presents a methodological problem. While one goal of sociolinguistic research is to base conclusions on conversation that is as "natural" as possible, one aspect of the basic method required for doing careful study of natural language use impinges on this goal. That is, the conversation being studied needs to be recorded, and yet the fact that the conversation is being recorded makes it less likely to be close to the vernacular use of the language. Labov (1972b) has called this problem the "Observer's Paradox". When considering sociolinguistic research in Deaf communities, this problem may be magnified. Videotaping is more intrusive than audiotaping. Equally important is the issue of anonymity. While voices on an audiotape cannot easily be connected to a face or a name, except by the researchers, faces on a videotape are not anonymous. The Deaf community is small, and signers may be concerned, with good reason, that what they say on videotape will be seen by others in the community and understood out of context. With videotaping, complete anonymity is impossible.

Conclusions

We return now to the questions that we posed at the beginning of this chapter. It would seem that the variation that we observe in all human languages, be they spoken or signed, is for the most part systematic. The linguistic factors that condition the variation have to do with features of the variable in question, the immediate linguistic environment in which it occurs, its function, or with features of the discourse in which it occurs. While many of the social factors that condition variation are the same for spoken and sign languages – e.g. region, age, gender, ethnicity, socioeconomic class – it seems that there are some factors, such as language use in the home, that are unique to sign language variation. Furthermore, it is clear that age and region need to be understood specifically within the context of Deaf education. While we see many similarities between the variable units and processes in spoken and sign languages, fundamental differences between the respective structures of spoken and sign languages are reflected in variation. We see this in the strong role that grammatical constraints play in phonological variation in sign languages. Continuing research on variation in a wide variety of sign languages can only enhance our understanding of variation in all languages.

Suggested readings

For spoken language variation, Wolfram's (1991) *Dialects and American English*, Trudgill's (1999) *The Dialects of England* and Wolfram and Schilling-Estes' (1998) *American English* all provide comprehensive and accessible discussions of the nature of variation, along with clear examples. A more philosophical discussion can be found in Milroy's (1992) *Linguistic Variation and Change*. For sign language variation, Lucas (1995) and Sutton-Spence and Woll (1999) provide good reviews of the literature, and individual articles on variation appear in various volumes of the *Sociolinguistics in Deaf Communities* series (ed. Ceil Lucas; published annually by Gallaudet University Press).

Exercises

1. What is variation? What is a sociolinguistic variable?
2. What is a linguistic variable?
3. Explain the concepts of internal constraints and external constraints on variation.
4. Does sign language variation resemble spoken language variation? If so, how?
5. Pick two signs, one which shows handshape variation and one which shows variation in palm orientation. Over the course of several weeks, keep a note of how signers are producing these two signs and of the characteristics of the signers, i.e male or female, old or young, African American or white, etc. Describe the patterns that emerge from your observations and discuss any external constraints (e.g. ethnic origin, religious affiliation) unique to your situation that may be contributing to the variation you observe.
6. Pick two signs which show regional variation, such as BIRTHDAY or PICNIC. Ask 20 signers what their signs are and make a note of where the signers are from. Again, describe the patterns that emerge from your observations.
7. Do a videotaped interview with two people (at the same time), asking them about topics of interest to the Deaf community, topics that are likely to elicit the sign DEAF. Describe the patterns that emerge, in terms of the sign being produced from ear to chin, from chin to ear, or as a contact on the cheek. If the sign DEAF does not display such variation in the sign language you are analyzing, substitute another sign that interests you.

NOTES

1 In accord with convention, English glosses of ASL signs are written in capitals.
2 In the notation that has become conventional in sociolinguistics, linguistic variables such as (ay) and (aw) are enclosed by parentheses. Thus, (r), for example, means "variable r". Chambers explains that "the parentheses are intended as equivalents to

slashes for phoneme(s) ... and square brackets for phone(s) .... Like the phonemes /r/ and /æ/, the variables (r) and (eh) represent abstract linguistic entities. Just as phonemes are actualized as one or more allophones, so variables are actualized as one or another of the variants" (1995: 17).

3 VARBRUL is a specialized application of the statistical procedure known as logistic regression. The program allows the researcher to investigate simultaneously the influence of the many factors that may potentially influence a language user's choice among variable linguistic forms. VARBRUL was developed by David Sankoff (Cedergren and Sankoff, 1974; Rousseau and Sankoff, 1978). For information on the mathematical basis of the program see Sankoff (1988). For a guide to the use of the program in studies of linguistic variation, see Young and Bayley (1996).

5   Discourse analysis

Melanie Metzger and Ben Bahan

Everyone knows that when individuals in the presence of others respond to events, their glances, looks, and postural shifts carry all kinds of implication and meaning. When in these settings words are spoken, then tone of voice, manner of uptake, restarts, and the variously positioned pauses similarly qualify. As does manner of listening. Every adult is wonderfully accomplished in producing all of these effects, and wonderfully perceptive in catching their significance when performed by accessible others. Everywhere and constantly this gestural resource is employed, yet rarely itself is systematically examined. In retelling events – an activity which occupies much of our speaking time – we are forced to sketch in these shadings a little, rendering a few movements and tones into words to do so. In addition to this folk transcription, we can employ discourse theatrics, vivifying the replay with caricaturized reenactments. In both cases, we can rely on our audience to take the part for the whole and cooperatively catch our meaning. Thus, in talk about how individuals acted or will act, we can get by with a small repertoire of alludings and simulations. Fiction writers and stage performers extend these everyday capacities, carrying the ability to reinvoke beyond that possessed by the rest of us.

Erving Goffman (1981: 1–2)

This phase of sign language behavior is of fundamental importance, and to the writers' knowledge has never been mentioned in the literature about American sign language. Many teachers and psychological counselors of the deaf who have been fairly successful in learning to make the signs and to finger spell and read the signing and spelling of deaf pupils and clients, have formed the impression that deaf persons are unresponsive, overly dependent, or lacking in self-reliance. What produced this impression seems to be a number of experiences of this kind: the teacher or counselor asks a question or gives a direction and gets no response but a watchful waiting attitude, often interpreted as the expectation of prompting or of help. But what has really happened in the linguistic situation is that the teacher's or counselor's utterance, correct enough in sign production and order, was followed by the kind of juncture that signals the end of a statement. The watcher is not unresponsive; on the contrary, he is responding perfectly correctly, waiting for the next utterance to follow, which the signer's "out of awareness" signal has told him is coming. When, however, the teacher or counselor holds his [or her] hands fixed in the last position reached in the sig of the ultimate sign or moves them toward the class or client still fixed in the dez configuration, he finds that his question has been perceived as a question and a signed answer or other appropriate answer is the response.

Stokoe *et al.* (1965: 275–6)

Discourse analysis is an interdisciplinary field of social inquiry that has recently come into its own right. For many years, scholars from a variety of fields including sociology, psychology, anthropology and cognitive science have pursued the study of human behavior in an effort to understand the patterns and rules that result in communicative interaction. Thanks to the work of scholars such as Schiffrin (1994) and van Dijk (1997a; 1997b), the diverse concerns these scholars have brought to their studies of discourse have been categorized and examined with the same scientific lens that has focused on discourse itself.

The first issue to be examined regards the definition of the very behavior that is to be studied. What is discourse? As van Dijk (1997a) points out, the term "discourse" has a variety of meanings, as diverse as the reference to a particular conversation or to broader social arenas, as in the phrase "political discourse". Fortunately, for the linguistic analysis of discourse, the term is at least somewhat constrained. Where linguists generally study language at many levels, from phonology to syntax, analysis of discourse refers to the study of language beyond the level of the grammatical sentence (Stubbs, 1983). In face-to-face interactions, sentences are not marked with capital letters or punctuation marks. One of the tasks of the discourse analyst is to identify the boundaries of units of discourse as it occurs when two or more people communicate. Another task is to determine what "grammatical" rules operate on the joining of these units into a coherent discourse, much like syntacticians study the rules by which grammatical sentences are formed. Discourse analysis distinguishes itself by focusing on language as it is used in real-world situations, regardless of whether the emphasis is on the structure of the discourse and the rules which constrain its construction, the actions accomplished through those constructions, or the contextual information that allows it to be both constructed and understood.

Discourse structure

Discourse can be examined in light of the rules that govern its organization. This organization can be analyzed regardless of whether the discourse is spoken, written or signed. The structural organization of discourse can be analyzed whether the discourse is monologic (as in lectures and narratives) or dialogic (as in conversations and interviews). The rules that operate on a given discourse can be studied based on whether the discourse is being jointly negotiated (as in face-to-face communication or in computerized chat rooms) or if it is less interactive (as in the pre-taping of a televized speech or the writing of a book).

Examination of the organization of discourse begins with the delineation of units of analysis, or discourse units. According to Schiffrin (1994), unlike the hierarchically structured phonological, morphological and syntactic units to which linguists are accustomed, discourse units do not clearly fit the notion of hierarchies. Discourse units have been described as being as large as entire encounters (see, for example, Schegloff, 1972; Schegloff and Sacks, 1973; Goffman, 1974). They have also been described as being as small as a single turn in conversation (Sacks *et al.*, 1974). Structural analyses of discourse can focus on propositions, reference and cohesion, topic and sub-topic organization, and even style issues. Regardless of the size of the unit of analysis, it is ultimately the examination of an utterance and its relationship to other utterances or types of utterances surrounding it that allow analysts to examine discourse structure.

Discourse action and interaction

Discourse can also be studied in terms of the impact it has on people and events. Through the use of a variety of linguistic tools, conversants are able to enact or comment upon real-world events. Language can affect social relationships at a macro-level. For example, an utterance such as "I hereby pronounce you husband and wife" is a linguistic behavior that changes social relationships for people from a variety of religious backgrounds. Language also affects interaction at the micro-level. For example, as Tannen (1986) points out, differences in conversational style can cause miscommunication and frustration between friends and family members.

When examining the acts conveyed through language, it can be seen that a single utterance can fulfill a variety of functions, including (but not limited to) requesting information, promising, or asserting. A single utterance can simultaneously fulfill more than one function. For example, uttering "Would you shut the door, please?" is both a question and a request. Likewise, a single function can be conveyed through more than one utterance. By focusing on function, it is possible to gain information about sequential structure mentioned above. For example, if one were heard to utter "Would you shut the door please? It's so cold in here!" then the assertion can be seen in relation to the request, i.e. as an explanation for it (van Dijk, 1997a: 14).

Acts conveyed by discourse can be direct or indirect. The request to close a door can be as direct as "Please shut the door" or as indirect as "Hmm, the door is open again ..." People use their knowledge of communication to respond appropriately (or inappropriately), with gravity or with humor. Whether or not an utterance conveys a certain intent can be subjective. A speaker might intend to insult an addressee but fails if the addressee does not feel insulted. Conversely, an addressee might feel insulted by an utterance, even though an insult is totally unintended by a speaker. In order to analyze how a particular utterance functions, one could analyze at least four aspects of the utterance:

- what happens just prior to the utterance and what a speaker or signer thinks is true about the addressee's thoughts and abilities;
- what the speaker/signer is thinking or intending;
- what is required in a given language for an utterance to be recognized functionally; and
- what is true about the world as put forth within the utterance.

This is one way of approaching the analysis of what conditions make utterances work between interlocutors. Discourse analysts can study the acts that are explicitly and implicitly conveyed by discourse, and the underlying rules that people bring to the uttering and interpretation of them.

Just as language provides a source for accomplishing certain acts, it is also a primary link allowing people to come together and interact with one another. Language is the behavior through which people communicate, and to do so they must have ways of beginning conversations (and ending them), initiating, maintaining and yielding turns, introducing or shifting topics, being polite (or rude) and, generally, conveying any of the myriad of acts alluded to above (such as insulting, requesting, agreeing, arguing, persuading, etc.). Analysts of discourse also study the ways in which people accomplish these aspects of interaction. If it is possible for a speaker or signer and an addressee to have different feelings about whether or not the addressee has been insulted, then interaction requires some cooperative effort focused on constructing and deconstructing the ideas and thoughts that are intended. That is, conversational partners work together to jointly negotiate their interactions. This is true regardless of whether the interaction is a casual conversation, an interview for a job or with a medical doctor, or a formal presentation in which the presence or absence of audience laughter and backchanneling causes the presenter to make adjustments to the style and content of the presentation.

Context and discourse

Unlike the objective principles and laws that govern the physical environment, human interaction is variable. In order to truly understand the structure of discourse, and the social factors that impact upon it, it is necessary to examine the context in which the discourse occurs. Yet, as van Dijk (1997b) points out, context is as difficult a construct to define as is discourse. Nevertheless, there seems to be some agreement that, in addition to the information provided by the sequential unfolding of utterances, context incorporates at least three factors. The physical environment includes not only the location in which the interaction is taking place (such as a doctor's office) but also the objects or props and actions that are happening there. A second contextual factor is the background knowledge that participants bring to the interaction. This background knowledge is the information about the world and how people are expected to behave in it; this knowledge has been acquired through natural interaction and through books and other media throughout a participant's lifetime. Finally, the social relationships and the situation in which the interaction takes place represent a third factor providing contextual clues that allow interlocutors to understand and interpret the meaning of the discourse as it unfolds. These factors work together to assist people in producing and interpreting utterances. For example, the response to the greeting below will likely vary, depending on whether it is uttered by a medical doctor in a doctor's office, or by a business associate in the hallway:

A: How are you doing?
B: Fine! How are you?

A: How are you doing?
B: Well, I still have a fever . . . my medicine doesn't seem to be working.

The different interpretations are based on the location of the interaction (conversations are usually short and quick in a hallway vs. a medical office), the background knowledge of participants (that doctors take medical histories and business associates use such statements as greetings) and social context (doctors are responsible for taking care of ailments, while business associates might not be so interested in such personal information). Recognition that context incorporates aspects of the physical environment, background knowledge of participants and social relationship of interlocutors provides an objective framework from which to analyze discourse.

Context is relevant to the analysis of discourse structure because it is through the use of particular expressions and utterances within specific contexts that people can convey and comprehend what is being communicated. The sequential structure of a particular discourse can be seen in terms of the relationship of utterances to the context within which they occur. It is relevant to the functions conveyed by discourse because the social actors, their relationships to one another, their background knowledge and the situation in which they communicate can all impact upon the effect of what is uttered. The utterance "I hereby pronounce you husband and wife" carries a specific function when uttered at a wedding by a preacher or justice of the peace. It cannot carry the same function when uttered in any other circumstance or by any other type of social actor.

Methodological approaches to discourse analysis

The notion of language as social interaction serves as the basis for the analysis of discourse above the sentence. Nevertheless, there are a variety of theoretical perspectives and methodological approaches that have been applied to the study of discourse. According to Schiffrin (1994), there are six approaches, each influenced by the theories and disciplines that originally motivated them. The six approaches that Schiffrin describes extensively are: speech act theory, interactional sociolinguistics, ethnography of communication, pragmatics, conversation analysis and variation analysis. These approaches have been applied to the study of sign language discourse, and so it is worth summarizing her description of them here.

Speech act theory

Speech act theory can be directly attributed to two philosophers, John Austin (1962) and John Searle (1962; 1969). In the mid-1950s, when Austin first discussed the principles of speech act theory, the prevailing philosophical thought about language was to analyze its truth value based on a formal system of logic. Austin, however, noticed that some utterances do not have a truth value, but are intended to accomplish certain functions. For example, to declare "I hereby name this ship the SS Linguistics" allows the smashing of a bottle against the bows of a ship to have meaning. Verbs within an utterance that actually state, or *perform*, the action to take place in particular circumstances are *performative* verbs. For example, a ship is *named* when the appropriate person says it is named, so the act of naming is performed by the uttering of the verb.

Austin divides speech acts into three parts: locutionary, illocutionary, and perlocutionary. The locutionary act refers to the actual process of producing a sensible utterance. The illocutionary act is the performative act that is being carried out. The perlocutionary act is the effect that the utterance has by having been uttered. These three together make up the speech act of an utterance. Searle applied Austin's work within linguistic theory and developed a set of rules that he felt are unconsciously learned by users of a language to determine what an utterance is intended to accomplish and whether or not it has been accomplished effectively.

Speech act theory was originated philosophically and developed theoretically. However, despite the fact that the theory does not focus on issues such as multiple speakers and overlaps so common in interactive discourse, its fundamental principles are extremely useful. A single utterance can incorporate more than one speech act. Similarly, a single speech act might involve more than one utterance (or more than one turn in a conversation) (Schiffrin, 1987: 33). The act or actions intended to be undertaken by an utterance may be indirect and veiled. For instance, a speaker might state a request directly as in "Please close

the door" or indirectly as in "It sure is cold in here!" Examination of directness and indirectness within utterances can provide useful information about
languages and social interaction. For example, Tannen (1986) discusses how
conversational style can vary based on factors such as regional background or
gender, and can have a tremendous impact on people's daily lives, even making or breaking personal relationships. Speech act theory provides a systematic
approach to analyzing the functions of utterances in discourse.

Despite the use of the term "speech", speech act theory is not limited to the
study of spoken languages. Native users of sign languages, like those of any
language, use language to perform such acts as asking, requesting, offering,
threatening, advising, etc. Although very little research directly applies speech
act theory to sign language discourse, Celo (1996) applies this theory to Italian Sign Language (LIS) and the use of interrogatives, and Roush (1999) to
indirectness in ASL. In his examination of the syntactic and pragmatic aspects
of *wh*-questions and *yes–no* questions, Celo finds that there is at least one performative sign in LIS that can be used to indicate interrogative intention for
yes–no questions. This manual sign is produced with a flat O handshape. This
handshape is articulated either in front of the signer or on the back of the other
hand (palm downward). There is no translation for this sign in Italian, but Celo
suggests it functions much like the upside-down question mark at the beginning
of written Spanish questions. In a similar way to the question mark in written
Spanish, the interrogative sign is produced at the beginning and end of the
signed LIS interrogative.

In his study of requests and refusals, Roush examines speech acts in terms
of politeness and conversational style. The application of speech act theory
provides a framework for Roush to challenge a stereotype about directness
within the American Deaf community. Interestingly, both Celo and Roush find
that non-manual signals play an important role in the analysis of illocutionary
and perlocutionary force in sign languages.

Interactional sociolinguistics

While speech act theory offers a philosophical approach to the study of discourse, anthropology and sociology combine with linguistic theory to provide
the interdisciplinary background for the approach Schiffrin (1994) identifies as
interactional sociolinguistics. Sociologist Erving Goffman provides the sociological perspective. In his extensive work he focuses on both the ritual and
systematic nature of interaction, and how this interacts with specific interactive
events. For example, in his work he applies the observations of Bateson (1972)
regarding animal interaction to humans. Bateson observes that monkeys are
able to engage in what is seemingly identical behavior (such as fighting), but
can determine when that behavior is intended as playful or serious. Goffman

discusses this ability to frame behavior in human interaction. Linguists then apply his analysis of how interaction is framed and how people frame their relationships to one another through their discourse.

Gumperz contributes an anthropological perspective. Like Goffman, he focuses on both the impact of society and the individual on a given encounter. Gumperz' work examines the ways an individual interprets an interaction. He describes a variety of contextualization cues that can be used as conversational strategies to aid in the interpretation of discourse within a particular interaction; these are based on the specific individuals who are present, and their cultural and subcultural backgrounds.

Because interactional sociolinguistics is focused on interpretations that are unique to a given encounter, the data are based on naturally occurring interactions. These data are recorded and transcribed, as a basis for analysis. A growing body of research on sign languages has applied this theoretical framework, including the work of:

- Mather (1987; 1989; 1990; 1994) regarding adult–child interaction;
- Mather (1991) as applied to tty (teletypewriter, a text telephone device) telephone conversations between deaf interlocutors;
- Winston (1991; 1992; 1993; 1995) as applied to the use of space in ASL monologic discourse; and
- Roy (1989a) and Metzger (1995; 1999) as applied to interpreted discourse.

These studies are addressed later in this chapter.

Ethnography of communication

Perhaps in keeping with its anthropological foundation, the ethnography of communication is one of the broader approaches to discourse. According to Schiffrin (1994: 137)

Not only does it focus upon a wider range of communicative behaviors than the other approaches, but built into its theory and methodology is an intentional openness to discovery of the variety of forms and functions available for communication, and to the way such forms and functions are part of different ways of life.

Developed by Dell Hymes (1972), the ethnography of communication includes both the notion of speech acts and the role of macro-level social, specifically cultural, experience in communication. Hymes refers to the knowledge that an individual brings to interaction regarding language use and structure as his or her "communicative competence". This communicative competence focuses on the ability to communicate in the situations of daily life. He contextualizes speech acts by associating them, in a given analysis, with the situation and event in which they occur. Data are collected via the ethnographic participant observation engaged in by anthropologists, and analysis is focused specifically by a set of issues identified as relevant by Hymes (1972) in his SPEAKING grid:

S   setting/scene
P   participants
E   ends
A   act sequence
K   key
I   instrumentalities
N   norms of interaction and interpretation
G   genre

This taxonomy assists in the analysis of the three units that Hymes deems essential:

- the speech situation, e.g. a medical encounter;
- the speech event, e.g. the medical history interview; and
- the speech act, e.g. a question.

By utilizing Hymes' taxonomy, analysis of discourse ethnographically yields a completely different perspective than other approaches to the analysis of discourse. This is because the ethnography of communication takes into account the participants in the interaction, their goals and the setting in which the discourse takes place.

The ethnography of communication as an approach to the study of signed discourse has been applied in a variety of studies, such as Erting (1982; 1994) and Ramsey (1997) in their examinations of the educational experiences of deaf children. Erting (1982; 1994) and Johnson and Erting (1989) examine the role of social identity in the interaction of deaf and hearing adults and children in a preschool for deaf children. The ethnographic approach to this research results in the recognition that, for at least some deaf people, their sense of identity is comparable to that of many ethnic groups, and that this sense of identity is the natural outcome of the use of a visual language in a visually-oriented cultural environment. This realization is found to have implications when hearing, non-native signers of ASL attempt simultaneously to sign and speak (or to use sign-supported speech, SSS) and end up producing a visually-incomplete or inaccurate utterance when comparing the signed portion of the utterance to the spoken one. This clearly has ramifications for the training and assessment of preschool teachers.

Ramsey (1997) finds, through her year long ethnographic study, that the public school mainstream class she examines does not provide the deaf children with an educational experience that is equitable to that provided to the hearing students. Interestingly, her findings indicate that this inequity is neither the result of malice nor apathy. That is, it is in spite of very good intentions (or, perhaps, because of them?) that the students receive an educational experience that is less than that of their hearing peers. Her study emphasizes the importance of focusing on the goals of education and development for deaf children as the priority within their classrooms.

Pragmatics

Pragmatics as a subfield within linguistics is so broad that it very nearly defies definition (Levinson, 1983). Generally, pragmatics distinguishes the meaning of utterances in interaction from their literal and conventional semantic meanings. Specifically, Schiffrin (1994) identifies Gricean pragmatics as a describable pragmatic approach to the analysis of discourse. H.P. Grice (1957; 1968; 1975) is attributed with two major contributions to the field of pragmatics. First, he analyzed "speaker meaning" (as opposed to "semantic meaning") and, therefore, raised the issue that an utterance can be made with a certain intent that could differ from the seemingly obvious conventional sense of the words. Second, he developed a description of the "Cooperative Principle" to account for the ways in which conversants take advantage of the expectation of conversational cooperation in order to try to satisfy their interactive goals. The cooperative principle essentially consists of four maxims regarding the quality, quantity, relevance and manner of utterances in a conversation. That is, conversational partners can generally be expected to share information, in a polite manner, that is factually correct, relevant and sufficient for the addressee's knowledge. Because of the underlying expectation for cooperation, conversationalists can flout the maxims. For example, if a child is concerned about his or her parents' reaction to a bad grade at school, he or she might respond as follows:

MOTHER: So, did you get your exam back today? How did you do?
CHILD: Oh, no, we didn't get our grades back this afternoon.

In this example, the child's utterance flouts only one of the four maxims in the Cooperative Principle: the maxim of quantity. His response is polite, relevant to the question, and factually correct, but does not include sufficient information for his mother: the exams were returned in the morning, not the afternoon. The child takes advantage of the expectation that what he says is enough information in order to conclude answers to the mother's requests for information. Any of the maxims of the cooperative principle can be flouted, and examples of it abound in many arenas, particularly in humor and advertising. Analysis of conversation provides insights into why people infer what an utterance – or a sequence of utterances – means.

Perhaps because of its roots in philosophy, Gricean pragmatics accepts constructed sentences in imagined real-world contexts as data. However, Schiffrin

(1994) suggests that to apply Gricean pragmatics to the study of discourse, it is necessary to apply it to utterances from real-world interactions. In fact, in her own sample analysis, she focuses on the questions Grice addresses regarding how people infer meaning by analyzing referring sequences within a spoken English narrative. She suggests that the application of Gricean pragmatics to the analysis of discourse helps in the examination of how addressees use discourse to infer what a speaker means. While listening to a pronoun in English, an addressee might depend on the maxim of relevance to infer the identity of the intended referent.

Although the number of analyses of pragmatics in sign language discourse is somewhat limited, there have been studies that incorporate issues related to Gricean pragmatics. For example, Johnson (1994) and Patrie and Johnson (in preparation) examine the role of first-time and second-time fingerspelled words in ASL discourse. This builds on Schiffrin's (1994) analysis of referring terms, and on the relevance of explicit vs. inexplicit reference. Johnson (1994) and Patrie and Johnson (in preparation) find that signers are often more explicit or clear in the articulation of first-time fingerspelled words. Since the phonological production of a fingerspelled word can convey a more or less explicit referring term, an addressee can use that information to assist him or her in interpreting the signer's intended meaning. That is, by recognizing that a fingerspelled word is articulated in a certain way, the addressee can identify that referring term as being a first-mention or as referring back to a previously mentioned referent. This kind of observation and analysis is exactly what pragmatic analysis of discourse is intended to uncover.

Roush (1999) examines the role of politeness in directness and indirectness in ASL, supporting Schiffrin's (1994) contention that politeness as referred to in the cooperative principle is culturally defined. Roush finds that ASL signers in conversation use both manual and non-manual signs to mitigate what might otherwise be construed as direct and even rude utterances. His research counters the previous perception of deaf Americans as being direct and rude. The application of a pragmatic approach to the analysis of a sign language provides useful information about how addressees can infer the intended meaning of a signer. In the two studies described here, it can be seen that two aspects of sign languages that are distinct from spoken language discourse – fingerspelling and non-manual signals – can play an important role in the pragmatics of signed discourse.

Conversation analysis

Harold Garfinkel's ethnomethodology (1967; 1974) provides the sociological foundation for the work of conversation analysts such as Sacks, Schegloff and Jefferson. Like some other approaches to the study of discourse, conversation analysis is concerned with both the structure of interaction and the knowledge that participants bring to it in order to communicate and understand one another effectively. However, conversation analysis is much more focused on the structural sequences within conversation. For example, the focus of analysis is on the description of events within a conversation, such as the opening up of the last phase of a conversation. In this sense, conversation analysis is less likely than other approaches to dwell on the competence of the participants. The focus is more on structural aspects of the conversation (which in turn reflect participants' knowledge and linguistic competence).

Schegloff (1972) and Schegloff and Sacks (1973) note that one event common in conversational discourse is the use of an utterance which requires a second part or a response of some sort to fill a next-position slot. Such "adjacency pairs" account for numerous aspects of interaction, including the manner in which people negotiate the beginning or ending of a conversation. One form of adjacency pair is the "summons–answer" sequence found in spoken telephone conversations (Schegloff, 1972). Adjacency pairs are found in greetings and also in conversational closings (Schegloff and Sacks, 1973). They provide evidence of the relationship between context and language use. That is, it is possible for contextual events, such as the flashing light of a telephone tty ringing, to provide the first part of a summons–answer sequence. In spoken language studies, this accounts for the seemingly three-part greeting exchange found in telephone conversations:

"Hello?"
"Hi! This is Dawson. How are you?"
"Oh, hi, I was just thinking about you!"

Adjacency pairs can also be used to negotiate the turn exchanges within a conversation. This happens explicitly to signal turn exchanges within a tty conversation, through the use of typed GA (Go ahead).

Recorded conversations and a transcription system are used to capture a conversation and to describe it in a manner that is unbiased about what is relevant. For example, pauses, inbreaths, etc. would all be transcribed by a spoken language conversation analyst. Although there is no conventional transcription system in place for the analysis of sign language following this approach, features that have been included in transcription include head and body movement, eye gaze, facial expression, spatial location of articulators (see Winston, 1993) and even gestures that are not linguistic *per se*, but are part of the gestured communication common to most languages, be they spoken or signed (see Liddell and Metzger, 1998). To gain insights into the relevant structural features, there is generally a preference toward analysis of a larger corpus of data.

This approach to the analysis of discourse can be found in a variety of sign language studies. For example, Dively (1998) applies the work of Schegloff *et al.* (1977) on conversational repair to the repairs in an ASL interview. Glaser (1999) examines the interaction of the constraints of written text and natural conversational features in tty conversations of an adult member of the British Deaf community. These two studies are discussed later in this chapter.

Variation analysis

The study of linguistic variation (i.e. alternate ways of saying the same thing) was developed by William Labov. Grounded in linguistics, variation analysis seeks to locate units of discourse that share a meaning, and to determine what social or linguistic factors contribute to the existence of multiple variants. Variation analysis can apply to units of discourse ranging in size from the smallest unit of contrast produced phonetically to entire segments, such as the narrative, which generally occurs within the larger context of interaction. In order to determine the environments in which certain variants occur, it is useful to gather a fairly large corpus of data and conduct quantitative analyses. In addition, when searching for social factors responsible for the variation, it is essential that the data include representation of these factors. That is, the data would include both male and female subjects when examining gender variation.

Lucas (1995) examines the ASL sign DEAF, and the phonological variation of location (chin-to-ear vs. ear-to-chin). She finds that the phonological variation is patterned in terms of the sign and its distribution in discourse (e.g. syntactically). Hoopes *et al.* (2001) focus on three different studies, including lexical variation, phonological variation and variation between visual and Tactile ASL. In what is likely the largest study of sociolinguistic variation in a sign language, Lucas *et al.* (2001) report on phonological, lexical, morphological and syntactic variation in ASL, based on videotaped conversations between native signers from seven locations in the USA, from three different age groups, including both white and African American signers.

Features of sign language discourse

There are many approaches to and motivations for the analysis of discourse, be it spoken, written or signed. Some research examines situated discourse with a focus on contexts and participants, and on their goals and how they use language to achieve them. Other studies focus on larger patterns of discourse that are identifiable within a particular genre of discourse (such as conversation or narrative) or on a particular language (such as a study of the role of eye gaze in Filipino Sign Language). Still others seek to find universal features of discourse that appear to be common for all languages, such as turntaking in conversational interaction.

Regardless of the motivation, theoretical framework, analytic approach or specific sign language being analyzed, the following sections describe features that researchers have found in their analyses of sign language discourse. The narrative in Figure 5.1 is used to provide examples of these features. This narrative is taken from a multiparty conversation including five deaf native signers of ASL between the ages of 25 and 55 from the American mid-west. The data are used with permission and taken from the study of Sociolinguistic Variation in ASL, conducted by Lucas *et al.* that has been supported in part by a grant from the National Science Foundation. Transcription is based on that used in the Vista ASL Series Transcription Convention (in Lentz *et al.*, 1988) with a translation into English provided in italics below each line of the narrative. The narrative occurs in the midst of a conversation about the bombing of a federal building in Oklahoma, and focuses on the signer's experience with the moment of silence that was held in respect for the many victims who were killed in that bombing. The narrative begins with the signer explaining that the moment of silence took place a week after the bombing, during a class he was teaching in an interpreter education program.

In this narrative, the signer begins his turn in the middle of the discussion about the bombing event. He takes only about 35 seconds to tell about his experience, but he includes many discourse-level features. The features that will be highlighted and discussed below include:

- the getting, maintenance and yielding of turns (turntaking);
- the occurrence of false starts and repairs within conversation (conversational repair);
- the use of discourse markers to provide information about what has been said or what is coming up next in the discourse (discourse markers);
- the acting out and "speaking for" others when describing events from other times and places (constructing dialogue and action);
- the ways in which people use discourse to coordinate what they say and make it more coherent (cohesion); and
- some of the strategies that are used to involve addressees more intently in what is being uttered (rhythm, rhyme and repetition).

Turntaking

One of the earliest studies of interactive sign language discourse focused on how deaf interlocutors get and yield turns (Baker, 1977). In order to examine how turntaking happens in discourse, it is necessary to identify relevant points for turn initiation and how these points are marked in the discourse. It can then be better understood why one person appears to have smoothly interjected a point, and why another person seems to be interrupting someone else's turn.

AWFUL! PRO-1 THINK
That reminds me of something awful

POSS-1 CLASS IX-loc
that happened in a class of mine.

PRO-1 TEACH INTERPRET TRAIN PROGRAM IX-loc
I teach in an interpreter training program

HAVE TWO STUDENT FROM O-K-A C-I-T-Y IX-loc
and I have two students who are from Oklahoma City.

THAT EXACT ONE WEEK – BOMB ONE WEEK LATER (head nod)
That week – a week after the bombing

ANNOUNCE HAVE TIME TIME-NINE-O'CLOCK IX SILENCE FOR ONE
  MINUTE. FINE.
we were all told that there was time set aside for a moment of silence, at nine o'clock.
  Okay . . .

DURING POSS-1 CLASS TIME EIGHT-T-(O) TEN. FINE.
That happened to be during the time I was teaching, since my class met from 8 to 10
  o'clock. Okay.

PRO-1 – (rs: PRO-3) PRO-3 WANT HONOR. FINE.
I – and they wanted to show respect. Okay.

WELL GET-UP (CL: people standing in semi-circle)
So, everyone stood-up

BE-QUIET. STAND. BE-QUIET . . .
and we were all standing there quietly,

#THEN FEW MINUTE PRO-1 OPEN-EYES THINK ENOUGH TIME. FINISH
then after a few minutes I opened my eyes because I thought it had been enough time
  and we were done.

PRO-1 CL:9 (eyes look up) (rs: startled) HOLD-IT. SILLY! STUDENT CRY+++
But when I opened my eyes and looked up at the class I was surprised to see someone
  crying.

LOOK-AT. WOW TOUCH-HEART.
And it really got to me . . .

(rs: IX-loc) FIND POSS-3 SEVERAL FRIENDS DIE PRO-3 (wh) IX-loc TOO
I found out they lost several friends that day.

S-O PRO-3 KNOW SOME PEOPLE IX-loc. WOW LOOK-AT WONDER. TOUCH-
  HEART WOW
So I had students who actually knew some of the people who died in the bombing. Really
  made me think!

Fig. 5.1   *Narrative from a multiparty conversation including five Deaf native*
signers of ASL
Notes: IX – index; loc – location; Poss – possessive; PRO – pronoun; rs – role
shift; CL – classifier; # – lexicalized fingerspelling.

Sacks *et al.* (1974) found in spoken conversations, a point in conversation they identify as the "turn relevance place". It is at that point in the conversation that a set of rules comes into play, governing the coordination of who gets a turn at talk. Turns can be allocated by a current speaker (and accepted or declined), requested by another speaker (and again, accepted by others or not), or the turn relevance place can be bypassed until the next opportunity arises. The identification of such rules is helpful not only in understanding the local organization of conversation, but also in examining what happens when conversations have "problems". That is, interruptions can be identified on the basis of a speaker "violating" the rules and attempting to elicit a turn at a place in the discourse that is not a turn relevance place. It is important to recognize, however, that conversational regulation, like any other aspect of discourse, is subject to sociolinguistic factors. It is possible to find that what one speaker considers to be an interruption may be seen by the "interrupter" to be a sign of rapport and interest (Tannen, 1984).

In the narrative in Figure 5.1, the five interlocutors are having a conversation about the bombing of a federal building in Oklahoma City. At the point that the narrative begins, the conversation has focused on how the experience might differ for surviving bomb victims who were stuck in the rubble, depending on whether they were hearing or deaf. After a comment about whether one would be better off hearing or not hearing rescue teams (especially if they were to come very close without making it in time), there is a pause in which all signers have their hands at rest. At this point the signer of the narrative raises his hands to begin, and the other conversants accept his turn in the conversation. This pause is an example of a turn relevance place. The signer took advantage of it and successfully took the floor. In research on sign language discourse, one way of taking the floor is to shift from a position in which the hands are at rest. This turntaking strategy and others were originally described in an early study of turntaking in sign language discourse (Baker, 1977). Baker's study of two videotaped, dyadic conversations examines the signaling of turn initiation, maintenance and shift in ASL. Baker discussed her findings in terms of both signer and addressee behaviors, and found that the majority of these regulators are articulated non-manually in ASL. Other studies have found additional features. These are the features that are discussed below:

- hand movements;
- indexing, touching, waving, tapping;
- postural/head shifts;
- use of eye gaze to or away from addressee;
- changes in pace of signing;
- filling pauses (by holding the preceding sign, furrowing brow, looking up, etc.);

- head nodding and facial expressions (such as smiling, expressing surprise, agreement, etc.);
- changing the size and frequency of head nodding;
- use of palm up or indexing addressee;
- shifting to or from hands at rest;
- repetition of signs.

Some of these features are used to elicit turns, others to continue or to shift turns. Some of these are employed by the signer whose turn it is, others by the addressee.

Baker's taxonomy of turn initiation regulators includes optional attention getting devices, such as indexing, touching or waving of a hand. Even without tactile initiation regulators or visual initiation regulators, Baker (1977) finds that the movement of a signer's arms out of a rest position is sufficient to mark the beginning of a turn, just as the signer did to initiate the telling of his Oklahoma City Bombing experience. The signer might also lean forward toward the addressee, and usually begins the turn without making eye contact, unless asking a question. Not surprisingly, addressee status is marked by eye gaze toward the signer and a lack of signing. This same eye gaze behavior has also been found in other sign languages, such as Filipino Sign Language (FSL) (Martinez, 1993; 1995).

The touching strategy in ASL, discussed in more detail by Baer (1991), can include various kinds of tapping. For example, Baer describes tapping on the top of the shoulder as indicating the request for a turn, as opposed to a tap on the side of the shoulder, which is an indication that the "addressee" is blocking the tapper's view. The weight and frequency of taps on the top of the shoulder convey information about the turn requestor's utterance-to-be, for instance, whether it is urgent or exciting information. Mather (1990) also examines attention getting strategies in ASL and distinguishes between what she terms tactile initiation regulators and visual initiation regulators. Mather and, later, FitzPatrick (1993) and Chen (1993), find that an additional strategy, used with young children, is moving into the line of sight of the addressee to elicit his or her attention. Mather finds this is most effective when the turn initiator waits for the child to settle into the eye contact before beginning the utterance. FitzPatrick finds that a combination of visual and tactile initiators seems to be most effective, when engaged in communication with a group of deaf children.

The signers maintain their turns at propositional boundaries or after brief pauses by maintaining a lack of eye contact, keeping their hands in the signing space (with possible fillers such as furrowing the brow or shaking an index finger slightly) or holding the last sign that was articulated while pausing. In addition, the signer might increase the speed of signs within their discourse. During turn maintenance the addressee maintains eye gaze at the signer, and responds through backchanneling, repetition of some of the signed utterance or indexing the signer after propositions.

Signers mark turn relevance places by making eye contact with the addressee (this has also been found in FSL; Martinez, 1993; 1995), slowing down the speed of their utterance near the end of their turn, returning to a rest position, or eliciting a response from the addressee through one of a variety of behaviors. Ways of eliciting a response include raising a palm with the heel of the hand raised up, indexing the addressee, raising or holding the last sign of a turn, or using other non-manual markers for question forms that indicate the expectation of a response. Addressees mark the desire to get a turn by moving the hands out of a rest position (and also possibly by using the attention getting devices previously mentioned), breaking eye contact from the signer (when the signer makes eye contact with the addressee) or interrupting the signer and repeating the beginning of his or her utterance until the signer makes eye contact and relinquishes the turn. In addition, the addressee might increase the frequency and size of head nodding or indexing the signer, or shift his or her palm to a raised position, palm up.

Baker also mentions that in her data, the use of overlap is different from that in spoken language, where overlaps are temporally relatively short. In more recent research, Thibeault (1993) examines the use of overlap in a videotaped, dyadic conversation in FSL. Thibeault finds that overlap in the FSL conversation occurs frequently, and that it apparently fulfills two functions. One is related to turntaking, as discussed by Baker, in which one participant uses overlap to "interrupt" the signer in successful attempts to initiate a turn. The other, following Tannen (1984), is the use of overlap as a high-involvement style, in which the signers overlap when they share knowledge of the topic. For example, the addressee overlaps with the signer to bypass the fingerspelling of a familiar name.

Conversational repair

Regardless of conversational style, every interaction is subject to the possibility of errors in need of repair. In fact, Schegloff et al. (1977) propose that repair is not limited to errors and corrections. They posit that repairs also take other forms, such as word searches when a speaker tries to remember someone's name. In their analysis of the organization of repair in English conversation, Sacks et al. (1974) describe the "repair-initiation opportunity space", a period of conversation lasting three turns and beginning with a trouble source. It is during this period that the speaker can self-initiate a repair, or that a repair can be initiated by another participant. They find that there is a preference for self-repair and describe in great detail what forms repairs take in their English data, and what options there may be regarding which participant completes an initiated repair. As Brown and Levinson (1987) point out, politeness and cooperation in interaction seem to be universal, although how this is accomplished varies culturally. It is quite likely that the preference for self-correction is an issue of politeness and saving face for the person with the floor.

In the Oklahoma City Bombing narrative in Figure 5.1 above, the signer produces at least one self-correction. At the point at which he is describing the announcement about the moment of silence he signs:

> THAT EXACT ONE WEEK – BOMB ONE WEEK LATER (head nod)
> *That week – a week after the bombing*

This self-correction is an example of what Sacks *et al.* call a replacement repair, in which the words (or signs) are intended to replace a prior utterance. Examples of replacement repairs, and other types of repairs described by Sacks *et al.*, are documented in an ethnographic interview with three deaf ASL signers (Dively, 1998). In addition to replacement repairs, Dively finds examples of self-initiated repair, self-completed repair, other-initiated repair, other-completed repair and word-search repair. She also finds some repair strategies that appear to be unique to sign language discourse. For example, she finds that lexical signs that are independent, free morphemes produced without the use of the hands (nonhanded signs) can be used for repair. One example of a nonhanded sign (NHS) used for repair is NHS-I-WRONG, which can be produced with a brief headshake or with the head moving from one side to the other and then back to neutral (p. 142). Dively also finds that space can be a repair issue in ASL. In one example from her data, the signer referred to her mother on the right side of the signing space. Later in her discourse, she replaced the right side with the left side of the signing space to indicate the same referent. Such a replacement could have been made as a result of the hand producing the remainder of utterances, since two hands can sign simultaneously (p. 157). Dively also finds that the signers use eye gaze and head turns to repair their ASL utterances. For example, Dively finds that eye gaze down and to the right or left of the signer combined with the turning of the head is used as a self-initiated word-search repair while the signer recalls information, such as the specific date of an event under discussion. Finally, the one type of repair that did not occur in Dively's data is other-initiated repair of ungrammatical utterances. Dively suggests that this is due to the fact that the three participants do not know one another very well. She also suggests that other-initiated repairs of grammaticality are more likely to occur in language learning environments. This is supported by research regarding the use of repair strategies as modeled by ASL teachers during ASL classes.

Strategies identified by Smith (1993) and Johnston (1993) include the ways in which the teacher would rephrase a question in order to assist a student in comprehending; for example, the teacher used a *wh*-question, followed by a more specific request which included lexicalized fingerspelling. When the student still did not understand, the teacher shifted to non-lexicalized fingerspelling and finally to a syntactic rephrasing of the original question (to a *yes–no* form). The teacher also used repetition of the students' lexical or fingerspelled utterances as a point of similarity upon which to build mutual understanding (Johnston, 1993). Smith (1993) suggests that, in this way, the teacher is modeling repair as a discourse strategy, based on students' own linguistic competence and for their future benefit as they become more fluent in the language.

Of the repair strategies identified in these studies, the use of "two-layered staff of utterances" is particularly interesting. By two-layered staff of utterances, Dively refers to the ability of signers to articulate more than one morpheme at the same time. That is, a signer can produce two separate one-handed signs simultaneously, one with the right hand, the other with the left. An example of this can be found in her data, in which one of the signers signs PRO.1 with the right hand while signing WAIT-A-MINUTE-hs-5-body with the left hand (Dively, 1998: 157). More commonly in her study, signers produce a two-handed manual sign concurrent with a nonhanded sign, as when one of the participants in her data signed what she categorizes as a fully lexical nonhanded sign NHS-UNSURE while signing manually DON'T-KNOW (p. 144). Dively calls for more research on the possible use of two-layered staff of utterances in spoken languages, perhaps through the use of spoken utterances combined with gestures such as thumbs up or down.

Discourse markers

Not surprisingly, the term "discourse markers" refers to units of discourse that mark or bracket segments of talking or signing. Schiffrin (1987) studies discourse markers as they occur in spoken English conversations, where they serve the speakers and addressees in producing and understanding interaction. She finds that discourse markers fulfill a variety of functions related to the exchange structure, the conveyance of actions, and framing the relationship between participants. Discourse markers help to connect sequences of utterances. For example, *and* joins two clauses by linking both prior and upcoming text, and *but* offers contrast between them (see also Tannen, 1993). In this manner, then, Schiffrin suggests that discourse markers coordinate discourse and provide coherence.

Discourse markers are not, however, limited to conversational discourse. For example, the use of *and* and *and then* in English narratives can be to sequence the description of events within the story:

1. **And then** we lived there for five years,
2. **and** we bought – we bought a triplex across the street.
3. **And** by that time we had two kids,

4. **and** we moved on the first floor,
5. **and** rented out the second.

(Schiffrin, 1987: 39)

In the Oklahoma City Bombing narrative, the signer also uses discourse markers to sequence the events that take place within his ASL narrative:

> THAT EXACT ONE WEEK – BOMB ONE WEEK LATER (head nod)
> *That week – a week after the bombing*

> ANNOUNCE HAVE TIME TIME-NINE-O'CLOCK IX SILENCE FOR ONE MINUTE. **FINE**.
> *we were all told that there was time set aside for a moment of silence, at nine o'clock. Okay ...*

> DURING POSS-1 CLASS TIME EIGHT-T-(O) TEN. **FINE**.
> *That happened to be during the time I was teaching, since my class met from 8 to 10 o'clock. Okay.*

> PRO-1– (rs: PRO-3) PRO-3 WANT HONOR. **FINE**.
> *I – and they wanted to show respect. Okay.*

In his narrative, the signer uses the sign FINE (produced with an open five handshape tapping on the signer's chest) to separate the events that lead up to his discovery that he teaches students who knew some of the victims killed in the bombing.

In an analysis of an ASL lecture, Roy (1989b) examines the role of discourse markers that segment the introductory, developmental and closing episodes. Similar to Schiffrin's (1987) findings regarding English markers of discourse, Roy finds that a single sign can have more than one function within the lecture. For example, she finds the sign NOW is used to convey temporal significance in the real world, as well as to mark temporally the beginning of topics or shifts to sub-topics within the lecture. She also observes use of a marker NOW-THAT, incorporating a one-handed sign for NOW with the other hand signing THAT, as in "that is the one I am talking about" (for a discussion of different signs that have been glossed as THAT, see Liddell, 1980). In the ASL lecture, NOW-THAT marks openings of new episodes while also referring back to a prior comment (as in "I am referring to that one"). While Roy finds several discourse markers that appear in gloss form to be similar to other languages (such as English *ok*, *anyway* and *know*), she also finds other markers, such as NOW-THAT (a two-handed sign produced in front of the body with a downward movement, with one Y-handshape palm up and the other palm down) and ON-TO-THE-NEXT-PART, that are clearly unique to ASL.

In a study of quotations and asides in ASL, Locker McKee (1992) finds the use of two lexical discourse markers: STOP (signed with the 5-handshape, palm facing forward away from the signer) and INDEX-HOLD. She also finds that the signer uses spatial location to mark aspects of discourse, such as marking an aside deviating from the main lecture by physically leaning or stepping to the side.

The study of discourse markers in sign languages indicates that, as in spoken languages, discourse markers in sign languages function to both bracket and link segments of discourse. Discourse markers in sign languages occur manually, non-manually and spatially.

Constructing dialogue and action

Varying accounts of the referential use of space exist, and these have evolved over time. Liddell (1980) and Winston (1991) have used the term "pantomime" as a descriptor for this aspect of discourse. While there have been many grammatical accounts of this spatial aspect of sign language discourse, many researchers describe the referential use of space as a pragmatic and discourse-level, rather than a grammatical, phenomenon (these include DeMatteo, 1977; Roy, 1989b; Winston, 1991; 1992; Liddell, 1995; Metzger, 1995; van Hoek, 1992; 1996; Liddell and Metzger, 1998). In particular, Roy (1989) follows Tannen (1989) and her observation that reported speech in discourse is seldom really a true report. Tannen suggests that speakers construct the dialogue of those in their stories, even dialogue originating from real conversations, adapting the discourse so that it fits appropriately the new social context, participants and the point that they hope to convey. For example, Tannen (1989), in her taxonomy of constructed dialogue, describes 10 different types. One type is choral dialogue in which the discourse represents the dialogue of many people – as in "And then all the Americans said, 'Oh, in that case, go ahead'" (Tannen, 1989: 113). Another is the dialogue of non-human speakers – as when, in speaking for a cat, someone utters, "She says, 'I see a beautiful world just waiting for me.'" (p. 118). In both of these cases, it is clear that the construction of discourse for others is not truly a representation of what was said, since rarely would one find a group of people uttering an identical sentence simultaneously, nor do we expect to hear speech from a cat.

Roy (1989b), Winston (1991; 1992), Metzger (1995) and Liddell and Metzger (1998) examine aspects of constructed dialogue in ASL, finding that, in sign language discourse, actions as well as discourse are constructed in narratives. Winston (1992) describes the construction of action and dialogue by signers as "performatives" that use space to "build" the elements of the narrative scene. Metzger (1995) builds on the analysis and uses Tannen's (1989) taxonomy to examine the occurrence of both constructed dialogue and constructed action in ASL in a series of sociolinguistic interviews. Metzger finds examples of six of the 10 types of constructed dialogue from Tannen's spoken language data occurring in Metzger's sign language data. Interestingly, seven out of eight of these categories that could pertain to constructing actions (such as constructing the actions of a cat) occur in the ASL data. Metzger finds that the signers utilize constructed action as a way of directly representing the actions of characters within a "storyworld", and that signers can indirectly represent the actions of characters through narration (such as using classifiers and/or gestures to describe rather than demonstrate the actions of characters within the narrative). In her data, signers also use a combination of both direct and indirect constructed action. For example, when a signer is describing a card game at which one of the seated players looks up to reply to someone who has just approached the card table, the signer both signs LOOK-UP and moves his head up and to the right, as he begins to construct the actions of that character (looking up and holding a handful of cards) as well as his dialogue (his response to the newcomer's utterance). While research suggests that constructed action plays a very prominent role in ASL narratives (see, for example, Mather and Winston, 1998; Liddell and Metzger, 1998), the construction of characters' actions is by no means limited to sign language discourse (see, for example, McNeill, 1992).

In the Oklahoma City Bombing narrative, the signer constructs his actions from the time within the "storyworld", demonstrating his actions at the moment he looked up and saw someone crying in his class:

> WELL GET-UP (CL: people standing in semi-circle)
> *So, everyone stood-up*
>
> BE-QUIET. STAND. BE-QUIET . . .
> *and we were all standing there quietly,*
>
> #THEN FEW MINUTE PRO-1 OPEN-EYES THINK ENOUGH TIME.
> FINISH
> *then after a few minutes I opened my eyes because I thought it had been enough time and we were done.*
>
> **PRO-1 CL: 9 (eyes look up) (rs: startled) HOLD-IT.** SILLY! STUDENT
> CRY+++
> *But when I opened my eyes and looked up at the class I was surprised to see someone crying*
>
> LOOK-AT. WOW TOUCH-HEART.
> *And it really got to me . . .*

When the signer uses the first person pronoun to indicate that he looks up and is surprised, he is not talking about the moment in which he is *telling* the story, but rather the moment within the story, at the time that he was teaching his class a week after the bombing took place. If his story were not a personal experience narrative, he would still be able to use a first person pronoun to refer to the person within the storyworld, even if that were a totally different person (and not simply himself at another time).

The use of constructed action and dialogue in ASL allows for discourse features, such as the conversational historical present (Wolfson, 1979), that are also found in other languages, albeit with different linguistic features. This aspect of sign language discourse has also been examined, following various theoretical perspectives, in many sign languages, including British Sign Language (Morgan, 1999), Danish Sign Language (Engberg-Pedersen, 1995), Swedish Sign Language (Ahlgren, 1990a) and Québec Sign Language (Poulin and Miller, 1995). Thus, the use of space for referential shift purposes is clearly an integral feature of the discourse of many sign languages.

Cohesion

Cohesion in discourse refers to those linguistic features that allow the discourse to be constructed and understood in a coherent manner. Cohesion can be identified based on linguistic structures that link different parts of discourse, such as referring terms (by using a pronoun to refer to a prior lexical noun, for example). In signed discourse, cohesion can be found not only lexically and grammatically, but also spatially. The analysis of the use of space for cohesive purposes in sign languages comes in large part from the work of Winston (1993; 1995) and her examination of cohesion in ASL, particularly the mapping of comparative discourse frames in an ASL lecture. In her examination of an ASL lecture on poetry, she finds that the signer establishes one side of the signing space to refer to poetry as art and the other side to refer to poetry as science. Once the concepts have been established in this way, the signer can refer to one or the other side of the signing space and the addressees can interpret him to be referring to the concepts and comparison he has previously established. In fact, the addressee finds that the signer refers to his introductory spatial map as many as 700 utterances later, even when it is embedded within a separate comparative discourse frame (Winston, 1995: 96).

In the Oklahoma City Bombing narrative, cohesion can be seen in the spatial reference that is first established with an index after the first mention of Oklahoma City:

> HAVE TWO STUDENT FROM O-K-A C-I-T-Y **IX-loc**
> *and I have two students who are from Oklahoma City.*

Then, at the end of the narrative, the signer refers twice to the same spatial location, indicating reference back to this prior spatial indexing:

> FIND POSS-3 SEVERAL FRIENDS DIE PRO-3 (wh) **IX-loc** TOO
> *I found out they lost several friends that day.*

> S-O PRO-3 KNOW SOME PEOPLE **IX-loc**. WOW LOOK-AT WONDER.
> TOUCH-HEART WOW

So I had students who actually knew some of the people who died in the bombing. Really made me think!

Pointing to places within the signing area for the purpose of referring to conceptual referents in the minds of addressees is referred to as "referential spatial mapping". According to Winston (1992), spatial mapping plays an extremely important role in the structuring of discourse and in involving addressees in making sense of the discourse that they see. Winston finds that spatial maps can be used for a variety of purposes, including comparisons, performatives (constructing actions and dialogue), and the mapping of events temporally. Mather and Winston (1998) find that spatial maps can be used to structure the entire telling of a story (translated from written English to ASL), as space is used to map the story's topics and to involve the addressees in the creation of the meaning of the story segments and the story as a whole.

The use of space is not the only feature of sign language discourse that reflects cohesive devices. Another example of cohesion in ASL can be found in the phonological production of fingerspelling. Rapid fingerspelling can be used for co-reference once careful fingerspelling has established a referent in the prior discourse (Johnson, 1994b; Patrie and Johnson, in preparation). Fingerspelling and the use of space are two examples of strategies that are unique to sign languages that incorporate the more universal discourse feature known as cohesion.

Rhythm, rhyme and repetition

Discourse markers, use of space for comparatives, performatives and fingerspelling all offer coordination and coherence in discourse between speakers and addressees. Many other aspects of discourse can be found to provide coherence and, further, to entice the addressee not only to attend to, but also to relate actively to what is being uttered. For example, Tannen (1989) discusses ways in which the rhythm of spoken discourse captures addressees, as well as the strategies by which utterers capture attention and involve them in the process of interpreting meaning. She suggests that spoken languages use phonology to create what she calls "music" with language, as a rhythmic way of engaging addressees.

In the Oklahoma City Bombing narrative, the use of repetition can be seen as a strategy that entices the addressees through the signer's own evaluation of the significance of what he experienced:

PRO-1 CL: 9 (eyes look up) (rs: startled) HOLD-IT. SILLY! STUDENT CRY+++
But when I opened my eyes and looked up at the class I was surprised to see someone crying.

LOOK-AT. WOW TOUCH-HEART.
And it really got to me ...

(rs: IX-loc) FIND POSS-3 SEVERAL FRIENDS DIE PRO-3 (wh) IX-loc
TOO
I found out they lost several friends that day.

S-O PRO-3 KNOW SOME PEOPLE IX-loc. **WOW LOOK-AT WONDER.
TOUCH-HEART WOW**
*So I had students who actually knew some of the people who died in the
bombing. Really made me think!*

In particular, the signer uses repetition to emphasize the impact of knowing
someone who had lost friends in the bombing incident. He also modulates
the speed of his signs during these sections, for instance by slowing down his
pronunciation of WONDER. These phonological involvement strategies have
been described in some detail in ASL by Winston (1998) in her discussion of
sign language prosody. She finds that nonmanual information conveyed by the
eyes, head, face, shoulders, torso and arms/hands can be altered qualitatively
in terms of their movement in space and in terms of features, such as speed,
tenseness, size, direction and repetition of movement. She suggests that these
can occur in combination and/or be combined with pauses, and that they impact the rhythmic production of signs, phrases, idea units and other units of
discourse.

These features have specifically been found in the examination of visual
rhythms in signed discourse. Mather (1989) examines the ways in which teachers sign stories from books to deaf students. In her study of a children's book,
The Three Little Kittens, she finds that a number of visual involvement strategies are used by the teacher who is a native signer of ASL. For example, the
teacher signs on the pages of the book using "miniature" signs, as a visual involvement strategy that represents a change at the phonological level (one that
is not possible in spoken language discourse). According to Mather (1989),
miniature signs are those produced by the teacher while resting the storybook
on her lap. By signing on the book, the teacher allows the students to see both
the illustrations and the ASL translation. Although the use of miniature signs
is only one of many strategies described by Mather, it is clearly one unique
to sign language discourse, and this allows the signer to draw the addressees
into the narrative by representing the actions of the characters illustrated on the
pages of the book. Another of the strategies used by the teacher is to translate
sound-related words from the English story to visual concepts, such as the *me-
ows* of the kittens being conveyed with the sign glossed as CRY. Mather (1996)
has also found that signers use space and repetition rhythmically as a strategy
to involve children in stories.

Repetition as an involvement strategy has also been found in ASL lecture
discourse (van Hoek *et al.*, 1989; Winston, 1991; 1993; 1994). Repetition can
happen at all linguistic levels. Winston (1991; 1993; 1994) examines repetition
of spatial reference as a cohesive device. That is, if a signer establishes two

concepts to be compared – one on the right side of the signing space and the other on the left – then signing using the hand on one particular side of the signing space is a way of indicating that that discourse is linked to the respective concept. Such repetition occurs through a variety of strategies on the part of the signer, not only by locating signs in a particular part of the signing space, but also by gazing toward a particular location, or by reversing hand dominance (Winston, 1994). The use of visual involvement strategies, constructed action and dialogue, and repetition have also been found in the translation of written English stories to ASL in Mather and Winston (1998).

Sign languages use visual rhythms, rhymes and repetition to create cohesive discourse and involve addressees. The fact that features such as rhythm and rhyme, originally described on the basis of spoken language discourse, can be seen to play a role in visual languages demonstrates that discourse-level features, like grammatical ones, constitute a rich and vital aspect of sign language discourse.

The relevance of discourse genre

The focus of this chapter has been on the description of discourse-level features that have been examined in sign language discourse. However, discourse takes many forms. While a variety of features have been discussed here, the function, frequency and types of features that occur in discourse can vary depending on whether the discourse is monologic or dialogic, or what genre of monologue – be it lecture, sermon, dialogue, meeting or classroom – is taking place, as well as on whether or not the interaction is interpreted.

Of the features discussed in this chapter, few can be clearly labeled as solely monologic or dialogic. For instance, one of the most strikingly conversational features is turntaking, since turntaking is generally a feature exclusive to discourse involving two or more participants. Nevertheless, as Tannen (1989) points out, conversation forms the basis from which narrative discourse is born. And, just as narratives creep into the midst of most human conversations – as people share their personal experiences and ideas as a part of work and daily life – so, too, the construction of conversations creeps into the midst of many narratives. As discussed earlier in this chapter, the use of constructed dialogue is a discourse strategy in which the signer "relives" or reenacts (or, really, "creates" as Tannen has pointed out) the discourse, including turntaking, between two or more characters in the narrative.

The notion of conversation as the foundation of discourse is intuitive if one considers social interaction itself: the desire to communicate through language is a direct outgrowth of interaction between two or more people. The result of this is that all of the features discussed in this chapter have a place in signed conversational discourse. It has been seen that conversational partners take turns and repair their discourse, they mark their place in their own discourse and within the conversation as a whole, they use space and other cohesive devices and involve their conversational partners with the use of narratives and involvement strategies such as rhythm, rhyme and repetition. Moreover, in addition to the research on signed conversations in face-to-face interaction (see, for example, Baker, 1977; Martinez, 1993; 1995; Thibeault, 1993; Dively, 1998), researchers have also examined the features of tty discourse in the text telephone conversations of members of Deaf communities. For example, Mather (1991) examines the role of discourse markers, such as OH, in tty conversations among deaf Americans. Similarly, Glaser (1999) analyzes the text conversations of British tty users, finding that mutual constraints of text-based communication and natural conversation result in a uniquely organized type of conversational encounter. The more research that is conducted on conversational features of signed discourse, the clearer it becomes that more research is necessary. A quick examination of one feature, turntaking, makes that very clear.

In Glaser's (1999) findings, the structure of turntaking in tty conversations is found to be well organized. As tty users are aware, turntaking in tty conversations is regulated by explicit markers, specifically the use of typed GA. Thus, the examination of the text-based telephone communication of Deaf communities provides one example of how a single feature, turntaking, can vary from its use in general (face-to-face) conversation.

Another example of an important distinction of a single feature, turntaking, can be studied in the context of the prevalent use of interpreters by members of Deaf communities when interacting with hearing interlocutors. For instance, Roy (1989a) has researched turntaking in an ASL–English interpreted interaction. She finds that the complex interrelationship between the two differently regulated languages results in a need for interpreters to act as regulators of turntaking, sometimes yielding a turn to one participant and other times holding a turn for another participant. Her ground-breaking research makes it clear that, despite frequent expectations to the contrary, interpreters cannot simply relay utterances when interpreting interactional discourse. In a follow up study, Sanheim (2000) finds similar results in an interpreted medical examination. Clearly, the study of turntaking regulators and other interactional features found in interpreted discourse in other settings might also yield new information about the structure of signed interaction.

Finally, while turntaking has features commonly found in face-to-face conversations, these features are likely to be used in special ways in particular settings, such as classrooms. For example, Mather (1987) finds that teachers working in classrooms with deaf children use two kinds of eye gaze to regulate turntaking. In her data, eye gaze directed at individual students preceding a gaze intended for the whole group is much more effective than simply starting with a group gaze. Moreover, she finds that the native signer in her research is the one to use the effective strategies, while a hearing non-native signing teacher does not. She finds that the teacher's communicative competence has a direct impact on the attentiveness and behavior of the students. Such information is useful in the training of teachers (as well as in the selection criteria for teachers being hired).

Taking a look at the varying structures of a single feature of conversational discourse, turntaking, when applied to a variety of contexts, makes it clear that the features of conversational discourse are quite dynamic. Fortunately, a growing pool of research addresses conversational discourse features, and, hopefully, even more research is yet to be done regarding each of these features in both two-party and multiparty conversations, in-person and on the telephone, both with and without interpreters, and in different settings, such as meetings, interviews and classrooms.

Like conversational discourse, monologic discourse takes many forms. For example, narratives, such as those that relate personal experiences, emerge in conversations. While much of the research on narratives in sign language discourse are analyses of elicited narratives (rather than videotaped as a part of conversations; see, for example, Gee and Kegl, 1983; Metzger, 1995; Emmorey and Falgier, 1999), Wilson (1996) has the opportunity to apply the conventional Labovian taxonomy of personal experience narratives to an ASL narrative that occurs during a videotaped conversation between six deaf signers. Labov (1972c) divides the structure of spoken personal experience narratives into five parts:

1. abstract: introductory summary of the story;
2. orientation: description of setting;
3. complicating action: events within the story;
4. evaluation: speaker's reasons for telling the story;
5. coda: the "punchline", the shift back from narrative-time to present time.

Wilson also includes in her analysis the narrative units identified by Gee (1986), dividing a narrative into lines and stanzas based on prosodic features such as intonation and pausing. Wilson finds that both approaches to the study of conversational narratives apply to the ASL data. Interestingly, she finds that in either approach, constructed dialogue is consistently relevant to the structure of the conversational, personal experience narrative.

More formal narratives are also examined in the literature on signed discourse. For example, Bahan and Supalla (1995) examine line segmentation and the role of eye gaze in the structure of a formal, commercially available narrative, *Bird of a Different Feather*. This analysis builds on Gee (1986) and breaks the narrative down into smaller units of discourse, from chapters, to sections, to strophes, to stanzas, to lines (1995: 173–176). In their examination of the smallest unit of narrative discourse (the line), they focus on eye gaze – rather than pausing (Gee and Kegl, 1983) or head nodding (Liddell, 1980) – applying the findings of Baker (1977) and Baker and Padden (1978) and the role of eye blinking and gazing in turntaking to the marking of line boundaries in the ASL narrative.

Bahan and Supalla find two basic types of eye gaze behavior in the narrative: gaze to the audience and character's gaze. Both of these types of eye gaze serve a particular function. For example, gazing to the audience is a marker of the fact that the signer is narrating the story. When the signer takes on the head posture (such as right or left head turning and eye gaze toward the imagined interlocutor) the signer is constructing the actions and/or dialogue of a character from the narrative. Bahan and Supalla find that the most common demarcation of lines in the segment of narrative that they examined is when there is alternation between these two types of eye gaze. In addition, the line boundaries are marked by a non-gaze behavior, either a pause, head nod or eye blink. They also find that the second type of eye gaze can occur at the end of two lines in a row, but in this case the line boundaries are not only marked with one of the three non-gaze behaviors, but also with either a brief gaze to the audience between lines or with a referential shift.

The study of narrative literary devices in sign languages is not only useful for its many practical applications, such as in ASL teaching and language arts classes, but also in the study of less formal narrative discourse. As Tannen (1989) points out, many of the typically literary devices in spoken languages, such as the use of imagery and detail, serve as involvement strategies in the discourse of everyday conversations. This appears to be true in sign language discourse as well. For example, in the study of ASL narratives, the role of constructed action and dialogue as a fundamental part of the narrative structure has been found to be true in literary narratives (Bahan and Supalla, 1995; Mather and Winston, 1998), conversational narratives (Wilson, 1996) and elicited narratives (Liddell and Metzger, 1998). Evidence suggests that this is also the case for other sign languages as well (for instance, for a discussion of Québec Sign Language, see Poulin and Miller, 1995; for Danish Sign Language, see Engberg-Pedersen, 1995; for British Sign Language, see Morgan, 1999).

Formal narratives are not the only literary genre of monologic discourse that has been examined. ASL poetry, BSL poetry and the poetry of other sign languages is a form of monologic discourse within the literary realm that has gained increasing recognition and research in recent years (see, for example, Valli, 1994; 1995; 1996). Such research has shown that many of the features of poetry found in spoken languages, including rhythm, rhyme and alliteration, are also prevalent in signed poetry, through such features as eye gaze, body shift, head shift and the selected use of handshapes and movements. This information, in turn, feeds the study of conversation, once again. As Tannen (1989) describes, the role of imagery and detail common to literature can often appear in daily conversational discourse.

In addition to the more literary monologic discourse found in ASL narratives and poetry, some analysis of formal lectures has also been conducted, as seen in the previous sections. For example, Roy (1989b) with a discussion of discourse markers and Winston (1993) with a discussion of cohesion are both based on the analysis of lectures in ASL. Some preliminary research has also been conducted on the discourse of sermons, as signed by deaf pastors. Richey (2000) finds that in ASL sermons, the use of questions to the congregation as an interactional involvement strategy is a unique feature not often found in the spoken English discourse of hearing pastors. Clearly, a wide variety of both conversational and monologic discourse genres has received the attention of sign language discourse analysts.

A word about sociolinguistic factors is also relevant here. Like all sociolinguistic research, sociolinguistic factors such as age, ethnicity and gender can play a role in the occurrence of such features. For example, Martinez (1995) finds that in FSL, the male signers in her study had longer turns than their female partners. Moreover, Bruce (1993) in a study of six deaf dyads, including both white and African American deaf signers, finds that the use of verbal and non-verbal backchanneling is different for the African American and the white deaf signers, and that African-American–African-American dyads used backchanneling differently from African-American–white dyads.

In addition to such sociolinguistic factors as gender and ethnicity, sign language communities generally include a unique variant used by deaf signers who are also blind. While sighted Deaf community members use a visual sign language, Deaf-Blind signers often use a tactile variety of that language. For example, Collins and Petronio (1998) find that Tactile ASL exhibits variation from visual ASL at a variety of linguistic levels, including phonological, in terms of movement, orientation and location, and morphological, in terms of the presence or absence of facial configuration with the co-occurring muscle tension and movement patterns that conveyed adverbial and adjectival information in their data.

Clearly, research regarding the impact of sociolinguistic factors on discourse suggests that a great amount of research remains to be done both across sign languages and within sign languages in order to study the features of signed discourse within different genres and based on a variety of sociolinguistic variables.

Conclusion

Discourse analyses of sign languages make clear the necessity for examination of sign language discourse at levels above the sentence, both for the improved understanding of sign language structure and for the understanding of language in general. These studies also have practical implications for professionals in a variety of fields. For example, for educators – regardless of whether they are engaged in first or second language teaching – developing discourse-level skills in learners is essential in order to be able to interact smoothly, coherently and successfully. It also has implications for the field of interpretation. Interpreters generally are expected to convey equivalent messages when translating between two languages. Interpreters who attempt to provide equivalence at a lexical or sentential level are potentially missing aspects of the discourse as a whole (such as cohesion). Discourse analysis of sign languages provides important information, both theoretical and practical.

A large portion of the linguistic work performed since Stokoe's ground breaking findings in the 1960s has focused on theoretical issues and formalist perspectives. Discourse analysis is grounded in the fact that language is used when people interact, and that the study of language in use can provide information to support or refute theories generated non-empirically. Sociolinguistic research by discourse analysts about visual languages and the Deaf communities that use them is increasing globally. This functional perspective is, perhaps, long overdue in the bulk of sign language research. It is likely that the analysis of signed discourse based on the approaches described here will contribute immensely in the years to come to our understanding of both sign languages and language in general.

Suggested readings

This chapter draws heavily from both the spoken language literature and the sign language literature on discourse analysis. For a general description of discourse analysis and issues that motivate this interdisciplinary field, van Dijk (1997a; 1997b) is an excellent source. Regarding the approaches to the analysis of spoken language discourse, Schiffrin (1994) provides a comprehensive overview of the six approaches summarized in this chapter. She not only provides detailed descriptions and comparisons of the approaches, but also includes sample analyses for each. These two books provide information about the field that is neither limited to one approach or to one theoretical perspective. For more specific information on a given approach or methodology, see the citations within that section of the chapter.

An exceptional source for the study of sign language discourse is Lucas' series *Sociolinguistics in Deaf Communities*, since every volume includes at least one chapter that focuses on sign language discourse. Specifically, volume 5 of the series, *Storytelling and Conversation: Discourse in Deaf Communities* (Winston, 1999) contains eight chapters that address the signed discourse of a variety of countries and is based on a variety of approaches. Additionally, for further information regarding the use of space in sign language discourse, Emmorey and Reilly's (1995) *Language, Gesture, and Space* includes 19 chapters that focus on spatial issues. While many of these focus more on the grammatical level than on the discourse level, several of the chapters in this book offer empirical analyses of sign languages above the level of the sentence.

Exercises

1. According to linguists, what is discourse?
2. What is discourse analysis?
3. What factors contribute to contextual information in which discourse occurs? Why is context important to discourse analysts?
4. Identify and describe two approaches to the analysis of discourse. From what discipline do these approaches evolve? What counts as data in each of these approaches?
5. How do people in conversations know when to take a turn? Identify at least three turntaking regulators in sign language discourse.
6. Identify and describe two forms of conversational repair.
7. To what does the term "discourse marker" refer?
8. Describe "constructed dialogue". Does it occur in sign language discourse? Does it occur in spoken language discourse?
9. Identify two features that provide cohesion in signed discourse.
10. What is the function of rhythm, rhyme and repetition in discourse?
11. Videotape a 3–5 minute signed conversation. View the videotape at least once through, and then transcribe it. Based on the features identified in this chapter:
    (a) Highlight and label at least two "turn relevance places" in the conversation. Which participant is responsible for who has each turn?
    (b) Highlight and label any instances of conversational repair.
    (c) Highlight and label any discourse markers that occur in the conversation.
    (d) Highlight and label any instances of constructed dialogue.
    (e) Highlight and label any instances of rhythm, rhyme or repetition.
12. Based on the discussion of discourse and discourse analysis in this chapter, describe why the features you have looked for did or did not occur in your three minutes of data.

6   Language planning and policy

Timothy Reagan

> Language planning refers to deliberate efforts to influence the behavior of others with respect to the acquisition, structure, or functional allocation of their language codes.
>
> Cooper (1989: 45)

> ... by analyzing [the sign system] SEE 2 as an instance of language planning, rather than as a more or less effective tool for teaching English to deaf children, we are forced to consider the broader issues that make SEE 2 and other [Manual Codes for English] controversial and problematic in relation to the complex sociolinguistic situation that surrounds deafness and the minority language community so engendered in the United States.
>
> Ramsey (1989: 144)

What is the correct spelling for a word? What is its correct pronunciation? What does a word mean? What kind of writing system should one use to write a particular language? For speakers of a language like English, which has been standardized for a relatively long period of time, these questions may seem to be relatively straightforward. With only rare exceptions, there are clear-cut answers to questions of these sorts. For the correct spelling, pronunciation and meaning of a word, we rely on a dictionary, which tells us what the socially accepted norms are. As for the writing system to be used, again, we rely on a socially agreed-upon system. Thus, English is written in the Latin alphabet rather than in the Cyrillic alphabet, which is used, for example, for Russian. English could, of course, be written in Cyrillic script – or in Arabic or Hebrew script, or even with Chinese characters. Although every writing system has its own advantages and disadvantages, any language could, in principle, be represented in any kind of orthography, and many languages have been written using different orthographies from time to time.[1]

For languages that are standardized, the socially accepted norms have been, at least in part, determined; they are widely shared and generally accepted by speakers of the languages. In societies with standardized languages, we tend to assume that such socially accepted norms are not only necessary and appropriate, but even that they represent the "real" language in some sense. This is, of course, not really the case at all; language is not static and fixed but is rather, by its very nature, complex, diverse and changing. Further, while some languages – such as French, Spanish, German, Russian, Japanese, Chinese, etc. – are standardized, the vast majority of languages spoken today are not standardized. Efforts to standardize language, including efforts to create new terminology where needed, are examples of "language planning activity". So, too, are efforts by institutions and governments to determine what language or languages can be used in particular spheres (for instance, in schools, courts, legislatures, business, etc.); in other words, attempts to institute particular "language policies". Such language planning activities are increasingly widespread today. They take place in some manner in most nations (Weinstein, 1990; Kaplan and Baldauf, 1997). In essence, a language policy is a deliberate effort to mandate specific language behaviors in particular contexts. Such policies can, and do, involve decisions about language development and allocation, language use, language rights, and a host of other important issues.

Language planning and language policy are activities of growing significance not only in terms of spoken languages around the world, but also with respect to sign languages. The broad framework within which sign language planning and sign language policies are developed and implemented is essentially the same as that for spoken languages. However, the exact details and challenges faced by sign language planners and policy makers differ from those faced by other language planners and policy makers in important ways, as we shall see below (see Covington, 1976; Erting, 1978; Deuchar, 1980; Ramsey, 1989; Reagan, 1990; Gutiérrez, 1994; Nover, 1995).

This chapter begins with a broad overview of the nature and purposes of language planning and language policy activities in general, including an examination of the role of ideology in language policy, issues of language rights in language policy debates, and the use (and misuse) of language planning and language policy to achieve social, political and educational ends. Throughout the chapter, examples of language policies and language planning activities are drawn from both spoken and sign languages.

The nature and purposes of language planning

Language planning and language policy formulation and implementation have been, and continue to be, important elements of social and educational policy in many societies. This has been especially true in the developing world as efforts are made to address the legacy of colonialism and, in many cases, the ongoing presence of considerable cultural and linguistic diversity (see, for example, Weinstein, 1990; Schiffman, 1996; Mazrui and Mazrui, 1998). Questions of national and official language selection, of orthographic selection and spelling standardization, of language use in government, judicial and educational settings, and of language status and power are rarely resolved easily. Such decisions seldom avoid a considerable degree of controversy and conflict. As Altbach observed:

Language is a key to the intellectual situation in many Third World nations. Language also plays a role in the distribution of knowledge, since the medium through which material is communicated determines accessibility. Many Third World nations are multilingual states in which questions of language policy are often politically volatile. (1984: 234)

Such controversy is especially common where language policies are concerned with the provision of education. This is understandable, since, as Kennedy has noted:

The close relationship between use of a language and political power, socioeconomic development, national and local identity, and cultural values has led to the increasing realization of the importance of language policies and planning in the life of a nation. Nowhere is this planning more crucial than in education, universally recognized as a powerful instrument of change. (1983: iii)

The role of language planning as a component of more general social and educational planning and policy analysis is, in short, an important facet of understanding development in many societies. Language planning as an element of national development strategy can best be understood as the deliberate attempt to change or in some way alter existing language usage, and thus to resolve various types of language problems and controversies (see, for example, Cobarrubias and Fishman, 1983; Kennedy, 1983; Christian, 1988; Cooper, 1989; Lambert, 1990; Tollefson, 1991). As Eastman cogently asserted: "Language planning is the activity of manipulating language as a social resource in order to reach objectives set out by planning agencies which, in general, are an area's governmental, educational, economic, and linguistic authorities" (1983: 29).

Language planning activities can focus on issues of language status (status planning), on issues of internal development (corpus planning), or on combinations of these two types of language planning activities (see Cobarrubias, 1983b; Williams, 1992: 123–147). Status planning refers to efforts by a government or institution to determine what language or languages are to be used in particular spheres of use. The identification of a country's "official language", for instance, constitutes status planning, as would a decision about what language should be used in schools. Corpus planning is often a result of status planning; it refers to efforts to standardize, elaborate and perhaps "purify" a language selected for use in a particular sphere of language use (see Cluver, 1993: 59).

Language planning activities – both status planning and corpus planning – serve a number of different, although sometimes overlapping, functions: language "purification", language revitalization, language reform, language standardization and language modernization (see Nahir, 1977; Eastman, 1983: 28). Furthermore, each of these functions of language planning and language policy can be reflected and manifested in virtually every sphere of human life. Language policies are reflected in:

- the political sphere: the language of political debate and discourse, etc.;
- the judicial sphere: the language of law, as well as the language used by the police and courts;
- the religious sphere: the language used for worship, as well as the language in which key religious texts are written;
- the cultural sphere;
- the commercial and economic sphere: the language of business and industry;
- the educational sphere: the language of instruction, additional languages studied by pupils, etc.; and
- the interpersonal and familial sphere: the language used in the home, with relatives, etc.

Language "purification" is a prescriptive effort on the part of policy makers to delimit "proper" or "correct" linguistic usage, often based on beliefs about what constitutes the historically "pure" variety of the language. Such efforts, which generally consist primarily of corpus planning, are often concerned with eliminating foreign or alien usages in both the spoken and written language, and are commonly tied to other manifestations of what might be termed "purist" or ethnocentric ideologies. They can also be outgrowths of anti-colonialist sentiments and movements. An example of a call for language "purification" in language planning is provided in Khalid (1977), in which a case is presented for the adoption of a "pure" variety of Swahili, uncontaminated by European influences. As Khalid commented, "Once our thinking has been freed from foreign domination, the reintroduction of the true Swahili language in the place of its colonialist falsification will follow as a matter of logic and self-respect" (1977: xiii). Language purists often have strong emotional attachments to the traditional form of their language, as Sibayan made clear in his discussion of Filipino in the Philippines:

> The purists are emotionally attached to Tagalog while the anti-purists do not hold such sentimental attachments. Generally, the purists are native speakers of Tagalog while most of the non-purists are non-native speakers. The purists would like to use original Tagalog words for many borrowed ones which are in general use and acceptance such as *guro* for the more generally used *maestra* (or *maestro*, if a man) "teacher", *aklat* for *libro* "book," and the now abandoned tease-word *salipawpaw* for what everyone calls *eroplano* "airplane". (1974: 233)

To some extent, one might hypothesize that purist movements are strongest in those instances in which national pride and self-confidence have suffered in some way. However, it is also important to note that even languages that have high economic and political status have on occasion been the objects of purist movements (see Jernudd and Shapiro, 1989). For example, there have been numerous efforts in recent years to stop the use of Anglicisms in modern French (which is critically referred to as *Franglais* in French), although terms like *le week-end* continue to be far more popular in daily speech than the historically preferred *la fin de semaine* (see Ball, 1997: 207–220). Similar phenomena have been noted in Spanish (Mar-Molinero, 1997: 168–170) and German (in which the equivalent of *Franglais* is now *Engleutsch*) (Stevenson, 1997: 212–216). Indeed, even in English there have been such purist efforts, as with the "Saxonist" movement in the late nineteenth century, which attempted (generally unsuccessfully) to reform English by replacing "foreign" terms borrowed from French and Latin roots with terms of Germanic origin (Baron, 1981).[2]

Language revitalization refers to various kinds of activities intended to promote the status and usage of a language that has been, in some sense, previously in decline (or even, in some instances, a dead language, i.e. one that has ceased to have native users). As King recently defined it, language revitalization is "the attempt to add new forms or functions to a threatened language with the ultimate aim of increasing its uses or users" (1999: 111). Language revitalization is primarily an example of status planning, although elements of corpus planning (especially in terms of lexical expansion) are also likely to be involved. Examples of the former abound: the use of Swahili in Tanzania is an example to which we return below, but other cases in the post-colonial world are common as colonial languages are replaced by (or are required to share official status with) previously dominant indigenous languages. The revival of dead languages is considerably rarer; the best example is the revival of Hebrew as a modern spoken language in Israel (see Nahir, 1988; Sáenz-Badillos, 1993).[3] Other instances of the revival of languages in advanced states of decline also exist: the revival of Irish Gaelic is well documented and is a powerful case in point (see Hindley, 1990; Ó Riagáin, 1997).[4]

Language reform takes place, both formally and informally, in many languages accorded official status in the modern world. This includes lexical and orthographic reform as well as occasional syntactic reform. Language reform as a type of language planning activity is, therefore, essentially corpus planning. The reform of written Chinese in the People's Republic of China is an instance of language reform (see Tai, 1988; Chen, 1999), as are the reforms of Ibo and other indigenous languages in Nigeria (Nwachukwu, 1983; Emenanjo, 1990), Turkish (Dogançay-Aktuna, 1995) and Norwegian (Haugen, 1966), among others. Indeed, there are relatively few official languages in the modern world that have not been subjected to deliberate efforts at language reform (see Cooper, 1989; Tollefson, 1991; Kaplan and Baldauf, 1997).

Language standardization involves both status planning (when it refers to the selection of a single variety of a language as the standard language) and corpus planning (when it refers to the codification of the language in a unified variety). Thus, the selection of Kiunguja, the Zanzibar dialect of Swahili, as the national linguistic norm in Tanzania would constitute an example of language standardization of the status planning type (see Harries, 1983: 127–128). Conversely, efforts to create a standardized spelling and grammar for a language would constitute a corpus planning approach to language standardization. Language standardization, it is important to note, can and often does overlap both language reform and lexical modernization in practice.

Finally, lexical modernization takes place as efforts are made to increase a language's lexicon in order to allow it to deal with new technological, political, economic, educational and social developments and concepts. Lexical modernization therefore constitutes a clear instance of corpus planning. All languages experience from time to time what can be termed lexical gaps; lexical modernization refers specifically to controlled and directed attempts to expand a given language's lexicon in a systematic manner (see Nahir, 1977: 117; Eastman, 1983: 232–237). As Jernudd noted, "A major activity of many language planning agencies . . . be they normal language academies, development boards or language committees, is the development of terminologies, particularly in technical fields" (1977: 215). Examples of lexical modernization abound; see, for example, Fodor and Hagège's multi-volume *Language Reform: History and Future* which includes studies of lexical (as well as orthographic and syntactic) modernization efforts in more than 60 different languages (Fodor and Hagège, 1983/84; 1990). While efforts at lexical modernization are quite common, the extent to which they are effective in mandating lexical usage is less clear. As Hinnebusch has commented with regard to lexical modernization in Swahili:

A serious question that has to be asked, however, is whether external planning, planning from the top, has any effect on actual usage. For example, in the list of astronomical terms, *mchota maji* (literally, "water bearer" from *-chota* "dip up" and *maji* "water") is suggested for "Aquarius", but a very popular astrologer in East Africa today uses *ndoo* (literally, "bucket, pail") for that sign; for "Sagittarius" he uses *mshale* (literally, "arrow"), while the suggested list gives *mpiga shaabaha* "shooter of the target" . . .

(1979: 288)

A particularly interesting contemporary case of both official and more informal lexical modernization has been taking place in Russia, as that society undergoes massive social, economic and political changes in the aftermath of the collapse of the Soviet Union. Examples of new terminology in modern Russian abound. The changes taking place in society have led to widespread lexical innovation, borrowing and creation, as new concepts, practices, technologies and institutions replace those of the Soviet state (see Ryazanova-Clarke and

Wade, 1999). Typical instances of such new lexical items in Russian would include:

Russian	English translation
тонер	"toner"
пейджер	"pager"
биг мак	"Big Mac"
сотка	"mobile telephone"
копирайт	"copyright"
маркетинг	"marketing"

Such examples of lexical modernization can be found in all languages. It is important to keep in mind that the need for new terminology to meet new needs in no way indicates any innate deficiency in the language itself; all human languages have lexical gaps, and all human languages have ways of filling those gaps.

The fundamental distinction between status planning and corpus planning applies to sign languages in a relatively straightforward manner. Efforts at status planning relating to sign languages involve decisions about whether to accord a particular sign language some sort of official or quasi-official status. Decisions of the first sort, which involve the official recognition of a sign language, remain relatively rare, although they do exist. Examples are found, in a fairly strong sense in Sweden (see Ahlgren, 1990b), in a more moderate sense in Denmark (see Hansen, 1990; Bergmann, 1994) and in a somewhat weak sense in France (see Mas, 1994); examples are also found in a variety of other countries. More telling, however, are the increasingly common efforts to recognize sign language in some official or constitutional sense. Such efforts have taken place in a number of settings; for instance, during the post-apartheid debates about language policy in South Africa, serious consideration was given to according South African Sign Language official status as an eleventh official language (see Reagan and Penn, 1997; Penn and Reagan, 1999). To some extent, efforts to gain recognition for American Sign Language (ASL) in various states in the USA also constitute attempts at language status planning. What is interesting about many of these attempts is that they are concerned not so much with recognition of ASL in an official capacity as with enabling the teaching of ASL and with the recognition of ASL as a "real language" (see Reagan, 1997). Certainly the "Statement on the Recognition of the National Sign Languages of the Deaf" – passed at the Third European Congress on Sign Language Research held in Hamburg in 1989 (see Appendix 6.1 at the end of this chapter) – is an important rhetorical statement of status planning. At the very least it is an important statement of the need for status planning, as was the World Federation of the Deaf's 1991 call for the recognition of sign languages (see Appendix 6.2).

At a more limited level, status planning efforts also take place with respect to the use of sign languages in judicial and educational settings. While the right of deaf individuals to be provided with competent interpretation into a sign language in legal proceedings is fairly widely (although by no means universally) recognized, the concomitant right to be educated in a sign language is far less commonly accorded (see Skutnabb-Kangas, 1994; Branson and Miller, 1998a), a point to which we return below. Indeed, it is interesting to observe that the vast majority of efforts at status planning for sign languages have clearly taken place, and continue to take place, primarily in the educational sphere. This is a sphere of language use that is often the target of language planners and policy makers, but perhaps nowhere more so than in the case of sign languages (see Corson, 1999).

If status planning for sign languages has taken place primarily in the educational sphere, corpus planning, at least formal corpus planning, has done so almost exclusively in educational contexts. The creation of lexical items for use in classroom settings has been one of the more important areas in which one can see corpus planning for various sign languages around the world, and the case of ASL provides a powerful example of the kind of lexical expansion that can be expected to occur as sign languages are employed to teach increasingly sophisticated content (see, for example, Battison, 1978; Collins-Ahlgren, 1990).

Corpus planning is also seen in efforts to create dictionaries of sign languages. Although sign language dictionaries around the world tend to be based on spoken language (for instance, most are organized alphabetically based on the spoken word), there are notable exceptions. For instance, there are now dictionaries of ASL (see Tennant and Brown, 1998), BSL (Brien, 1992) and Australian Sign Language (Johnston, 1989) that use as their organizing principle handshape. Similarly, efforts to develop textbooks for specific sign languages are also examples of corpus planning (see Wilcox and Wilcox, 1997).

Perhaps the most extreme example of both status and corpus planning for sign language, however, has been provided in the USA by the creation of what are called manual sign codes, that is, visual/gestural communication systems intended to allow the representation of spoken language in a sign modality (manual sign codes in the US context are often called Manually Coded English, or MCE). Such efforts are, as we shall see, highly questionable on a number of grounds, but they do represent a compelling example of language planning in action, and so we turn now to an examination of the history of such manual sign codes.

The education of deaf children has, since the mid-nineteenth century, been characterized by a deep division between educators favoring an oral approach, in which signing is generally forbidden, and those supporting a manual approach in which signing of some sort is allowed in conjunction with speech (see Winefield, 1987; Reagan, 1989); indeed, some educators of the Deaf talk about two competing, bipolar educational philosophies in Deaf education (see Paul and Quigley, 1990: 5–7; Paul and Jackson, 1993). Although oralism remains a powerful force in Deaf education, manualism, often under the more contemporary label "total communication", is the dominant philosophical approach to Deaf education today. Since the 1960s, however, there has been a growing debate among manualists about what type of signing should be employed in the education of deaf children (Woodward, 1982; Reagan, 1985; Bornstein, 1990). At the heart of this debate has been the creation and use of manual sign codes for spoken languages.

Although the development of manual sign codes for spoken language is an international phenomenon (see, for example, Paget, 1951; Kyle, 1987; Penn and Reagan, 1990; Serpell and Mbewe, 1990), the emergence and educational implementation of manual sign codes has taken place primarily in the USA, where the strongest commitment to their use remains. In the US context, several distinct approaches to the creation of artificial manual sign codes currently exist, although the major systems are closely related, sharing both common historical roots and underlying social and linguistic assumptions. Further, artificially constructed systems of signing all have as their principal target population deaf children at school, and all of the systems rely on teachers of the Deaf and, to a lesser extent, parents of deaf children, for their successful implementation.

The first artificially constructed manual sign code to be developed in the USA was created by a young deaf immigrant from Britain, David Anthony, in 1966. This system, initially intended for use with mentally retarded deaf children (Wilbur, 1979: 204), was no doubt inspired in part by the Paget– Gorman system in use in Britain (see Crystal and Craig, 1978). Anthony's system provided the base for what was eventually to become Seeing Essential English (SEE-I). Beginning in January 1969, groups of deaf and hearing people began meeting in Southern California to develop signs and guidelines for Seeing Essential English. As Gustason and Woodward recount, "a working committee of five [were] elected. Sign classes were taught by these five, and papers with written descriptions of each sign were utilized in these classes. The papers were mailed to interested persons" (1973: v). Disagreements and differences of opinion about certain features of manual signing, however, led to the breakup of this original group in 1971 and, as a consequence, SEE-I now coexists with both Signing Exact English (SEE-II) and Linguistics of Visual English (LOVE) (see Wilbur, 1979: 204–205; Schein, 1984: 66–67; Ramsey, 1989). A further addition to the array of artificial manual sign codes in the USA has been Signed English, designed for use with preschool children, which shares a number of the general characteristics of SEE-I and its progeny while attempting to remain relatively simple syntactically, semantically and structurally (see Bornstein *et al.*, 1975: 295–296). In fact, this expanding diversity of artificial sign systems has even been the subject of humor in the Deaf community, as can be seen in the ASL play, "Sign Me Alice", written by the deaf playwright Gilbert Eastman (1974).

The differences among the various manual sign codes are nevertheless significant, since those systems which more closely parallel the structure of English appear to have greater educational benefits for deaf students (see Luetke-Stahlman, 1988). Among the more important variations among the different manual sign codes are the rules for producing and creating new signs and sign markers (e.g. inflectional suffixes), the use of past tense markers in the different systems, and the view of what constitutes a base or root word, as well as how one deals with compound and complex words (see Paul and Quigley, 1990). Despite these differences, however, the various American manual sign codes are similar in terms of both their philosophical underpinnings and their guiding structural principles. For example, all of the different artificial systems utilize at least some signs borrowed from ASL (although not necessarily with the same semantic space as that identified with the sign in ASL). The different sign codes operate with radically different morphological principles than does ASL, and all require the use of various prefixes and suffixes to convey specific English syntactic information. For example, there are some 74 affixes listed in one of the basic handbooks for SEE-II (Gustason *et al.*, 1980), as well as an additional seven contractions for which there are separate signs. Further, all of the different manual sign codes not only allow the use of fingerspelling, but also employ widespread initialization, although, again, the parameters within which such linguistic behaviors are appropriate vary among the different manual code systems. Finally, word order in the different sign codes is always, as a matter of principle, the same as that found in English. These features taken together make clear the fundamental objective of the creators of the various manual sign codes: to represent English in a visual/manual modality. As Gustason *et al.* explicitly noted, "The most important principle in Signing Exact English is that English should be signed in a manner that is as consistent as possible with how it is spoken or written in order to constitute a language input for the deaf child that will result in his [or her] mastery of English" (1980: xiii).

Although widely accepted as a legitimate goal by both teachers of the Deaf and hearing parents of deaf children (see Ramsey, 1989: 143–154), such an objective is at best highly questionable from a linguistic perspective. The problem here is that the manual sign codes, in essence, seek to represent the lexical items of an oral/aural language in a gestural/visual linguistic context. The result is a type of signed communication that is, in essence, "neither fish nor fowl". Sign systems such as SEE-I, SEE-II, LOVE and Signed English tend to be both awkward and confusing, and often entail violations of the structural and morphological rules and norms of ASL. Insofar as these systems are efforts to represent spoken English visually this is, of course, hardly a problem, especially where they are used with students who are postlingually deaf (i.e. those whose deafness occurred after the acquisition of speech and spoken language) or with students with a reasonable degree of residual hearing. For prelingually deaf students (i.e. those whose deafness was present at birth or at least before the development of spoken language), however, for whom ASL is effectively the linguistic base from which they operate, such violations can present serious problems. For example, Cokely and Gawlik (1973) and Woodward (1973b) have discussed the morphological and chirological (phonological) problems of different manual sign codes in considerable detail, as well as some of the syntactic problems that arise in their use. As Padden and Humphries argue, the efforts to devise manual sign codes, "however well-intentioned, rest on the pervasive belief that signed languages are essentially 'incomplete' systems and amenable to modification for educational purposes. They ignore the fact that individual signs, like words, are inseparable parts of a larger grammatical system" (1988: 64).

One of the more important criticisms lodged against manual sign codes is that while they may help hearing people to learn to sign – and hence improve communication between deaf children and some hearing people – at that same time such codes inevitably create semantic and syntactic gaps (and even chasms) between deaf children and parts of the adult Deaf community. It was just such gaps caused by the impact of manual sign codes with which one elderly deaf man was concerned when interviewed by Carol Padden:

Nowadays, signs are different. Back then, signs were better, you know, more natural, but now with all this IS kind of signs and all that . . . Nowadays, with IS and all those things, you get these long drawn-out sentences that take forever to sign. It's a waste of time, I tell you.[5] (Quoted in Padden and Humphries, 1988: 63)

The fundamental issue here is that faced by other non-English-speaking groups in American society, although it is somewhat more complicated due to the fact that the vast majority of deaf children have hearing (and generally non-signing) parents, who are likely to have hearing children as well. The tension here is between those individuals in the group who have access to the dominant language of the society and those who do not. In the case of deaf adults in American society, the views of English, manual sign codes, pidgin sign and ASL vary markedly, and there is no clear consensus about what kind of language is most appropriate for the education of deaf children. Within the Deaf culture itself, however, this is less true, with most members of the cultural community strongly supporting ASL and rejecting manual sign codes. In short, there are both linguistic and sociocultural limitations imposed by the development and use of various manual sign codes. As Woodward commented:

Normal standardization attempts, not to mention imposition of one language upon another, are considered impossible by many linguists. There are good reasons for this in the history and structure of languages. With the added burden of imposing English (a language with an oral channel) on ASL (a language with a visual channel), one can legitimately question the possibility of success for Manual English systems. (1973b: 8)

From the discussion thus far, it should be clear that the various artificial sign codes that have been devised and constructed for use in the education of the Deaf are, at least in certain respects, examples of language planning activity. As Ramsey noted:

The development of SEE 2 [SEE-II] and other MCEs [Manual Codes for English] bears a resemblance to the language-planning activities carried out on a national scale that appear to require instrumental solutions. Rather than attempt to create standard written norms, SEE 2 planners aimed to mold another language (ASL) into a system of signs that recode the standard. This is a unique problem in language planning. (1989: 144)

While those involved in the creation and development of the manual sign codes would dispute Ramsey's claim that they are trying to mold ASL into an English framework, arguing instead that they are merely trying to represent spoken English as accurately as possible in a visual modality, Ramsey's observation about such efforts as language planning activity is certainly correct. Further, the creation and development of the manual sign codes has involved both status planning and corpus planning. Efforts to employ SEE-I, SEE-II, LOVE and Signed English in classrooms, whether as a result of teacher training, the availability of texts, dictionaries and curricular materials or school policy, constitute examples of status planning. The mere existence of the different artificial sign systems, as well as the publication of texts, dictionaries and so on, on the other hand, exemplifies corpus planning.

It is important to note that such efforts in the USA have been largely informal and local in nature, and that no formal policy by any state or national agency recognizes such codes or mandates their use. However, many individual schools do have explicit policies in this regard (see Nover, 1995; Corson, 1999). The nature and focus of these policies is often problematic in nature, as Stephen Nover has pointed out:

In the United States, there exist seven manual codes of English none of which express the real, authentic perspective of the Deaf community. These were developed and implemented by those who lacked knowledge and expertise in general linguistics, the linguistics and sociolinguistics of ASL, or language planning processes . . . these invented, ad hoc codes have inadequate bases in the systematic conventions for representing manually either oral or written English, yet are widely recognized by English-only educators for instructional purposes. [Research] indicates that these language development and planning processes do not take into account the expressions of the Deaf community. (1995: 128)

While much language planning activity clearly takes place in the USA and elsewhere with respect to the creation and dissemination of artificial manual sign codes, it is important to note that what is taking place is not the same as language creation *per se*. The creation of an artificial spoken language, such as Esperanto (see Janton, 1993; Eco, 1995; Nuessel, 2000), is interesting in part because what is being undertaken is the creation of a *new* language. The development of the manual sign codes is, instead, an effort to codify an already existent spoken language in a different modality. In short, the creation of SEE-I, SEE-II, LOVE, Signed English, etc. is most appropriately compared with the creation of an orthography rather than with the establishment of a new language. This is an important distinction, because it emphasizes the difference between a signed language (such as ASL, BSL, etc.) and a manual sign code for a particular spoken language (such as SEE-I, SEE-II, LOVE and Signed English for English).

As has already been noted, language planning as an applied sociolinguistic activity has the potential to function either as a tool for empowerment and liberation or as a means of oppression and domination. This is the case, in part, because language planning and language policy activities often involve both implicit and explicit goals and objectives. As Robert Cooper noted:

That language planning should serve so many covert goals is not surprising. Language is the fundamental institution of society, not only because it is the first institution experienced by the individual but also because all other institutions are built upon its regulatory patterns . . . To plan language is to plan society. A satisfactory theory of language planning, therefore, awaits a satisfactory theory of social change. (1989: 182)

Further, and closely related to the presence of both implicit and explicit goals and objectives in language planning and language policy, is the fundamentally ideological nature of such activities (see Cobarrubias, 1983a). As Tollefson explained:

Language policy is a form of disciplinary power. Its success depends in part upon the ability of the state to structure into the institutions of society the differentiation of individuals into "insiders" and "outsiders" . . . To a large degree, this occurs through the close association between language and nationalism. By making language a mechanism for the expression of nationalism, the state can manipulate feelings of security and belonging . . . the state uses language policy to discipline and control its workers by establishing language-based limitations on education, employment, and political participation. This is one sense in which language policy is inherently ideological. (1991: 207–208)

The development of artificial manual sign codes for use in Deaf education provides us with an interesting case in which language planning activities have been argued to have promoted both an explicit agenda (i.e. the teaching of English to deaf children) and an implicit agenda (i.e. the devaluation of natural sign languages and continued hearing hegemony in Deaf education) (Ramsey, 1989). In addition to the promotion of these two agendas, the development of manual sign codes for spoken languages could also be argued to have supported social and ideological positions related to the nature of deafness and the status and role of the Deaf community in Deaf education (see, for example, Woodward, 1982; Padden and Humphries, 1988; Sacks, 1989; Schein, 1989; Lane, 1992; Parasnis, 1998).

Central to the ideological and political positions about deafness and the Deaf that seem to be embedded in the efforts to create the various manual sign codes has been a tacit rejection of what has been called the sociocultural paradigm of deafness (see Woodward, 1982; Reagan, 1985; Johnson *et al.*, 1989; Lane, 1992; Paul and Jackson, 1993). Rather than conceptualizing the Deaf as a distinctive cultural and linguistic community, advocates of the various manual sign codes in effect adopt the medical, or pathological, view of deafness (although, to be fair, few do so explicitly, and some claim to accept elements of the sociocultural paradigm). The result has been a situation in which educators of the Deaf can see the acquisition of English as not only pragmatically appropriate, but also as ideologically legitimized, since deaf children are seen as learning not a second language, but rather as acquiring their own language and gaining access to their own culture. The problem with such a view, in essence, is that it could be taken to delegitimize the presence and status of the Deaf cultural community, as well as the language of that community.

The construction of artificial manual sign codes can thus be argued to constitute, in short, a series of efforts to impose languages on a dominated and oppressed cultural and linguistic minority group. Efforts to encourage the use of various manual sign codes in Deaf education can, on this account, be seen as attempts to reinforce the subservient role of the Deaf even in the matters most important to them and their survival as a community. Further, the creation of artificial sign codes to allow spoken languages to be presented in a visual/manual modality suggests not only assumptions about the superiority of spoken languages, but also demonstrates the continued pattern of hearing hegemony found in the education of the Deaf. In short, the development, presence, and use of manual sign codes in the education of deaf children can be seen as a typical pattern of colonial oppression, in which the dominant group (in this case, the hearing culture) utilizes language and language policy as a tool to maintain its cultural and linguistic dominance, and all in the name of "doing good" for the oppressed, and presumably "disadvantaged", group (see Woodward, 1982; Reagan, 1988; Johnson *et al.*, 1989; Gregory and Hartley, 1991; Gregory, 1992; Lane, 1992; Branson and Miller, 1993).

Having said this, it is important to note that such a view is very much a minority one, not only in the Deaf community but also among those involved, both personally and professionally, in the education of deaf children. Complicating the picture is the tension between members of the core Deaf cultural community, who identify themselves as an oppressed cultural community trying to protect their language and culture from outsiders, and the hearing parents of deaf children, who wish their children to have access to their home language and the dominant language of the society in which they will live. Both positions are understandable, of course, and a middle ground, in which both ASL and English (in whatever representation works best pedagogically) can play a role in the education of the deaf child, is certainly a viable alternative.

The creators and advocates of manual sign codes have been sincere in their efforts to help deaf children; they have also utilized language planning activities to achieve their ends. What they have failed to do, however, is to take into account the complexity of the issue surrounding the language rights of the Deaf (in whatever way one defines this), and to recognize that both of the communities to which the language planning activities are directed – that is, members of the Deaf cultural community and the parents of deaf children – must be involved in that language planning activity (see Annamalai, 1986). The problem, in a nutshell, is the perception that "the solution offered by MCEs serves the symbolic needs of the hearing society much better than it does the linguistic and educational needs of deaf children" (Ramsey, 1989: 146). This is an important lesson not only for those working with the Deaf, but also for those engaged in other types of language planning activities for historically oppressed and dominated populations. Language planning efforts, if they are to be defensible, must entail the active involvement and participation of those for whom they are intended. Only when emerging in such a context can language planning efforts contribute to the creation of more just, humane and legitimate social and educational policies. And, indeed, as of this writing, there are many educational programs in the USA and other countries that are implementing bilingual education programs for deaf children, in which instruction is offered in the sign language indigenous to the situation (e.g. ASL, Swedish Sign Language, Venezuelan Sign Language) and literacy is provided in the written form of the spoken language of the majority community (see Nover and Andrews, 1998).

Ideologies of language policy

Language planning activities and specific language policies not only perform different functions, as we have seen, but also fall into different ideological orientations with respect to their underlying assumptions as well as their social and educational goals and objectives (see, for example, Joseph and Taylor, 1990; Phillipson, 1992). Cobarrubias (1983a: 63–66) identified four broadly conceived ideologies of language that guide and orientate language policies. As Cobarrubias explained:

Language ideologies reflect a mode of treatment of one language group with respect to another and ordinarily involve judgments as to what is right or wrong. Also, ideologies involve frames of reference pertaining to an ideal social group that will evolve, at some future time, from the segment of reality to which the ideology is being applied. The ideological aspect related to language-status planning is perhaps the most neglected area of language planning, in spite of the fact that ideologies underlie all forms of status planning. It is because ideologies involve value judgments and direct a certain mode of treatment that status decisions raise ethical issues. (1983a: 63)

The four ideologies of language identified by Cobarrubias are linguistic assimilation, linguistic pluralism, vernacularization and internationalization, each of which is briefly discussed here.

Linguistic assimilation as an ideology of language is based on the assumption that linguistic (and, presumably, cultural) unity is at the very least desirable in a society; it may also be necessary to some extent. Thus, language policies grounded in the ideology of linguistic assimilation tend to favor monolingual models of society. An important component of linguistic assimilation is that advocates of such policies are concerned not merely with individuals and groups acquiring competence in a specific, common language, but also with the rejection and replacement of other languages in the society, at least in the public sphere. The ideology of linguistic assimilation also tends, in practice, to encourage a belief in the superiority of the dominant language in a society; in practice, this often results in the denial of language rights to speakers of languages other than the dominant language (see Cobarrubias, 1983a: 63–64). In the context of developing countries, language policies based on the ideology of linguistic assimilation were most common during the colonial era. As Cobarrubias noted, "Instances of linguistic assimilation through colonization can be found in Guam, the Philippines under American rule . . . and to some degree Puerto Rico prior to the 1952 Constitution" (1983a: 64). Educationally, language policies grounded in the ideology of linguistic assimilation most often entail formal schooling in the selected national language, and the exclusion of other indigenous languages at least in official settings. Thus, the use of French in Francophone Africa in virtually all educational settings (save, notably, in Qur'anic schools) would be an example of the ideology of linguistic assimilation in educational practice (see Weinstein, 1980; Djité, 1990; 1991). In such cases, a necessary (and, often, sufficient) condition for being "educated" is competence in the dominant language.

Unlike the ideology of linguistic assimilation, that of linguistic pluralism emphasizes the language rights of minority groups and, in general, tends not only to accept but also to support language diversity in a society. Linguistic pluralism in practice exists in a variety of forms, ranging from relatively weak toleration of diversity to strong support for multiple languages, even to the extent of granting official status to two or more languages in a society. Examples of countries in which official status is granted to more than one language include Nigeria (Afolayan, 1988; Akinnaso, 1989; Akinnaso and Ogunbiyi, 1990),

India (Khubchandani, 1983; Srivastava, 1988), South Africa (Reagan, 1987; 1995a; Young, 1988; Alexander, 1989) and Canada (Genesee, 1988; Ricento and Burnaby, 1998); in each of these cases, educational policy tends to mirror language policy. While policies of linguistic pluralism are often politically the easiest solution for developing societies since they appear to avoid problems related to the domination of less powerful groups by more powerful ones, the trade off that such policies entail is both an economic one and a political one. This is the case because multilingualism is inevitably more expensive than monolingualism, and because such policies can encourage the development of insular pluralistic communities within a society (Bullivant, 1981; see also Edwards, 1984b; Beer and Jacob, 1985).

Closely related to the ideology of linguistic pluralism is the ideology of vernacularization, which entails the selection of one or more indigenous languages in a society to serve in an official capacity. Such selection almost always involves considerable language engineering, as discussed above, and such engineering inevitably focuses on the educational sphere, with the production of textbooks, curricular materials, matriculation examinations and so on. Further, vernacularization can focus on a single indigenous language, as in the case of Swahili in Tanzania, or on multiple languages, as has been the case in South Africa (see Louw, 1983/84; Reagan, 1987; 1995a). As Cobarrubias noted:

> Vernacularization involves the restoration and/or elaboration of an indigenous language and its adoption as an official language. There are also several processes of vernacularization which include the revival of a dead language (Hebrew in Israel), the restoration of a classical language (the Arabization process in Syria, Egypt, and Morocco), the promotion of an indigenous language to official status and its eventual standardization (Tagalog in the Philippines and Quechua in Peru). (1983a: 66)

Finally, the ideology of internationalization involves the selection of a language of wider communication, such as English or French, for use as the society's official language. Such selections are quite common throughout the developing world, and almost always reflect the colonial past of a country. Thus, the division between Anglophone and Francophone Africa largely reflects differences not only in official languages but also in terms of the colonial past (although other ideologies of language also exist in the African context, especially in Anglophone Africa, as both Nigeria and Tanzania make clear).

In his discussion of the different ideologies of language, Cobarrubias emphasizes the diversity of options within each ideology, as well as noting that this taxonomy is in no way an exhaustive one (see Cobarrubias, 1983a: 63). It should also be noted that these ideologies can occur not only independently, but can also co-occur. Such co-occurrence of different ideologies of language is especially common in developing countries, as can be seen in the inclusion of language and educational policies in Francophone Africa under both the ideologies of assimilation and internationalization (see also Reagan, 1986b).

In the case of sign languages, evidence can be offered of the existence, and indeed the co-existence, of all four of the ideologies identified by Cobarrubias. Linguistic assimilation, which presupposes the desirability of a monolingual norm in society, applies to the case of sign language planning in two distinct ways. First, efforts to encourage the use of the spoken, national language of a society through a sign modality (as in the case of the manual sign codes discussed earlier) are examples of the ideology of linguistic assimilation. Second, in societies in which there are multiple natural sign languages utilized by the Deaf, efforts to unite these sign languages into a single norm would also constitute linguistic assimilation in practice. This second kind of linguistic assimilation is especially common in developing societies in which the Deaf population has been historically scattered and disempowered.

The ideology of linguistic pluralism is found in efforts to recognize and encourage the diversity of sign languages in a society. In the US context, studies of regional variations in ASL serve to contribute to the ideology of linguistic pluralism (see Shroyer and Shroyer, 1984). Another example of an effort to recognize the internal linguistic diversity of the Deaf community is provided in the case of the development of the five-volume *Dictionary of Southern African Signs*, which documents the broad diversity of lexical items in Southern African sign languages. In that context, in the process of collecting signs for some 2,500 lexical items, only two percent of all the words represented had a single, common sign across all the different Deaf groups, and roughly 10 percent of the words had as few as one or two signed variants. These words tended to be represented by iconic and indexic signs (e.g. CAP, CREEP, HAIR, NOSE, SPRAY, THAT, etc.). On average, six variants per word were found and the range went as high as 11 variants, each informant having a different sign (e.g. BRICKLAYER, CEMENT and FUNNY, with 11 variants each, and FEATHER, HURRY, SHOULD and SNOWMAN, with 10 variants). A significant number of words with large numbers of sign variants were in fact compound words and words involving the use of person markers in signing (e.g. TEACHER, PASSENGER, UNDERTAKER, etc.). There were also a considerable number of terms for which some informants did not have a sign (e.g. Northern Transvaal Tswana had no sign for MAYOR, and four of the groups had no sign for LIBRARIAN). This diversity, although not unexpected, exceeded the original expectations of both the researchers and the deaf individuals involved with the South African Sign Language Research Program (see Penn and Reagan, 1991; 1994; 1995).

Vernacularization as an ideology of sign language planning can be seen in attempts to develop new signs within the structural framework of an existing natural sign language. In other words, rather than simply accepting artificial signs created by hearing educators, members of the Deaf community can develop their own meaningful signs as part of the process of lexical modernization. In practice, of course, such developments parallel each other, and both are likely to involve a number of very similar processes (lexical adaptation, lexical borrowing, initializing, etc.).

Finally, the ideology of internationalization is seen in the relative dominance of ASL in the international Deaf community, due to the size of its speaker community, its extensively developed vocabulary and the role of Gallaudet University, Washington DC as the premier educational institution of the Deaf in the world. There is also the example of Gestuno, an international sign language devised under the auspices of the World Federation of the Deaf (see World Federation of the Deaf, 1975; Schein and Stewart, 1995: 83–86). This undertaking, which again combines status and corpus planning, although intriguing in a number of ways, is nevertheless somewhat quixotic. As Schein and Stewart, seeking to present Gestuno in its most positive light, argued:

Gestuno is not a true language in the sense of national sign languages of the world; it arose from the choices of a committee, not naturally like the languages from which it drew most of its signs. But the group selecting the signs consisted of potential users, of deaf people accustomed to signing who would be dependent on their decisions in future international meetings. Perhaps these differences explain why, unlike Manual Codes for English, Gestuno appears viable over the long run. (1995: 86)

Ideology, in short, plays a key role in both status and corpus planning for sign languages, just as it does for spoken languages.

The language planning process

Language planning efforts can be conceptualized as consisting of four interrelated, and to some extent overlapping, components:

1. the initial fact-finding phase;
2. the establishment and articulation of goals, desired outcomes and the strategies to be employed in achieving these goals and outcomes;
3. the implementation process; and
4. the evaluation of all aspects of the language planning process (see Reagan, 1983).

During the first stage of the language planning process, information about the setting in which the language policy is to be implemented is gathered. Clearly, the more information that is available to the language planner, the better. In any event, two sorts of information must be gathered if the language policy is expected to have a significant and positive impact. The first of these is a clear understanding of the sociolinguistic setting in which the language policy is to be implemented. Especially important in this context are the common patterns of linguistic usage. The second sort of necessary information is that which would provide a proper understanding of other social, economic and political processes and developments. It is only with a combination of these two kinds of information that a realistic perspective on need determination and assessment of needs and wants can be gained by the language planner.

The second step in the language planning process involves the determination and articulation of goals, strategies and outcomes. This process will take place on several levels and will require a variety of skilled personnel. Goals, both linguistic and extra-linguistic, will be set based on the assessment of needs and wants determined in the information-gathering phase within the parameters made possible by the political and socioeconomic context. The goals, in turn, will serve to define and delineate the expected (and desired) outcomes of the language policy to be effected. The strategies for achieving these outcomes, which are normally seen as primarily a technical matter, will provide the basis and direction for the implementation of the language policy.

The implementation of the language policy, which is the third step in the language planning process, is in many ways the central focus of much of the language planning literature. This phase entails the mobilization of resources, general finance and personnel management, motivation and supervision of those concerned both with the management of the language policy program and with its target populations, and preparation, sequencing and coordination of related aspects of the language policy (such as the development of textbooks, etc.) (Rubin and Jernudd, 1971).

The last step in the process of language planning, and often the most neglected, is that of evaluation. Evaluation of the language policy should take place in two senses: both as an integral, ongoing component of all phases of the language planning process, and as a final, cumulative examination of the successes and failures of the language policy (mainly, although not exclusively, in terms of the correlation of goals and outcomes). Insofar as the predicted outcomes are still considered valid ones, the actual outcomes ought to be, as a consequence of evaluation, brought continually closer to the articulated goals of the language policy.

The model of the process of language planning presented here is essentially a normative one, which is to say that this is how language planners and policy makers would generally advocate that policies related to language be made. However, as our earlier discussion of the development and implementation of manual sign codes made clear, such a model often does not describe or reflect reality accurately. In fact, language policies and related language planning decisions are frequently made solely or primarily on the basis of short-term political expediency, misguided assumptions and beliefs, and a range of extra-linguistic factors. It is also true, however, that language policies and language planning activities are often unsuccessful, usually because of the way in which they were designed and implemented. This is an important topic to which we return when we discuss the evaluation of language policies.

Language rights and language policy

At the start of the twenty-first century, the world in which we live is very different from how it was a mere century ago. The changes of the past hundred years are probably nowhere more visible, recognized and utilized than in the scientific and technological spheres. So, too, have our social, cultural and political realities changed, although not always in such obvious ways. One area in which we can clearly see significant evolution in social thought is with respect to the discourse on human rights. As the British philosopher Brenda Almond noted:

The Second World War involved violations of human rights on an unprecedented scale but its ending saw the dawn of a new era for rights. Following their heyday in the seventeenth century . . . rights played a crucial role in the revolutions of the late eighteenth century. In the nineteenth and early twentieth centuries, however, appeal to rights was eclipsed by movements such as utilitarianism and Marxism which could not, or would not, accommodate them . . . The contemporary period has seen a further shift in their fortunes and today they provide an accepted international currency for moral and political debate. In many parts of the world, irrespective of cultural or religious traditions, when issues of torture or terrorism, poverty or power are debated, the argument is very often conducted in terms of rights and their violation. (1993: 259)

Indeed, the latter half of the twentieth century has witnessed a veritable explosion of interest in and concern with human rights. To some extent, of course, such interest and concern has been self-serving. As with young children who master the concept of "unfairness" when it applies to them far more quickly than when it applies to others, we tend to be more aware of violations of our own rights than of our violations of others' rights. Discourse about human rights, and on the violation of human rights, in the international realm also serves multiple purposes, and is often used as a convenient weapon to distract or to delegitimize a political opponent.

The use and misuse of rights discourse to achieve other kinds of ends sometimes, quite understandably, leads to a tendency simply to ignore or dismiss the issue altogether as merely another sort of meaningless political rhetoric. However, rights do matter, as does discourse about rights. Discussions and debates about rights impact legislation, social policy and, ultimately, the quality of life of both groups and individuals. As Robert Phillipson, Mart Rannut and Tove Skutnabb-Kangas have argued, "The history of human rights shows that the concept of human rights is not static. It is constantly evolving in response to changed perceptions of how humans have their fundamental freedoms restricted, and the challenge to the international community to counteract injustice" (1995: 16).

The twentieth century, then, has witnessed not only challenges to and abrogations of human rights, but also growing awareness and articulation of such rights. One area in which such awareness has been relatively late to develop, in spite of ongoing and often egregious violations of group and individual rights, is that of language. As recently as 1985, Gomes de Matos could write that "Although ours has been said to be 'the age of rights' . . . there has not yet been a thorough, well-documented, carefully thought out discussion of the crucial problem of the human being's linguistic rights" (1985: 1–2). Given the centrality of language to self-identification and to our sense of who we are and where we fit in the broader world, it is interesting that a concern with language rights has taken so long to emerge. And yet, such concern *has* emerged in recent decades, and the scholarly and political literature dealing with issues of language rights has increased dramatically both quantitatively and qualitatively (see, for example, Skutnabb-Kangas and Phillipson, 1995; Herriman and Burnaby, 1996; Benson *et al.*, in press). Although it is clear that we have a long way to go in terms of raising consciousness about language rights, and while such rights are far from universally recognized (let alone observed), the fact that the issue itself has been put on the table for discussion and debate is itself a promising development.

The fundamental challenge presented by debates about language and language policy is essentially one of achieving balance between the competing goods of social unity and access, on the one hand, and respect for and toleration of diversity, on the other. Basically, the question that policy makers are trying to address in such debates is the extent to which pluralism, as a necessary condition for a democratic social order, applies to the issue of language. At the heart of this discussion, of course, is the issue of language rights. In other words, to what extent, and in what ways, are *language* rights *human* rights? Also relevant here is the related question of whether rights (in this case, language rights) apply only to the individual, or whether there are rights which are "group rights" (that is, rights which apply to a community rather than solely to the members of that community by virtue of some common, shared feature of the individuals in the community) (see Tollefson, 1991: 167–200; Coulombe, 1993). This issue is far more complex than it might at first seem, since language rights are "preeminently *social*, in that they are only comprehensible in relation to a group of other human beings with whom the language is shared and from which personal and cultural identity is achieved" (MacMillan, 1982: 420). In other words, debates about language rights are unique in that, as Kenneth McRae argued, "societies characterized by linguistic pluralism differ from those characterized by racial, religious, class or ideological divisions in one essential respect, which stems from the pervasive nature of language as a general vehicle of communication" (1978: 331). This having been said, the concept of group rights is itself somewhat problematic, potentially leading to an apartheid-style mandate of ethnic obligation (for a compelling discussion of the concept of group rights, see Degenaar, 1987), even as the alternative of linguistic imperialism looms large (see Phillipson, 1992; Pennycook, 1994; 1998). The challenge, in short, is a very real one, with very real and significant outcomes for people's lives.

In working toward a conception of "language rights", a good place to begin the discussion is with The UN Declaration on the Rights of Persons Belonging to National or Ethnic, Religious and Linguistic Minorities (18 December 1992), in which the international community attempted to articulate the nature of the human and civil rights which ought to be accorded members of minority groups (see Skutnabb-Kangas, 1994). This Declaration was a follow-up to the Universal Declaration of Human Rights, necessitated by the widespread violation of the second article of the Universal Declaration of Human Rights which prohibits discrimination against individuals based on language. Specifically, three articles of the Declaration are relevant here. First, Article 2.1 prohibits what might be termed active discrimination against members of minority groups:

Persons belonging to national or ethnic, religious and linguistic minorities (hereinafter referred to as persons belonging to minorities) have the right to enjoy their own culture, to profess and practice their own religion, *and to use their own language, in private and in public, freely and without interference or any form of discrimination.* (Article 2.1; my emphasis)

This, in a sense, is the negative force of the Declaration, in that it focuses on simply prohibiting actions and policies that unfairly target minority groups. The Declaration goes far beyond this negative constraint, however, and in Articles 4.2 and 4.3 specify what can be called positive language rights:

States shall take measures to create favorable conditions to enable persons belonging to minorities to express their characteristics and to develop their culture, language, religion, traditions and customs, except where specific practices are in violation of national and contrary to international standards. (Article 4.2)

States should take appropriate measures so that, whenever possible, persons belonging to minorities have adequate opportunities to learn their mother tongue or to have instruction in their mother tongue. (Article 4.3)

These explicit statements of both negative and positive aspects of language rights differ in significant ways from the constitutional provisions governing the issue of language rights in the United States[6] and, indeed, of those in many countries. They differ even more, in many instances, from government policies and practices.

This discussion brings us to the issue of language rights and the Deaf. The medical and sociocultural perspectives of deafness not only lead to different understandings of deafness and the Deaf, and to different social and educational policies for the Deaf (see Johnson *et al.*, 1989; Walworth *et al.*, 1992; Baynton, 1996; Safford and Safford, 1996: 90–121), but also lead to very different approaches to the issue of language rights in the Deaf community. For those accepting a medical model of deafness, discussions of language rights are, basically, irrelevant. The Deaf do not constitute a minority group in the sense intended in the passages but, rather, are seen as disadvantaged members of a particular spoken language community. Thus, the medical perspective leads to what is essentially a compensatory view of language rights, which focuses on ensuring access through what is assumed to be a common language. This means that interpreting services and similar support will be provided to the Deaf, because this is a way of compensating for a deficit. Although certainly well meaning, such an approach is profoundly paternalistic, and is clearly grounded in an understanding of deafness as a disability. The alternative conceptualization of language rights and the Deaf, which has been forcefully articulated by Tove Skutnabb-Kangas (1994; see also Reagan, in press) among others, is grounded in the sociocultural view of deafness. The sociocultural view of deafness leads to an empowerment approach to language rights for the Deaf, in which signed language and other supports are called for not as a means to correct a disability, but rather because the Deaf, as a cultural and linguistic minority, should be entitled to them as basic human rights (see Nover, 1995). Also at issue here is the matter of how one defines "mother tongue" in the context of the deaf child; a matter of no little complexity, to be sure (for a very thorough discussion of this topic, see Bouvet, 1990: 119–133). Here, then, The UN Declaration of the Rights of Persons Belonging to National or Ethnic, Religious and Linguistic Minorities is clearly relevant, even though, as Harlan Lane and his colleagues have argued, internationally recognized language rights are "almost universally violated when it comes to signed language minorities" (Lane *et al.*, 1996: 422).

In recent years, for example, there have been ongoing debates in many parts of the USA about whether ASL should be offered as a foreign language in secondary schools and in colleges and universities. Central to these debates has been the question of whether ASL is in some sense less "real" or "legitimate" than spoken languages. This is a position that ignores more than 30 years of linguistic research on the nature, structure and uses of ASL (see Wilcox, 1988; Reagan, 1997; Wilcox and Wilcox, 1997). The recognition of ASL as a "real" language, generally for purposes of academic foreign language credit (especially with respect to secondary schools), is one that has been gradually taking place in the USA on a state-by-state basis (see Wilcox, 1988). Jacobs (1996: 217–226) provides a detailed analysis of the status of ASL in each of the 50 states of the USA. Although well-intended and clearly supported by the Deaf themselves, such efforts have the potential to do positive harm as well as good. As Jeffrey Nash has argued:

Since ASL has been maintained in spite of and perhaps to a degree because of oppressive language policies, such official recognition of ASL may not be necessary, and could even have unintended consequences of changing the social functions of ASL. ASL functions as the cement of the community because of the symbolic identity it offers to deaf people – an identity which contrasts markedly with those they receive from having been members of educational institutions . . . As long as deaf people feel a need to create for themselves distinctive identities, they will rely on ASL as their medium for social contact. Conversely, if ASL were to become an official language of instruction in special education programs in the United States, it might lose some of its power as a device for accomplishing a distinctive social identity. (1987: 20)

Such efforts legislatively to declare ASL a "real language" and discussion in South Africa about the possibility of South African Sign Language being recognized in the new constitution as a twelfth official language in South Africa[7] are both illustrative of manifestations of this empowerment perspective on language rights for the deaf. Implicit in this empowerment perspective on language rights for the deaf is a rejection of the compensatory perspective as either a sort of linguistic imperialism, or perhaps even cultural and linguistic genocide (see Skutnabb-Kangas, 1994; 2000).

Thus far I have suggested that compensatory and empowerment approaches to language rights for the Deaf are representative of basically incompatible views of both deafness and language rights. Although a case might be made for these two perspectives constituting what philosophers of science sometimes call "incommensurable paradigms", political practice in the real world is somewhat more complex and confused. This is the case in part because resources in many societies tend to be more readily available for disabled groups than they are for cultural and linguistic minorities (and especially for very small cultural and linguistic minorities). Thus, in the case of the Deaf it is often politically and financially expedient to accept the status and labels of disability, even while advocating recognition of the Deaf as a non-disabled cultural and linguistic community. In short, there is a generally unarticulated tension with respect to the rights of the Deaf: the cost of political recognition as a cultural and linguistic minority group may well be far greater, for the average deaf person, than the benefits of tolerating the paternalism (and even pity) of the hearing majority (see J. Shapiro, 1993; Wrigley, 1997). Compensatory approaches to language rights may, then, in some circumstances, be somewhat empowering, even as empowerment approaches may prove to be disempowering.

Evaluating language policies

An important point that is often minimized, or even overlooked entirely, in discussions of language planning is that such activity is profoundly political in nature (see Phillipson 1992; McKay 1993; Pennycook 1994; 1998; van Dijk, 1995). Language planning involves public decisions about language, its use, status and development. These are decisions which have overwhelming significance socially, economically, educationally and politically for both society and the individual. Language planning cannot be separated from such concerns, nor, indeed, would it be appropriate to try to do so. Language planning efforts are, in short, inevitably ideological and political in nature, and this fact must be taken into account in trying to understand them (see Tollefson, 1991: 22–42).

The philosopher Donna Kerr (1976) has suggested four "tests" that any good public policy must pass. These four tests, and the fundamental questions that they seek to raise, are:

- The desirability test: Is the goal of the policy one that the community as a whole believes to be desirable?
- The justness test: Is the policy just and fair? That is, does it treat all people in an equitable and appropriate manner?
- The effectiveness test: Is the policy effective? Does it achieve its objectives?
- The tolerability test: Is the policy resource-sensitive? Is it viable in the context in which it is to be effected?

These four tests are useful in evaluating language policies and can serve as a working model for analyzing different language planning processes, providing us with a series of questions that can be used in evaluating different language policy options. A powerful example of how these tests can be applied to a specific context of language policy can be seen in the case of South Africa under the apartheid regime.

The *taalstryd* ("language struggle") has been a central point of disagreement and debate throughout the history of South Africa, especially in the educational sphere. Under the apartheid regime, the language medium question was most controversial in black education, where the policy of initial mother tongue instruction was widely denounced as an attempt to retribalize black South Africans (Hirson, 1981; Reagan, 1987; 1995a; Alexander, 1989; Beukes, 1991). To some extent it is important to remember that the mother tongue policy was, however, a reflection of the historical language struggle which took place in the white community of South Africa in the nineteenth and early twentieth centuries, since that struggle deeply influenced both white perceptions and government policy with regard to language policies in education. This earlier language struggle had focused in part on the rights of Afrikaners to educate their children in their mother tongue, in the face of

ongoing efforts at Anglicization (see Steyn, 1980). Although the tensions between English and Afrikaans were never eliminated, government policies of
what might be termed active official bilingualism, coupled with English and
Afrikaans speakers attending their own-medium schools, mitigated what tensions existed. However, language remained a highly controversial issue in black
education (Reagan, 1984; 1986b; 1987; 1991; 1995a; Hartshorne, 1987; Marivate, 1993). Somewhat ironically, it was the Afrikaner government which supported mother tongue schooling for blacks, while blacks themselves, for the
most part, opposed such schooling. It is this irony that provides, at least in part,
a key to understanding the apartheid-era debate on language policy in South
African education. The apartheid regime consistently favored mother tongue
schooling for blacks (and, in fact, for almost all children in the country), but
for arguably quite different reasons from those used to defend mother tongue
instruction for white children. It is clear that mother tongue programs for blacks
were not only consistent with the ideology of apartheid, but that they functioned
as one of the pillars of apartheid in perpetuating both racial and ethnolinguistic
divisions in South African society (see Reagan, 1987). Mother tongue schooling
for blacks was employed from the passage of the Bantu Education Act of 1953
to the end of the apartheid era to support the social and educational goals of
Verwoerdian-style apartheid. The apartheid regime used such programs to reinforce ethnic and tribal identity among black schoolchildren, seeking to "divide
and conquer" by encouraging ethnolinguistic divisions within the black community (see Heugh, 1985; Hartshorne, 1987; 1992). As Barnard perceptively
noted:

Moedertaalonderwys . . . is not the Afrikaans term for mother-tongue instruction. It is
a political concept which has its roots in the dogma of Christian National Education.
According to this dogma, each "race" or "volk" has its own identity which sets it apart
from all others . . . Surely one has to wonder and become suspicious when there is
this insistence on the part of the authorities to force upon all children, against the
wishes of their parents, a particular language . . . What is being attempted is certainly
not mother-tongue education in the interests of the children but the enforcement of
"moedertaalonderwys" as an instrument of social control and subjugation, as a means
to an end . . . (Quoted in Heugh, 1987: 143–144)

Given this historical background, it is easy to understand the resistance to mother
tongue education, as well as to mandatory instruction in Afrikaans (see Reagan, 1987), found in many parts of the black community during the apartheid
era. Indeed, schooling designed to emphasize ethnic and cultural differences
often falls prey to this sort of "pluralist dilemma". As the Australian scholar
Brian Bullivant observed, programs designed and intended to encourage ethnic
identification, including various kinds of multicultural education programs in
many western societies, "are ideal methods of controlling knowledge/power,
while appearing through symbolic political language to be acting solely from

the best of motives in the interests of the ethnic groups themselves" (Bullivant, 1981: 291).

This was clearly the case in the South African instance, and while few blacks were taken in by the rhetoric of pluralism, the same cannot be said for much of the South African educational establishment, which began utilizing the language of multiculturalism and cultural pluralism toward the end of the apartheid era (see van Zijl, 1987). The real problem which now confronts educators and language planners alike in the South African context is how the realities of cultural and linguistic diversity can be dealt with in an equitable and just manner.

A fascinating footnote with respect to the South African experience in language planning and language policy implementation is provided by the case of sign language in the education of the Deaf. Under apartheid, all schooling in the country was segregated by race, and this included schools serving special populations, including those that were explicitly intended to serve the Deaf and hard-of-hearing. Schools serving white students were historically strongly oral in orientation, while those serving black deaf children were generally far more accommodating with respect to the use of signing – although the latter encouraged and promoted the use of an artificially constructed sign code rather than a natural sign language (see Penn and Reagan, 1990; 1991; 1995; 1999; Reagan and Penn, 1997). In any event, the irony in this case is that, to some extent, the black Deaf were provided a somewhat more appropriate education (at least with respect to the toleration and use of sign language) than were other deaf children in South Africa.

Conclusions

It is clear that language planning and language policies can and do serve a variety of quite different ends. Language planning can serve as a tool for empowering groups and individuals, for creating and strengthening national bonds and ties, and for maximizing educational and economic development. However, it can also be used (and has been used) to maintain and perpetuate oppression, social class discrimination, and social and educational inequity (see Fairclough, 1989; Pennycook, 1994, 1998; Skutnabb-Kangas, 2000). This is true both in the case of spoken languages and in the case of sign languages. Returning to our earlier discussion of the development of manual sign codes, for instance, it is important to recall that, while the creators and advocates of manual sign codes may have been sincere in their efforts to help deaf children, and while they utilized language planning activities to achieve their ends, they also failed to take into account the complexity of the issue surrounding the language rights of the Deaf (however one defines this), and to recognize that both of the communities to which the language planning activities are directed must be involved in that language planning activity. Language planning efforts, if they are to be defensible, must entail the active involvement and participation of those for whom they are intended. Only when emerging in such a context can language planning efforts contribute to the creation of more just, humane and legitimate social and educational policies. As James Tollefson argued quite powerfully, "the foundation for rights is *power* and . . . constant *struggle* is necessary to sustain language rights" (1991: 167). This is true in the case of sign languages as well as for other languages, as the history of the Deaf community makes clear (see Lane, 1984; Fischer and Lane, 1993; van Cleve, 1993; Baynton, 1996; Rée, 1999).

Suggested readings

The single best work on language planning in general is Kaplan and Baldauf's *Language Planning: From Practice to Theory* (1997). Two other outstanding books that deal explicitly with a range of language planning and language policy issues are Cooper's *Language Planning and Social Change* (1989) and Tollefson's *Planning Language, Planning Inequality: Language Policy in the Community* (1991). For those interested in language policy in the school context, David Corson's *Language Policy in Schools: A Resource for Teachers and Administrators* (1999) is invaluable. For those interested specifically in works on language planning and policy with respect to sign languages, the best works available are chapters on these topics found in Ceil Lucas, ed., *The Sociolinguistics of the Deaf Community* (1989) and Ceil Lucas, ed., *Sociolinguistics in Deaf Communities* (1995). Finally, there is the *magnum opus* of Tove Skutnabb-Kangas – *Linguistic Genocide in Education: Or Worldwide Diversity and Human Rights?* (2000) – which is perhaps the most powerful book ever written on language planning and language policy issues. This book contains extensive discussions about language planning and policy issues as they relate to sign languages.

Exercises

1. Many people are uncomfortable when they hear about efforts to "plan language". When do you believe that language planning as an applied sociolinguistic activity is necessary? When, and why, is it defensible? In what kinds of situations and settings is language planning either not necessary or not defensible? Why?
2. What kinds of language policies are you familiar with? Who is responsible for implementing these policies? For evaluating them? Who decides how and when these language policies are implemented?
3. What does the phrase "language rights" mean to you? What are the implications of this concept for educators? For policy makers?

4. Imagine that you have been asked to develop a language policy for a particular school. What kinds of background information would you need to complete this task? What are some of the social and educational issues that you would need to address? What would the role of the recognition of language rights be in the language policy you develop?
5. There has been extensive discussion and debate in the USA in recent years about the possibility of adopting English as the country's official language. What do you believe the implications of such an action would be in the case of deaf people and their language? Would the effect be positive or negative? Why?

NOTES

1 Turkish, for instance, was historically written using Arabic orthography, but now uses the Roman alphabet. In an extremely interesting case, the languages of Central Asia under the control first of the Russian Empire and later the Soviet Union underwent multiple orthographic shifts in the twentieth century. Originally written in Arabic script, these languages were written in the Roman script in the early years of the Soviet Union and then, later, in the Cyrillic script. Some former Soviet states are again changing the script used. Such changes, of course, mirror changes in political and ideological realities (see Shorish, 1984).

2 Baron (1981) provides numerous examples of proposals for language reform offered by various "Saxonist" scholars. For example, in the late nineteenth century, Elias Molee proposed the following alternatives:

English	Saxonist alternative
village	dorf
because	forthat
enmity	findship
nation	gefolk
dentist	toothhealer

Saxonist alternatives were generally drawn either from historical roots, with an emphasis on Old English roots, or from comparable German roots (the assumption being, apparently, that modern German was "purer" and closer to its Germanic roots than is modern English).

3 The creation of modern Hebrew is sometimes described as an instance of a "dead" language being restored to daily use, but this is not entirely accurate. Although Hebrew was not used as a vernacular language by Jews, it had remained their religious language and the language of scholarship. In this role it was very much alive. Nevertheless, its revitalization as a language of daily life is a very impressive example of successful language revival.

4 The Irish case is an interesting one from a number of perspectives, not the least of which is that of how one evaluates language policies. In terms of revitalizing Irish to the point where it functions as the common, daily vernacular language in Ireland, language planning and policy efforts cannot be considered to have been very successful. However, in many other ways, including attitudes toward Irish and the

growth of fluent second-language users of Irish (who can, perhaps, be said to constitute a "speech network" more than a "speech community"), the movement has been far more successful (see Edwards, 1984a; Hindley, 1990; Maguire, 1991; O'Huallacháin, 1991; 1994; Ó Riagáin, 1997).

5 By "IS kind of signs", this informant is referring to the use in manual sign codes of the ASL sign REALLY, in initialized forms, to function in place of the English verb *to be*. Since ASL does not employ the copula, the use of variations of REALLY where English would use *am*, *is* and *are* strikes many ASL users as slow, awkward and, on occasion, confusing, as this quote indicates.

6 At the present time, the US Constitution makes no direct reference to language or to language rights. Such rights are presumed to be inherent in other legal and constitutional protections. Indeed, it is this lack of specific mention of language rights that is, to some extent, at issue in contemporary debates about adopting English as the official language of the USA (see Baron, 1990; Crawford, 1992a; 1992b).

7 Increased recognition of the Deaf in South Africa is rapidly developing. For example, early in 1996 the Language Plan Task Group was established by the Minister of Arts, Culture, Science and Technology for the purpose of advising him on the development of a coherent National Language Plan for South Africa. Eight subcommittees were appointed, and a policy document was published later that year. During this process, South African Sign Language emerged as a significant topic of discussion. Such was the prominence of the issues related to South African Sign Language that the entire final summit conference, which was attended by a number of deaf delegates, was interpreted in sign language. Further, sign language was explicitly mentioned in five out of eight subcommittee reports of the final report (Language Plan Task Group, 1996). Although there was considerable discussion about the status of South African Sign Language in the constitutional discussions, the constitution that was eventually approved, although recognizing South African Sign Language as a South African language, did not accord it official status.

APPENDIX 6.1   STATEMENT ON THE RECOGNITION OF THE NATIONAL
SIGN LANGUAGES OF THE DEAF PASSED AT THE THIRD EUROPEAN
CONGRESS ON SIGN LANGUAGE RESEARCH, HAMBURG (1989)

Comment

From 26–29 July, the *Third European Congress on Sign Language Research* took place in Hamburg. This international linguistic congress was arranged by the *International Sign Language Association* (ISLA) and attended by about 200 professionals from 21 countries.

In the closing session the participants unanimously declared sign languages to be full and equal languages. They strongly demanded the national sign languages of the deaf be recognized by society.

In this context, the following statement was, again unanimously, agreed on. It could serve as the basis for another international resolution to be worked out by *ISLA* and the *World Federation of the Deaf*. It should be passed at the *International Symposium on Sign Language Research* in 1991 at the latest.

The statement

Prejudices and attitudes towards sign language rooted in educational philosophy have deeply influenced the living conditions of deaf people and their chances of personal development. Due to the grave consequences that negative perception of sign language have in deaf people's lives, we consider it our duty to go beyond the realm of scientific discourse and with this resolution bring to the public's attention the social and political implications of our research.

Earlier opinions of sign language.   In Milan, 1880, the hearing participants of the International Congress of Educators of the Deaf approved a resolution in which sign language was officially banned and virtually eliminated from deaf education. Sign language was no longer recognized as the language of deaf people but was seen, at best, as suitable only for the most elementary communication needs, as a mixture of simple pantomime and primitive gesturing incapable of conveying abstract concepts and complex ideas, as a form more closely related to subhuman forms of communication.

Recent scientific research on sign language.   In recent years, there has been a dramatic change in how sign language has been perceived. Scientific investigations of a number of national sign languages over the past 30 years have produced ample evidence that sign languages are full and complex language systems equivalent to spoken languages in functional and structural respects. These studies have demonstrated that sign languages possess sophisticated grammars and large vocabularies; linguists have described the basic linguistic structures, rules, and functions of these languages.

Sign languages, however, are more than just abstract linguistic systems. Psychological, psycholinguistic and sociolinguistic studies have also shown that the use of sign language promotes emotional, social, and mental development in deaf children. Early use of sign language facilitates concept formation, developmentally appropriate acquisition of knowledge, of social values and norms of behavior, and a high degree of overall communicative competence. There is evidence that even acquisition of the spoken and written language may be strengthened by the early acquisition of sign language. In general, early and consistent use of sign language by deaf children results in more effective learning both in and out of school.

The Deaf as a linguistic community.   For the deaf adult, sign language is a prerequisite to social integration. It is not physical disability but sign language which unites deaf people in a social community that exhibits all the traits of a language community. The sign language community is the deaf person's safeguard against the fate of living isolated in a hearing world; the deaf community is a guarantee for the individual's social and psychological well-being.

Public recognition of the Deaf community and their language. The society should recognize the sign language of the deaf and the community of the deaf. Deaf people must be able to decide themselves all questions directly concerning themselves and their community.

In particular, the policy-making agencies must no longer ignore deaf people's demand for bilingual education, which explicitly recognizes the importance of sign language and the deaf community for the deaf person.

Sign language is also a means of meaningful integration of the deaf into hearing society. Through provision of adequate, qualified interpreting services, deaf people can benefit from all existing sources of information as well as make themselves heard within the larger society.

WE DEMAND THE FOLLOWING POLITICAL ACTION NECESSARY TO ALTER THE CURRENT SITUATION:

- **Recognition of sign languages and recognition of the deaf as a language minority** by national parliaments in accordance with the resolution unanimously passed by the European Parliament on 12 June 1988. Translation into action of this decision through appropriate legislative and administrative measures.
- **Public financing of interpreting services** and all ensuing costs including interpreter training. Elimination of discrimination against deaf persons by making academic instruction and vocational training for the deaf more available through the provision of qualified interpreters. Increased use of interpreters in public institutions and on television.
- **Support of a sign language environment for the deaf baby and young deaf child**, to begin from the time when deafness is first diagnosed, by supporting the study and use of sign language within the family, as well as outside of the family (play groups, day-care centers, kindergartens), by making possible regular contact by developing sign language materials for this age group.
- **Introduction of a bilingual curriculum** in cultural and educational institutions for the deaf by creation of appropriate prerequisites (e.g. training of qualified deaf teachers and educators; further training of existing hearing staff; production of suitable teaching materials).
- **Support of autonomous cultural activities of the deaf** through support for sign language courses and development of appropriate teaching methods; access to visual media; production of television programs by and for deaf people.

- **Support for further basic theoretical and applied research** towards the attainment of these goals.

APPENDIX 6.2   WORLD FEDERATION OF THE DEAF CALLS FOR RECOGNITION
OF SIGN LANGUAGES

The World Federation of the Deaf (WFD) Commission on Sign Language puts forward the following recommendations:

1. We recommend that the WFD call for the recognition of sign languages and of the right to use sign languages around the world.

   A. This calls on every government to propose (if not already implemented) official recognition of the sign language(s) used by deaf people in their country as one of the country's indigenous languages.
   B. This calls on every government to abolish any remaining obstacles to the use of sign language as the primary and everyday language of deaf people.

2. We recommend that the WFD call for the right of deaf children to have full early exposure to sign language, and to be educated as bilinguals or multilinguals with regard to reading and writing.

   A. A sign language should be recognized and treated as the first language of a deaf child.
      (a) The sign language in question must be the national sign language, that is, the natural sign language of the adult Deaf community in that region.
      (b) In order for the deaf children to acquire their first language early and with full fluency, they must be guaranteed the right to be exposed to sign language early in life, in an environment which includes highly skilled signers.
   B. Deaf children have the right to be educated, particularly with regard to reading and writing, in a bilingual (or multilingual) environment.
      (a) The national sign language should be the language of instruction for most academic subjects.
      (b) Instruction in the national spoken and written language should occur separately but in parallel, as is common in bilingual/multilingual educational programs for other languages.
   C. Sign language teaching programs should be established and further developed for parents and personnel working with deaf children.
   D. Teachers of the deaf must be expected to learn and use the accepted natural sign language as the primary language of instruction.
   E. In order to achieve A–D above, the national sign language must be included as an academic subject in the curriculum of programs for the deaf, including both the programs which deaf students attend and the programs which train teachers of the deaf.

3. We recommend that the WFD call for substantially increased government support for research on the native sign languages, with fluent deaf users of sign language prominently included at every level.

   A. Research on sign language must be established at universities, research institutes, and educational institutions in every country.

B. Because deaf individuals are the primary fluent users of sign language, Deaf individuals and national Deaf associations must be closely involved with the research and its dissemination.

   (a) Deaf individuals who are fluent native users of their national sign language should be recognized as the legitimate arbiters in the correct usage of the indigenous sign language and should hold significant positions in research efforts.

   (b) Funds must be provided for advanced training of deaf individuals in sign language research, so that adequate numbers of Deaf researchers are available.

   (c) Deaf individuals should be encouraged to attend meetings concerning sign language in national and international settings.

C. Research findings should be disseminated to deaf people around the world, through the national Deaf associations, as well as through other means which will inform Deaf people about research on their languages.

D. Research findings on sign language should be used to guide the teaching of sign language, the training of interpreters, and the training of parents and professionals. Training and teaching programs established for these purposes should be encouraged to combine research with training and teaching.

4. We recommend that the WFD call for massive expansion of sign language instruction in every country.

A. Programs offering sign language instruction must be available to all of the following groups:

   (a) Relatives and friends of deaf children.

   (b) All professionals working with deaf children and adults.

   (c) Deaf people with no prior knowledge of sign language.

   (d) Deafened and severely hard of hearing individuals with poor lip-reading skills.

B. Programs offering broader training in sign language studies must be available to the above groups, as well as to all deaf children, deaf adults, and teachers of the deaf. Sign language studies curricula should include training in the structure of natural sign languages, as well as in the culture of the Deaf communities in which these sign languages are used.

C. Training programs must be available for sign language instructors, including both training in language instruction and broader academic training in sign language studies.

D. Specialized programs must be offered for those dealing with deaf-blind individuals.

E. All of the above programs should be initially established in cooperation with the national organization of the deaf to maximize the academic quality of the program. This cooperation and supervision should occur with governmental or non-governmental organizations according to the traditions in each country.

5. We recommend that the WFD call for the right of all deaf individuals to have access to high quality interpreting between the spoken language of the hearing community and the sign language of the Deaf community. This in turn requires the establishment of qualified interpreter training programs, and the establishment of mechanisms in every country for making professional interpreters widely available to deaf individuals.

    A. It must be recognized that sign language interpreters are the principal means by which deaf individuals gain access to the facilities, services, and information of the larger communities in which they live. Sign language interpreters are thus a crucial mechanism by which deaf individuals obtain equal access and opportunities as the hearing individual in any society.

    B. Interpreting between sign language and spoken language must involve full translation between two different languages.

    C. In order to fulfill A and B above, sign language interpreting must be recognized as a highly skilled profession requiring both extensive training and extensive well-funded employment mechanisms. (See the recommendations from the Commission on Interpreting for further details.)

6. We recommend that the WFD call for Government support of widespread availability of the media through sign language.

    A. Broadcasting authorities must include translation into sign language of TV news programs, programs of political interest, and to the extent possible, a selection of programs of cultural or general interest.

    B. Broadcasting authorities must include sign language programs for deaf adults and children, and sign language teaching programs for the general public.

    C. Written materials of the same types as described in A and B (e.g. newspapers, news or political documents and information) should be translated into sign language and made available in video form.

    D. Support should be provided for the expansion of TV, video, film and books which are developed in sign language (e.g. materials to inform the deaf communities about their sign languages or materials to be used in teaching sign language).

*Sarah Burns, Patrick Matthews
and Evelyn Nolan-Conroy*

> Which reminds me that the funniest thing I saw over the whole holiday period
> was the Queen's Speech as interpreted into sign language by a splendid blonde
> lady in a long blue dress. Her hands flew like birds to convey the message to
> the deaf; all the relevant emotions crossed her face in a constant flux of sun
> and cloud. It was an Oscar winner among sign language mimes and nailed
> alongside her by the miracle of TV technology, the royal visage spoke and
> stared out in granite immobility. I hope HM and millions of the deaf enjoyed
> it as much as we did. But my guess is some back-room electronic wizard is
> making urgent inquiries about emigration.
>> Reference to British Sign Language in *The Guardian*, 2 January 1989, reprinted in
>> Gregory and Miles (1991)

> The language stands for being Irish, the whole ethnic component, and it stands
> for one other thing. It stands for what is old-fashioned, agricultural, archaic,
> not entirely of this world or this time, and that doesn't help.
>> Reference to Irish in an interview with Joshua Fishman, 1975,
>> reprinted in Ó Murchú (1994)

We all form attitudes and opinions – sometimes positive, sometimes negative – about languages, such as British Sign Language (BSL) or Irish referred
to above, and varieties of languages, such as African American Vernacular
English (AAVE) or Received Pronunciation (RP).[1] We may feel that one language or variety is "elegant", "expressive", and "musical", while another is
"vulgar", "backward" and "ugly". All levels of language use, whole languages,
language varieties, pragmatics and discourse, the meaning and structure of
words and sentences, and pronunciation and accent, are subject to such opinions and we endow some language forms with prestige, while we stigmatize
others.

From the linguistic viewpoint, all languages and all varieties of languages
are equal. Evaluative judgments are socially conditioned; the languages, varieties and features that receive less favorable evaluation do so because the
individuals who use them are socially stigmatized (Romaine, 1989). Coupland
and Jaworski (1997), therefore, warn us that in the examination of language

attitudes, linguistic facts may be less important than people's beliefs, especially where beliefs can be shown to be regularly and systematically held.

Anecdotal and popular evidence from the media, and academic surveys of language attitudes, tend to reveal the same underlying and recurrent patterns of values and value judgments. Some academic studies have been limited to examining attitudes toward a language itself. More often, however, the definition of language attitudes has been broadened to include attitudes toward the users of a language or language variety. It is extremely difficult to separate the two since attitudes toward a language are often intimately connected with those toward its users. We develop opinions about languages that reflect our views about those who use them and the contexts and functions with which they are associated.

Language attitudes are complex psychological entities. Individuals seldom choose what attitudes to have toward a language or variety – instead, we acquire them as a factor of group membership (Saville-Troike, 1989). Indeed, our evaluations may be unconscious or subconscious: most people are unaware that they are making judgments about how other people speak, write or sign until they are forced to confront them or articulate them in some manner. Almost always these attitudes are held resolutely. Lippi-Green (1997: xv) equates them with religious beliefs, when she says that "beliefs about the way language should be used are passed down and protected in much the same way that religious beliefs are passed along and cherished".

Clearly, researchers cannot directly observe or measure a person's attitudes. As Baker (1992) states, in his evaluation of the study of spoken language attitudes, a person's thoughts, processing system and feelings are hidden and we therefore have to infer attitudes from the direction and persistence of external behavior. Researchers have had to be creative and imaginative in devising methods to evaluate language attitudes. In interpreting the results of these studies, we need to be aware of the fact that most are time specific. As societies change, so too do our attitudes. The results of past studies, and the attitudes suggested by the quotes opening this chapter, may not be true today. Moreover, the findings of the most recent studies will very likely change in the future.

We discuss these and other language attitude issues in this chapter. We begin by asking why language attitudes are studied and by examining some definitions of the term. We then look back at some of the early research and the evolution of the field since the early 1960s. We explore how the research has been carried out, some of the questions addressed by various studies, as well as some of the answers advanced and theories that have been developed. Finally, the consequences of language attitudes, and changes in how languages and their users are perceived over time, are considered.

Why study language attitudes?

The evaluation of language attitudes "is recognised as a central concern in socio-linguistics" (Garrett *et al.*, 1999: 321) and is a thread that runs through many of the issues discussed in the earlier chapters of this book. Evaluative data may help explain, for example, the nature of the distribution of language variation (for classic examples, see Labov, 1966; 1972b; Trudgill, 1974; 1983) and are of vital importance when considering language restoration, maintenance, shift or death. Negative or positive attitudes can determine the level of knowledge speakers have of their first language, as well as their level of everyday use of it. Similarly, they may predict whether or not a language is learned as a second language and the degree of competence likely to be attained. Attitude surveys may also provide valuable information for language planners as they make decisions about which language or variety to use as the official language of government or in education.

Negative or positive attitudes can have real and profound effects on a broad range of spheres including: medical, occupational, legal and educational. We explore these consequences of language attitudes below. In short, attitudes may summarize, explain, or even predict behavior. It is for these reasons that studies of language attitudes are extremely important and that within Deaf communities, attitudes towards sign languages, and particularly their use in education, are a major issue worldwide.

Definitions

The study of language attitudes originated in the discipline of social psychol-ogy, but fields such as ethnography, sociology and sociolinguistics have also influenced it. It is perhaps because of the influence of these different traditions that definitions of the term "language attitudes" abound in the literature; the definitions vary according to the theoretical orientation of the writer. Fasold (1984) argues that most researchers working in the area view attitude as a state of readiness or an intervening variable between a stimulus affecting a person and that person's response. This "mentalist" viewpoint is voiced in the frequently cited definitions of attitude offered by, for example, Allport (1935: 810) – "a mental or neural state of readiness, organised through experience, exerting a directive or dynamic influence upon the individual's response to all objects and situations with which it is related" – Sarnoff (1970: 279) – "a disposition to react favourably or unfavourably to a class of objects" – and Williams (1974: 21) – "an internal state aroused by stimulation of some type and which may mediate the organism's subsequent response". From this perspective, attitudes can be used as a tool to predict future behaviors, which is one of the factors that distinguishes it from a second "behaviorist" view. Behaviorists hold that attitudes are to be found only in the responses people make to social situations (Fasold, 1984). Osgood *et al.*'s (1957: 190) definition of attitude as a "quantified set of responses to bipolar scales" is a typical example.

Another factor which differentiates the mentalist and behaviorist positions is that the latter considers attitudes as single units, while the former holds that it is important that a distinction be made between three components: affective (feelings), cognitive (knowledge) and conative (action) (Agheyisi and Fishman, 1970; Cooper and Fishman, 1974). Broadly speaking, there is an interrelationship between, on the one hand, the feelings or attitudes toward a language, knowledge or ability to speak it and, on the other hand, its actual use. As Baker (1992) points out, these three components may not always be in harmony; this is a relevant consideration when interpreting studies. In Ireland, for instance, where a considerable corpus of survey data on public attitudes toward Irish and Irish language policies has been gathered since the early 1960s, one paradoxical finding has permeated all of the results. Although the majority of the Irish population have continued to support the maintenance of the Irish language over the years, a much smaller proportion claim high levels of ability in it, and an even smaller proportion use the language frequently. Support for a displacement policy has remained low, never rising above 20 percent, over the period when the studies were carried out, yet only about 13 percent of the national samples regard themselves as competent Irish speakers (Ó Riagáin and Ó Gliasáin, 1984; 1994; Bord na Gaeilge, 1989).

The distinction between attitudes, knowledge and use can also be readily observed in sign languages. In the classroom, for example, use of natural sign language has traditionally been viewed negatively and considered unworthy in the education of deaf children. Numerous studies have reported that where hearing teachers do use sign, they are not fluent in the natural sign language, and typically develop a contact code that intermixes spoken and sign language grammatical elements (for examples, see La Bue, 1995; Oviedo, 1996). It is possible that these teachers' limited sign language skills lead to misconceptions about the validity of the grammar of sign languages, which in turn may impact the level of skill they are likely to achieve in the language. We return to the topic of language attitudes in education below.

Early research on language attitudes

Wallace Lambert, a Canadian psychologist, and his colleagues are generally accredited with having carried out the first contemporary study of language attitudes (Lambert *et al.*, 1960). They set about examining listeners' evaluative reactions to English and French in Montreal, Quebec. Bilingual French and English speakers were audiotaped reading a passage of prose, first in one of their languages and then in the other; in other words, for each language the voice samples were "matched" for content and speaker. The voices and the languages on the tapes were randomized. Two groups of students, one English-speaking and the other French-speaking, were then asked to evaluate the personality characteristics of the French and English speakers. The "guises" or speakers' identities, and the fact that the same individual produced both language samples were concealed from the judges. Fourteen traits, including leadership, intelligence, character and kindness, were evaluated on a semantic-differential scale; this was a six point bipolar scale with "very little" at one end and "very much" at the other. Because the judges did not know that the same person produced the samples, differences in the judges' evaluations of the guises could be said to be the result of different attitudes to the two languages. Surprisingly, the study found that both the English and French speaking respondents perceived the speakers of the English versions as having higher status than French speakers and rated them more favorably on several traits, such as intelligence and kindness. The research team concluded that the findings demonstrated not only favorable reactions from members of the high-status group toward their own speech, but also that these reactions had been adopted by members of the lower-status group (Lambert *et al.*, 1960).

The "matched guise" technique described here was developed by Lambert *et al.*, in an attempt to exert some experimental control over speaker variables. It has been replicated and modified by many researchers since the early 1960s. Indeed, Bradac (1990), in his review of language attitude research up to the late 1980s, states that the earliest studies established themes and procedures that are still with us today. He comments that this is either a testament to their excellence or a sign of stagnation in the field. The main focus of the language attitude research in the early 1960s was to explore the evaluative consequences of language variation among groups of speakers differentiated mainly by their geographical location. During the 1970s, researchers continued this work, but began to recognize variation and its consequences, not only between languages and language varieties, but also within them. In addition, they became interested in examining language variation based upon between-group differences reflecting social roles. Research carried out in the 1980s and 1990s has typically striven to develop theories to explain results and to explore applications of these theories in various domains. Efforts have also been made to address some methodological concerns and to tighten the validity of studies carried out in more naturalistic settings.

Compared to the study of spoken languages, there has been relatively little empirical research of attitudes toward sign languages and their users. Kannapell (1989), referring specifically to American Sign Language (ASL), states that most of the research that has been carried out on sign languages, focuses on their structural analysis and variation. To date, there is a significant lack of research on language attitudes among deaf people. Of the studies that have been completed, most have focused on the area of education, investigating the attitudes of deaf students (see, for example, Kannapell, 1989; Fenn, 1992; McDonnell, 1992; Matthews, 1996) and teachers of the Deaf and other professionals (see, for example, Ward Trotter, 1989; La Bue, 1995) toward natural sign languages, majority spoken languages and manual codes for spoken language. Other topics that have been explored include attitudes toward the outcome of language contact (see, for example, Lucas and Valli, 1989; 1991; 1992; Matthews, 1996) and attitudes toward the invention and introduction of new signs (see, for example, Woll, 1994; Kleinfeld and Warner, 1996). The attitudes about sign languages parallel, to a great extent, the attitudes about spoken minority languages and so, as is true in many other areas of linguistic and sociolinguistic investigation, we can learn many valuable lessons and borrow useful techniques from the work already carried out on spoken languages.

How are language attitudes studied?

As we noted above, language attitudes are subjective in nature. They are, consequently, extremely difficult to measure. There are many reasons why attitude measurement is rarely, if ever, completely valid (see Baker, 1992). Labov (1972b) coined the term "Observer's Paradox" to refer to one of the biggest obstacles facing researchers. He states that in order "to obtain the data most important for linguistic theory, we have to observe how people speak when they are not being observed" (1972b: 113). Similarly, once people are aware their attitudes are under investigation, their responses and behaviors tend to change. Consciously or unconsciously, they usually provide what they perceive to be a socially desirable answer. This phenomenon is known as the "halo effect" or the "principle of subordinate shift" (Labov, 1972b). Their perception of the researcher and the purpose of the research also impacts their responses.

Researchers have worked hard to devise methods that might overcome these difficulties. As a result, experimental approaches, where subjects are unaware that their attitudes are being measured, have dominated the field. In turn, the limitations of these experimental approaches have become apparent over the years and have inspired researchers to seek yet other ways of collecting and interpreting data. Greater use is now made of descriptive and inclusive research designs in an effort to collect qualitative, as well as quantitative information. There is a new emphasis on multiple variables and the search for interactions between them, multiple pathways of causality and bi-directional cause–effect links (see Baker, 1992).

Language attitude measurement techniques have been divided into three categories: content analysis, direct measurement and indirect measurement (Bouchard Ryan *et al.*, 1982).

Content analysis

Content analysis involves various forms of observation, including autobiograph-
ical, case study, and participant observation. The greatest advantage of this
method is that it is unobtrusive and yields the most naturalistic data. It has been
faulted for its obvious subjectivity; the researcher must make inferences on the
basis of the observed behavior. In the study of spoken language, Lesley Milroy
has made extensive use of participant observation within the context of social
network theory. The researcher presents himself (or herself) as "a friend of a
friend" to the community being investigated. By attaching himself to a group
in this way, the researcher can obtain much larger amounts of naturalistic data
than is generally possible in interaction with a single individual who is isolated
from his or her own social network (see Milroy, 1987a; 1987b). Deuchar (1984)
recommends the application of this method in the study of sign languages. She
chose observation as her main method of data collection in her investigation
of BSL. In the USA, Carol Erting has also made use of participant observation in her examination of the relationship between sign language and ethnicity
(Johnson and Erting, 1989; Erting, 1994).

Direct measurement

Direct measurement usually requires subjects to answer questions designed
to explore their language attitudes either through questionnaire or interview
format. A questionnaire may be made up of open or closed questions. Open
questions allow respondents maximum freedom to present their views but,
because it is possible for them to stray from the subject, they are difficult to score.
In a closed question format, respondents are more restricted in the responses
they can offer. Examples include: *yes–no* answers, multiple choice, ranking
schemes and the semantic-differential. Charles Osgood developed the former,
which is frequently used in conjunction with the matched guise technique and is
referred to above. The respondent is typically asked to judge entities or concepts
by means of a series of bipolar scales (for examples, see Fasold, 1984; Fenn,
1992). Closed questions are easier and quicker for subjects to respond to and are
easy for the researcher to score; however, they encourage the subject to answer
in the researcher's terms rather than their own (Fasold, 1984).

Overall, the advantages of questionnaires are that they are relatively easy to
distribute and collect which means that a much greater number of people can be
surveyed than it is practical to observe or interview. In addition, comparisons
can be made between informants' responses. The principle disadvantage to their
use is that the researcher can lose a significant degree of control over the results.
For example, they may not know whether the person to whom the questionnaire is given is the person who completes it. Neither does the researcher have
the opportunity to clarify terms or misunderstandings. In many communities,

questionnaires may be unfamiliar and may be perceived as threatening or intimidating (Romaine, 1989). They may also be written in a language that is not the first language of the potential respondents. Romaine cites some examples of studies where these difficulties arose and suggests that such problems may be alleviated by having informants complete the questionnaire as part of a face-to-face interview. Matthews (1996) did exactly this in his study of Irish Sign Language (ISL). Postal questionnaires distributed by him met with a very poor response from his Deaf informants. As a result, he decided to travel around Ireland to meet with members of the Deaf community on a personal level. At various centers, he gave lectures outlining the aims and objectives of his research project. He explained the kind of information he and his team wanted to collect and the reasons why they were gathering it. His lectures were delivered in ISL, which was more accessible to deaf people than information in written English. After each lecture, Matthews and his team had an opportunity to meet the deaf people present, distribute the questionnaire and have it completed on the spot. Informants were given the option of providing their responses in ISL, which was recorded on videotape and later transcribed onto the questionnaires. This method was obviously much slower, but Matthews reports that the overall results in terms of completed questionnaires returned at each meeting made his efforts worthwhile.

Indirect measurement

Indirect measurement techniques are designed to keep informants from knowing that their language attitudes are under investigation. The classic example is the matched guise technique described above. The most significant advantage of this technique is that it aims to control for all variables except language. It also lends itself particularly well to the application of statistical measures. It has been criticized, however, mainly because of its artificiality and sterility. The use of a tape-recording sets up an artificial situation, while no text is ever completely neutral (see Fasold, 1984; Giles and Coupland, 1991). Ward Trotter (1989) and Fenn (1992) have both successfully used modified versions of the matched guise technique to examine attitudes toward ASL.

A critical issue with regard to all of these methods is that of validity. Demonstrating validity in the case of language attitudes is extremely difficult. Fishman devised an ingenious technique known as "commitment measure" to tackle this problem. He asked questions involving the attitudes of Puerto Ricans in the New York City area about their ethnicity. In addition, he invited them to a Puerto Rican dance and cultural evening. It was then possible to compare the responses to questionnaires with whether or not the respondent replied to his invitation, said they would attend, and actually did (Fishman, 1968).

There are a number of special issues that arise when carrying out language attitude research among Deaf communities. The most obvious is the visual nature of sign language that necessitates the use of video rather than audio recording. The use of videotape is more intrusive than audiotape and, consequently, Deaf informants may be reluctant to participate in research. Matthews (1996) found that some of his respondents were hesitant or refused to give information on video. Some people felt that they were giving personal details and were worried that others, including unauthorized personnel, might gain access to this information without their consent, especially after completion of the research project.

The visual nature of sign languages also limits the application of a classic or pure version of the matched guise technique. A judge cannot be shown the same piece of data twice and be given different information about the signer each time as hearing judges can with audiotapes (Ward Trotter, 1989; Lucas and Valli, 1991; Fenn, 1992). Fenn attempted to overcome this difficulty by selecting signers that were fluent ASL users, were dressed in a similar fashion and were physically similar. Another difficulty that he encountered was that many of his subjects recognized the actors presenting the language samples. The Deaf community is a small one, and so there is always the danger that this may bias results. It is critical that signers are not chosen from the same pool as the judges.

A second issue is the nature of the research team. In the past, hearing people, whose first language was not a natural sign language, typically carried out sign language research. These researchers were obviously limited by their lack of insider knowledge and fluency in the language. As a result, there was a move to include deaf people as research assistants. More recently, it is not uncommon to find deaf people leading these teams. Deaf and hearing researchers come from different linguistic and cultural backgrounds. Consequently, there will be differences in approach and even in presentation styles (see Lawrence, 1998) and they will bring different skills and insights to their work. Deaf researchers are native sign language users and share many of the experiences of their subjects. Deaf informants are likely to feel more comfortable sharing their feelings with another deaf person. Hearing researchers, on the other hand, often process useful skills and experience from their involvement in spoken language research. They may be less likely to know the subjects and, as a result, may find it easier to maintain an objective stance. Ideally, sign language research needs to be conducted by bilingual/bicultural teams, led by deaf researchers in partnership with fluent hearing signers. Members of such teams need to tease out issues of language difference and power and to develop trust and understanding.

It is clear that there is an enormous need for methods of language attitude research to be improved so that the factors that have biased the work to date can be minimized. This need is particularly critical with regard to sign language research. The measurement of attitudes is unlikely to warrant one style of approach. The techniques that are adopted will depend on factors, such as the topic of research and the researcher's preference in methodology. In order to ensure maximum control on the part of the researcher, a combination of various types of data collection and analysis – or what Edwards (1985: 150) refers to as an "eclectic, triangulation approach" – seems the most desirable.

Questions addressed by language attitude studies

The questions addressed by language attitude studies fall broadly into three categories:

1. those which explore attitudes toward a language, variety, dialect or speech style (for example, do you think a given variety is beautiful, expressive and logical or ungrammatical, concrete and coarse?);
2. those which explore stereotyped impressions toward languages, their speakers and their functions (for example, do you think the speakers of a given variety are intelligent, attractive and friendly or uneducated, linguistically and cognitively deficient, and aloof?); and
3. those which focus on applied concerns (for example, do you think a given variety is appropriate for use in the classroom or on television?).

We discuss some studies that investigate the first two questions below, and look at the third question in a later section dealing with the consequences and applications of language attitudes.

Attitudes toward languages

In situations where two languages are in contact, the majority language is usually attributed positive qualities, while the non-dominant minority language is often viewed negatively (Romaine, 1989). These derogatory attitudes may originate within the more powerful, dominant language group and can be slowly adopted by the minority group, so that in the end its members feel they are speaking or using an "impoverished" language. There are numerous references to this phenomenon in the literature. For example, Edwards and Ladd (1983), referring to the linguistic status of West Indian Creole in Britain, cite a report in which teachers describe the language of their West Indian students as "babyish", "careless and slovenly", "lacking proper grammar", and "very relaxed like the way they walk". Edwards and Ladd continue that West Indians, and particularly educated West Indians, are among the severest critics of their own speech. In fact, many deny all knowledge of Creole. Wassink (1999: 58), discussing another creole language, Jamaican Creole, states that until relatively recently Creole was considered as the "fragmented language of a fragmented people".

With regard to sign languages, a number of powerful and influential hearing people have argued that they are not real languages, and that they are merely gesture and cannot be used to express abstract thought (Bloomfield, 1933; van Uden, 1986; Griffey, 1994). Bloomfield (1933: 39) believed that "gesture languages" were "merely developments of ordinary gestures and that any and all complicated or not immediately intelligible gestures are based on the conveniences of speech". He argued (1933: 144), therefore, that "elaborate systems of gesture, deaf-and-dumb language, signalling codes, the use of writing, telegraphy and so on, turn out, upon inspection, to be merely derivatives of language". More recently, van Uden (1986), a leading educationalist at Sint Michielsgestel Institute for the Deaf in the Netherlands, has claimed that linguistic phonology and functional morphology are not to be found in sign languages and that a linguistic syntax does not exist either. Similarly, Griffey, an influential educator of deaf children in Ireland over a 50-year period, has contended that "sign language is quite dependent on concrete situations and mime. Its informative power can be very limited without knowledge of a majority language such as English, French, etc." (1994: 28). Even the Abbé de l'Epée, the man often referred to as "the Father of Sign Language", believed that the sign system his students were already using should be converted to follow the grammar of spoken French (Lane, 1985). In the last chapter of a book such as this, it may seem asinine to state that the linguistic status of natural sign languages has been established without doubt, but it is this point which has been missed by those who perceive sign languages to be deficient or deviant.

The attitude of most governments is one of tolerance and indifference to the existence of sign languages. At the time of writing, there are just eight countries in the world whose indigenous sign language is recognized in their written constitution. A further 13 countries approximately have some legal reference to sign language.[2] Describing the situation in Britain, Turner et al. (1998: 146) are not optimistic that official recognition will be given to BSL in the near future. They quote from a statement made by the British Education Minister (Secretary) in 1993, which perhaps reflects the attitudes of government officials in other countries:

A language needs to have a cultural heritage and generally a written form permitting access to a body of expression and ideas, literature and common values, which when taken together, are characteristic of it. I could not agree that British Sign Language is comparable to English, French, or any other language in regular use.

While most governments tend not to interfere with the Deaf community's own promotion of its language, neither do they actively support the maintenance or development of sign languages. Edwards (1985) points out that lack of response is itself a government action. Use of sign languages in the domains of administration, business, education and the mass media continues to be limited (World Federation of the Deaf, 1993; Kyle and Allsop, 1997). Public awareness of the existence of sign languages is growing, but the concept of a complex language is not yet understood. A recent study examining the status of sign languages in 17 European countries found that hearing people view sign language "as a 'need' of Deaf people, something which might be assessed (and costed) and as a device by which Deaf people can be supported". In other words, their responses reflect a "service-orientated view" (Kyle and Allsop, 1997: 4).

The results of studies investigating the attitudes of deaf people themselves toward natural sign language and the majority spoken language parallel those investigating attitudes to minority spoken languages, in that deaf people frequently perceive their language negatively. Kyle and Woll (1983), describing the situation in Britain, state that when research into BSL began, deaf people had no label for the language apart from "signing" and did not realize it was a language. Likewise, in Ireland, a study by Burns (1998) found that only two-thirds of the deaf subjects recognized Irish Sign Language as a real language. Terms such as "broken", "ugly", "telegraphic" (Edwards and Ladd, 1983), "short-hand for English", "broken English" (Swisher and McKee, 1989), "dumb language" and "street language" (Lentz, 1977) have all been reported in the literature as having been used by deaf people to describe their language.

A number of studies have addressed attitudes of deaf people toward the type of signing that results from contact between natural sign language and spoken language.[3] The interaction between the languages has often been viewed in terms of a continuum (Woodward, 1972; 1973c; Baker and Cokely, 1980; Woodward and Markowicz, 1980; Lawson, 1981). Choice of the appropriate variety from along the continuum is made depending on a number of factors such as topic, purpose and participants. The deaf person takes into account not only the status or role of the participants in the conversation, but also factors such as whether or not they are deaf, and whether or not they use any form of manual communication. This type of signing has been said to be used particularly in Deaf-Hearing interaction. It has been suggested that deaf people not only sign differently with other deaf people than with hearing people, but that they may initiate a conversation in one language and then radically switch when the interlocutor's hearing status is revealed. Indeed, it has been postulated that contact signing serves to prevent significant intrusions of dominant language patterns into a Deaf community, and that it, therefore, functions as a device for maintaining an ethnic boundary between hearing and deaf people (Woodward and Markowicz, 1980; Woodward, 1987, Johnson and Erting, 1989).

More recent studies have challenged these traditional perspectives on language contact in the Deaf community (see Lucas and Valli, 1989; 1991; 1992). Lucas and Valli provide evidence that deaf native ASL signers use contact signing with each other and use ASL in the presence of hearing people. They argue that their choice to do so is motivated by sociolinguistic factors, such as the desire to establish one's social identity as a bone fide member of the Deaf community, the formality of the interview situation, and the participant's lack of familiarity with the interviewer and other informants. They also propose that an individual may be perceived as using ASL because of what is known about his or her background, even if they are not in fact using ASL.[4] Lucas and Valli (1989) conclude that the choice of varieties "other than ASL", and the view that ASL is not appropriate for certain situations, are the direct result of a sociolinguistic situation in which ASL has been suppressed, and in which the focus has traditionally been on the instruction and use of spoken and signed English. They suggest that, as sign language becomes more highly valued and recognized, the outcome of language contact in the Deaf community will change noticeably. Deaf people may become more inclined to use natural sign language more consistently with hearing second language learners.

There are frequent references in the literature to the attitudes of deaf people toward the invention and introduction of new signs, and in particular to those invented and introduced by hearing people. Various efforts have been made by hearing educators to engineer manual codes that would give the fullest possible representation of the structure of spoken language. Rarely have they gained acceptance by members of the Deaf community. Examples include: Seeing Essential English (Anthony, 1971), Signing Exact English (Gustason et al., 1975) and Signed English (Bornstein et al., 1975) in North America, Signed Swedish (Bergman, 1979) in Sweden, and the Paget–Gorman Sign System (Paget and Gorman, 1976) in Britain. Johnson (1990: 313), among others in the USA, has reported the testimony of deaf students that lectures given in simultaneous communication using signs from these manual codes are "difficult and often exhausting to follow", while lectures in ASL are "easy on the eyes and much easier to understand". Baker and Cokely (1980) report that these codes are viewed as intrusions on sign language, and that they are not considered "real Sign". In Britain, Lawson (1981: 33) reports that "most native signers are opposed to the notion of hearing educationalists inventing or creating signs specifically for classroom teaching, or borrowing words from English which are supposed to have no equivalent in the BSL vocabulary". She continues that native signers regard these signs as "odd or even ridiculous". Also in Britain, Sutton-Spence and Woll (1999) report that some deaf people do not consider the manual alphabet a "natural" part of BSL. They state that since the manual alphabet was invented by hearing people, and that fingerspelling is always derived from English, it may be perceived as a threat to BSL because of the power of English.

Signs introduced and used by deaf people themselves do not always meet with widespread approval. Sutton-Spence and Woll (1999) describe how in Britain, when *The Dictionary of British Sign Language/English* (Brien, 1992) was published, some people were offended by a sign it contained glossed as JEW. The linguists provide other examples of old-fashioned signs in BSL, such as DISABLED, CHINESE and GAY that are increasingly perceived as unacceptable, particularly by younger members of the Deaf community. In Ireland, a constitutional referendum on abortion was held in the early 1990s. Some disagreement arose among Deaf television presenters of the daily "News for the Deaf" broadcast as to the most appropriate sign for the word ABOR-TION. One presenter used a sign that appeared to represent the removing and dropping or disposing of the fetus from the stomach area, while the other suggested a stabbing movement. The national press reported the controversy about the two signs. Over time the former sign has become more prevalent among younger deaf people while older deaf people rarely use either sign, as abortion remains a taboo subject for them (Conama, personal communication). Similar examples of signs that are considered offensive can be found in other sign languages. New "politically correct" signs are introduced that are more widely acceptable. In many cases, it has become common practice when naming a country to borrow the sign from the natural sign language of that country. Other signs that are considered distasteful are sometimes replaced by fingerspelling. In the USA, the sign meaning "gay" is often fingerspelled for this reason (Kleinfeld and Warner, 1996).

Attitudes toward language groups

In situations where two language groups exist in close proximity, the negative attitudes of the majority group to the group without power and prestige can be adopted by the minority group to such a degree that members downgrade themselves. Lambert refers to this as "subtractive bilingualism". We mentioned his matched guise technique and his 1960 study above, which found that both English-speaking and French-speaking respondents in Canada rated the speakers of English more favorably. Although it may seem remarkable that the French speakers would evaluate the English speakers more highly, this study clearly illustrates the type of attitudes that exist within and between two language groups, where one is dominant politically, economically and culturally.

Further studies carried out in Canada, and in other countries such as Britain, Israel, Mexico, Paraguay, Peru, Spain, Switzerland and the USA, have revealed similar results. A study by Giles (1970), examining the reactions of British students to a variety of accents, found that in terms of status, aesthetic quality and communicative content, Received Pronunciation was rated most favorably, regional accents were in the middle ranks and urban accents were rated least favorably. Carranza and Ryan (1975) investigated the reactions of Mexican Americans and Anglo-American students to speakers of English and Spanish and discovered that English speakers were rated more favorably on scales of integrity and attractiveness by both groups of students. In Paraguay, Rubin (1968) found that speakers of Guaraní were considered to be "ill-bred", "less intelligent" and "less cultured", particularly by the Spanish-speaking upper-classes.

Traditionally, hearing society – including the professionals who work with deaf people – have viewed deaf people and their language negatively. Deafness has been considered "a medical, educational and linguistic emergency" (Ramsey, 1989: 141). Lane and Philip (1984) state that, compared to speakers of other minority languages, those who use sign language have been particularly oppressed because their language was so alien to speakers of spoken language, and their varying degrees of hearing loss seemed to justify viewing them as deficient. Hearing people have emphasized what is lacking in deaf people, have made "normalization" their top priority, and have labeled them as linguistically deficient, culturally deprived and socially isolated. By use of their own native sign language, deaf people have been regarded as "inferior, undesirable and even sub-human" (Erting, 1978: 140).

Many deaf people have adopted the negative attitudes of hearing society and have downgraded themselves. Instead of relying on sign, they may be anxious to improve their skills in spoken language, believing it necessary for social and economic success. In a collection of essays written by students at Gallaudet University (Valli and Lucas, 1992: 10), Esmé Farb writes: "I knew that there was ASL, but somehow, I felt that I had to sign more the English way to show that I was smart." The degree to which deaf people have adopted these negative attitudes varies considerably from country to country, and even within countries. Deaf people's self-image and the situation of their communities are related to factors such as economic growth and political status. For a more detailed account of the situation in individual countries in Europe and around the world, see reports compiled by the World Federation of the Deaf (1993) and Kyle and Allsop (1997).

It is interesting to compare the attitudes toward deaf people in most Western industrialized societies where the incidence of deafness is low, with societies which have been isolated over time and where much higher incidences have occurred (Groce, 1985; Washabaugh, 1986; Branson et al., 1996). The best-known and best-documented case is that of the island community of Martha's Vineyard, Massachusetts, USA (Groce, 1985). It is thought that some of the original settlers, who came from Kent in England, carried a recessive gene for deafness and the interrelationships of the islanders increased the risk that the trait was expressed in the population. The ratio of deaf to hearing was 1 in 155 for the island as a whole and 1 in 25 for the most isolated town on the island in the mid-nineteenth century. Vineyard residents, both deaf and hearing, compensated for their condition by inventing or borrowing an efficient sign language which was used by almost everybody on the island. Groce reports that although the last hereditary deaf person on the island died in 1952, some of the older residents still remember the days when everybody used sign. Deaf people were full participants in the island community. They were never thought of or referred to as a group or "the Deaf".

Perhaps the best description of the status of deaf individuals on the Vineyard was given to me by an island woman in her eighties, when I asked her about those who were handicapped by deafness when she was a girl. "Oh" she said emphatically, "those people weren't handicapped. They were just deaf". Groce (1985: 5)

There is much less written in the literature about deaf people's perceptions of hearing people than there is about hearing people's perceptions of deaf people. Given the negative experiences imposed on deaf people by well-intentioned parents, teachers and professionals, it is not surprising that deaf people view their distance from hearing behavior as a key criterion of their membership of the Deaf community. The lack of power of deaf people outside the Deaf community can lead to a more determined effort to maintain power within the community. Deaf people live and function in an essentially hearing world: they attend schools managed by hearing educators, they work for hearing employers and they are governed by a hearing government. As a result, they have to accept the hearing way to a large extent, but there tends to be a mistrust and sometimes resentment of hearing society (Kyle and Allsop, 1997).

Language and identity

Up to this point, we have mainly focused on negative attitudes toward minority languages, but it is not always the case that a minority language is viewed negatively by its users. Speakers of a minority language may have reservations about the status of their language; yet it may hold significant social value to them, and they may attribute to it qualities such as intimacy and homeliness. Ambivalent feelings are common among users of minority languages. We mentioned a study above carried out by Carranza and Ryan (1975), who found that English was generally rated more favorably than Spanish on status-related and solidarity dimensions by Mexican-American and Anglo-American students. However, Spanish was seen more favorably on the traits of solidarity than on status. In Catalonia, studies by Woolard have established that speakers of Catalan feel greater solidarity when speaking or hearing their own language. It is considered "polite" to speak Catalan only to those who are identified as native speakers or for whom there are fairly clear signals of this identity, such as physical or accent clues (Woolard, 1985). Speakers of Yiddish in America consistently associate the language with "yiddish-keit", the essence of being Jewish (Peltz, 1991).

Deaf people often ascribe emotional or aesthetic values to sign language. In their study of BSL, for example, Edwards and Ladd (1983) found that while, on the one hand, deaf people recognize the prestige of spoken and signed versions of the majority language and the low status of their own, on the other hand they consider BSL to be more sincere and socially attractive than signed varieties of spoken language. Comments about the "truthfulness", "trustworthiness", and "lack of pompousness" of BSL users have been elicited from deaf subjects who viewed video recordings of the same monologue in BSL and Signed English (Llewellyn-Jones *et al.*, 1979). Adjectives such as "creative", "pleasant", "expressive", "exciting", "flexible", "powerful" (Benson, 1979) and "beautiful", "lovely" and "graceful" (Padden and Humphries, 1988) have all been used in studies to describe ASL. Natural sign language is sometimes even considered to be an art form by its users:

It is implied that good signing is like a beautiful painting or sculpture: there is order in how the parts come together. The result of correct signing is aesthetically pleasing and satisfying. Bad signing, in contrast, is jarring and unpleasant. Padden and Humphries (1988: 62)

In the case of the Deaf community, Kannapell (1989) suggests that these ambivalent or conflicting feelings are a product of deaf people's experience of growing up, and that they are based on misconceptions about the languages. Both at home and at school, natural sign language is generally not used or encouraged. Deaf children rarely have exposure to adult deaf or native sign role models. They are not "taught" their native language, either naturally or formally, unlike their hearing peers.[5] At school, native sign languages have been considered the "last resort" in cases of "oral failure". In some situations deaf children have been punished for using them (McDonnell and Saunders, 1993). It is not surprising, therefore, that many deaf people have negative feelings toward their native sign language and may even refuse to use it, particularly with hearing people. Some believe that it is only appropriate for use with other profoundly deaf individuals (Woodward and Markowicz, 1980; Kannapell, 1982; Padden, 1987). Most deaf people are bilingual to some degree, but few are equally fluent in both the spoken and sign language of their country, and they may vary along a continuum such as that offered by Kannapell (1982) for the American Deaf community. A deaf person's position on the continuum may have some impact on their language attitudes. Typically, there is a tension between the two languages: on the one hand, the spoken majority language is needed for social and economic survival or advancement; on the other hand, deaf people continue to use natural sign language because it plays a most important function in their lives.

All languages and language varieties can serve a bonding or solidarity function; they can act as a symbol of group identity. Knowledge of a language involves a personal sense of unity with, and a set of attitudes toward the community that uses the language. Language and identity are intimately linked (Tabouret-Keller, 1997). Use of natural sign language is the primary identifying criterion for membership of the Deaf community. Kannapell (1993 [1985]: 29) states that "an individual's choice of language and his or her expressed language attitudes serve to indicate, construct and maintain Deaf or hearing social identity during social interaction with others". By choosing to use one language over another, deaf people make a statement about their identity. They indicate whether or not they consider themselves to be a member of the Deaf community. In an earlier publication, the same American deaf researcher writes:

If a deaf person behaves like a hearing person, other deaf people will sign "hearing" on the forehead to show "he thinks like a hearing person". Thus, he is on the fringe of the Deaf community, depending on his/her attitudes. Conversely, if a deaf person behaves like a deaf person, other deaf people may sign "strong deaf" or "fluent ASL", which means that the person is culturally deaf. Thus, he or she is admitted to the core of the Deaf community. Kannapell (1982: 24)

In addition, by choosing to use their natural sign language deaf people exert a certain power over hearing people who cannot understand them.

ASL serves as a way for deaf people to communicate with each other, but there is much more to it than just a function of language. There is a symbolic function in relation to identity and power, and we often keep our use of ASL limited to ourselves to preserve these factors of identity and power. Kannapell (1982: 25)

Perhaps the most significant difference between Deaf communities and other linguistic minorities is the relationship between language and identity. For most linguistic minorities, language is a meaningful but disposable feature of their identity. The decline of the Irish language, for example, has not resulted in a loss of ethnic identity for Irish people. In the case of Deaf communities, however, language is crucial. Use of natural sign language is a defining and non-disposable part of being "ethnically" Deaf. The prognosis for the maintenance of sign languages around the globe may appear poor when we examine the negative attitudes toward them, and when expressed in terms of community resources such as schools, religion and the mass media; yet they have been maintained through the centuries because of the role they play in the definition of Deaf communities. Sign languages will continue to be maintained as long as there are biologically deaf people who need to use them to communicate, and as long as these people come together to form Deaf communities. Indeed, it can be postulated that if language were to play such a critical role in the ethnic identity of any other linguistic minority, then that language would be an unassailable one.

Theories of language attitudes: Answers to the questions

From the wealth of linguistic data now gathered, a number of generalizations or principles can be drawn about language attitudes. The early research tended to look at single relationships, such as the link between age and the use of Welsh, or gender and Received Pronunciation. More contemporary work has investigated the joint influences of two or more linguistic variables. In addition, there has been a move away from describing attitudinal differences to put more emphasis on explaining results. Some researchers have developed theories around their findings in an effort to interpret and account for the complex and multivariate nature of language attitudes. We briefly summarize what we consider to be some of the most significant of these principles and theories here. Nine generalizations are listed that are applicable to both the situation of spoken and sign languages, and many of these are illustrated by the studies mentioned above. For a more in-depth review, specifically referring to spoken language research, see Bradac (1990) or Giles and Coupland (1991). It is important to point out that many more questions remain unanswered.

1. Language use can evoke stereotyped reactions that reflect different social perceptions. Listeners in spoken language conversations employ speech cues to make inferences regarding an individual's personal characteristics, social group membership and psychological states. Sign language users also make such inferences about participants in a conversation based on their signing.
2. Evaluations of speakers typically fall into two or three broad categories:
    (a) competence: includes traits such as intelligence, confidence and ambition;
    (b) personal integrity: traits such as trustworthiness and helpfulness;
    (c) social attractiveness: traits such as friendliness and sense of humor.

    Some researchers have condensed these three categories into two markedly salient ones:
    (a) social status: basically equivalent to competence;
    (b) solidarity: roughly combines integrity and attractiveness (Edwards, 1999).
3. Majority languages and standard varieties are most often associated with high socioeconomic status, power and overt prestige. Users of high status languages/varieties are typically evaluated favorably, particularly on traits relating to competence.
4. Minority languages and non-standard, ethnic, regional and lower class varieties are usually associated with low status and lack overt prestige. Users of low status languages/varieties are generally downgraded – even by the users themselves – particularly on traits relating to competence.
5. Minority languages/varieties and their users are sometimes attributed positive connotations, particularly on traits relating to integrity and attractiveness.

Table 7.1 *Factors that influence judgments*

User characteristics	Language characteristics
Age	Official status
Gender	Government support
Socioeconomic status	Political and economic status
Linguistic background and ability	Social status
Cultural background	Demographics: number and distribution
Educational background	Institutional support: use in community organizations, education, religious services, the mass media, business transactions

In other words, certain languages/varieties may be assigned covert prestige, and may be valued by their users as part of their identity. The link between language and identity helps explain why people continue to use the languages/varieties they profess to despise.

6. All language users regularly make decisions about which form to use. Users of minority languages/varieties are, however, often faced with the most difficult decisions. They must choose between the opportunity to gain social mobility by adopting the linguistic forms of the dominant group, or to maintain their group identity by preserving their own linguistic forms.

7. Numerous factors influence the judgments that we make about languages/ varieties and their users. Some of these factors are listed under the headings "user characteristics" and "language characteristics" in Table 7.1. Individuals' attitudes to a language may be determined by their age, gender, the school they attended, the language they use at home, etc. The status of a language is also influenced by many factors outside of the individual, including the number and distribution of users and political, economic and institutional support.

8. The factors that impact language judgments are not isolated: they may interact. Bouchard Ryan *et al.* (1982) have proposed a two-dimensional model that gives prominence to this interaction. They suggest that there are two critical determinants of language perceptions: standardization and vitality. Standardization refers to a set of norms defining "correct" usage that has been codified and accepted by the linguistic community. Vitality concerns the number and importance of functions served by the language/variety, and includes such socio-cultural factors as status, demography and institutional support. The position of languages plotted on the model is determined by increasing or

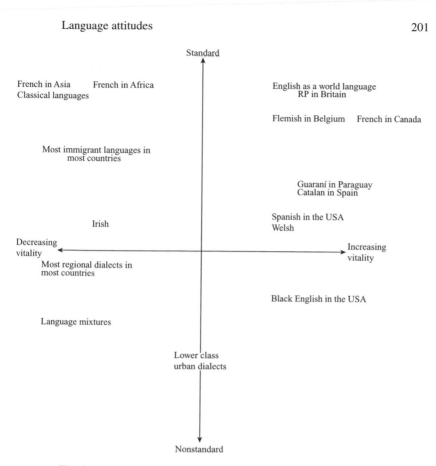

Fig. 7.1 *The two primary sociostructural factors affecting language attitudes: Standardization and vitality*
Source: after Bouchard Ryan *et al.*, 1982.

decreasing standardization and vitality (see Figure 7.1). Bouchard Ryan *et al.* explain that standardization contributes significantly to the vitality of a language/variety, while strong vitality increases its potential for achieving standardization. There are also contexts in which increasing vitality occurs for non-standard varieties, as well as those in which standard varieties lose vitality. In addition, they note that "the standard–non-standard dimension is a relatively static, readily documentable determinant of language attitudes, whereas the extent to which a particular language variety is increasing or decreasing in vitality is much more variable across time and location, as well as more difficult to assess comprehensively" (1982: 5).

9. Users of a language may consciously or unconsciously alter their speech/ signing in an effort to achieve social approval. "Speech accommodation

theory" was initially proposed by Giles (1973) and Giles and Powesland (1975) in an effort to explain this phenomenon. Giles and Powesland describe how a speaker can move toward (convergence) or away from (divergence) the accent or dialect of the other participants in a conversation. Changes may be observed across several areas of language, including syntax, vocabulary, pronunciation and speech rate. Convergence reduces the difference between speakers, thus facilitating interaction and obtaining the listener's social approval. Linguistic accommodation carries risks as well as possible benefits – such as the loss of personal or group identity, or the perceived loss of integrity – so much so that a listener may react against the speaker's new style. Accommodation behavior will, therefore, only be initiated if potential rewards are available. Divergence may take place when speakers want to emphasize their personal or group identity, show their dislike of a listener's appearance or behavior or disassociate themselves from a particular group.

Consequences and applications

Second language

Numerous studies have addressed the broad range of consequences and applications of language attitudes. For instance, language attitudes may predict the degree of competence likely to be achieved in a second language. Studies have repeatedly found that positive attitudes toward the language and the culture of its users are likely to facilitate second language acquisition. Much of the early work in this area was carried out by Gardner and Lambert who were interested in the language attitudes of Anglophone and Francophone Canadians toward French and English (Gardner and Lambert, 1972; Gardner, 1985). Gardner developed a comprehensive model of second language acquisition in school settings, and his work continues to influence contemporary thinking. More recently, researchers such as McGroarty (1996) have argued that the relationships between the learner's prior linguistic and academic experience, the social context of instruction and the results of formal language instruction are complex, and that positive attitudes about language and language learning may be as much the result of success as the cause.

Attitudes toward sign language similarly impact a learner's ability to acquire it as a second language. Jacobs (1996) emphasizes the point that natural sign languages such as ASL are real languages that take time and effort to acquire. Yet, natural sign languages are frequently perceived as being "easier" to learn than spoken languages. She argues that as a result, in the USA, the structure and length of ASL programs, the entrance requirements for ASL–English interpreting programs, the standards for teacher qualification and the information presented to those aspiring to a career in interpretation are inadequate. The availability of materials and resources to support the teaching and learning of a language also has an effect on its perceived status. A language that is well represented and presented has a better chance of being well received. To date, the availability of such resources to teachers and learners of sign languages has been limited, although a number have now been published or are currently under development.

Employers' hiring practices

Another consequence of language attitudes is that they may impact employers' hiring practices. Research in Britain, Canada and the USA indicates that people with low-status accents are regarded negatively for employment in high-status jobs, but positively for employment in low-status jobs (Bradac, 1990; Giles and Coupland, 1991). For example, in the USA de la Zerda and Hopper (1979) found that potential employers were more likely to assign speakers exhibiting a Mexican-American accent to low-status positions than to positions of high status, and the opposite was true for speakers exhibiting a standard American accent. Kalin and Rayko (1980) found that speakers exhibiting a variety of foreign accents were perceived to be well suited for relatively low-status positions, whereas speakers exhibiting an English Canadian accent were viewed as better suited for high-status positions, by Canadian university students. Giles *et al.* (1981) obtained a similar result for Welsh vs. Received Pronunciation accents. In a more recent study of racial and ethnic minorities in the workplace in Britain, Roberts *et al.* (1992) provide numerous examples of discrimination focused on language.

Studies in a number of countries have indicated that, in general, deaf people are in a subordinated position compared to their hearing colleagues at work (Foster, 1986; Schein, 1987; Jones and Pullen, 1990; Matthews, 1996; Kyle and Allsop, 1997). They are likely to be underemployed, have factory jobs, be more poorly paid, have considerably less chance of promotion and be supervised by hearing people. Rarely do hearing supervisors have any knowledge of sign language, and communication often breaks down. Interpreters who could provide access to the spoken language are often not made available to deaf employees, although there is significant discrepancy on this point in different countries. Deaf people have even, traditionally, been underemployed by the organizations claiming to represent them (Taylor and Mason, 1991). Consequently, deaf people often have a much lower position in society and, without the financial base and the associated social standing, their views and their language are frequently lacking in recognition.

Mass media

The mass media play a major role in the communication and transmission of social values, and the propagation and defense of national culture

(Lippi-Green, 1997). It is easy to find examples of evaluative judgments of languages and language varieties on radio and television and in newspapers and magazines. Within the print and broadcast media, one group which has particularly drawn on and benefited from stereotypical ideas about people on the basis of their language is advertisers. Advertisers have used, for example, rural accents to indicate the wholesome nature of food products, or more prestigious accents to promote financial services (Thomas, 1999).

Sign languages are visual languages and can, therefore, gain exposure only through the visual media. Radio is completely inaccessible to deaf people, and access to the print media is limited by their knowledge of the language in which it is written. Deaf people are aware that, by having sign language channeled through the very powerful medium of television and film, the status of the language may be considerably advanced. Movements such as the Deaf Broadcasting Campaign established in Britain in the early 1980s (see Woolley, 1981) have been launched in a number of countries with the aim of pressing for improvement in broadcasting provisions for deaf people. Most have met with at least limited success (see, for example, Jensen, 1995; Stachlewitz and Rundfunk, 1995), although a report on the status of sign languages worldwide found that use of sign language in the general media remains at a disappointing level. The availability of film and videotape preserving literary forms developed within sign languages themselves is also very limited (World Federation of the Deaf, 1993). Schuchman (1988) carried out a survey of film and television in the USA; he reports that the Hollywood stereotype of a deaf person is invariably someone who speaks clearly and reads lips accurately. Films portraying deaf people often end with a cure through an experimental drug or operation.

Education

It is in the area of education, however, that in our opinion language attitudes have the greatest influence. They are often the basis for selecting a communication mode, for choosing teaching materials, and may be an indirect way of evaluating students (Ward Trotter, 1989). As Adegbija (1994: 96) states:

Education language planning in any nation impinges simultaneously on the economy, the political structure, the pedagogical framework, the level of technological development, the socio-historical and cultural heritage and the socio-linguistic scenario. Stances in each of these areas can tilt attitudes towards language use in education in one direction rather than another.

It is this issue which has been addressed not only by studies of spoken languages, but most extensively by the studies of attitudes toward sign languages. The attitudes of two main groups of people have been investigated: teachers and students. Teachers fulfill a highly significant "gate-keeping function" through the judgments, both formal and informal, that they make about young people, while students are at "a particularly salient period of social sensitisation", as they establish social identities and positions that will influence their employment and relational decisions in the future (Garrett *et al.*, 1999: 324–325).

Studies have posed a number of questions, including:

1. How do teachers evaluate the language/variety used by their students? For spoken language, see, for example, Williams, 1973; 1974; H. Edwards, 1978; 1983; for sign language, see Ward Trotter, 1989; La Bue, 1995.
2. How do students evaluate their own minority language or variety, and the dominant majority language/variety used by their teachers? For spoken language, see, for example, Rosenthal, 1974; Giles and Powesland, 1975; for sign language see, for example, Bergman, 1976; Lentz, 1977; Berke, 1978; Curry and Curry, 1978; Meath-Lang, 1978; Meath-Lang *et al.*, 1984; Kannapell, 1989; Fenn, 1992; McDonnell, 1992; Valli and Lucas, 1992.
3. Can stereotypical attitudes influence teachers' interaction with, and evaluation of their students? For spoken language, see, for example, Seligman *et al.*, 1972; Frender and Lambert, 1973.
4. Can stereotypical attitudes affect students' perceptions of their teachers? For spoken language, see, for example, Rubin and Smith, 1990; Rubin, 1992.
5. What is the most appropriate language or variety for use in the classroom? For spoken language see, for example, Cummins and Swain, 1986; Baker, 1993; for sign languages, see Johnson *et al.*, 1989; Mahshie, 1995.

The studies referred to above, and numerous others, have repeatedly found that the answer to the first four questions is "yes". Teachers, like other members of the population, do maintain stereotyped and often negative views of certain languages/varieties and their users. These stereotypes can and do impact teachers' evaluation of their students. Researchers such as Ward Trotter (1989) and La Bue (1995) have examined attitudes of teachers of the Deaf toward sign and spoken language. Reviewing the literature, Ward Trotter states that these attitudes vary widely but that, whatever the stand, "attitudes seem to be deeply ingrained and are vehemently defended" (1989: 217). Most prospective teachers of the Deaf enter teacher-training programs with little to no knowledge of Deaf culture, deaf people or sign language. Based on her own direct experience in such a training program, Ward Trotter (1989: 218) reports that students were instructed that:

(1) the biggest obstacle of deaf people was their lack of language (in contrast to lack of skills in the English language); (2) all deaf children enter school with no language (similar to the prevalent view in the 1960s that black children enter school with no language; see Labov, 1972: 201); (3) those deaf persons who use sign language still operate at a deficit, because sign language, with its limited vocabulary, is incapable of

discussing abstract ideas; and (4) it is the rare and brilliant deaf person who is capable of abstract thought.

Ward Trotter used a modified version of the matched guise technique to examine the covert and overt language attitudes of her subjects. She found that in general Signed English was rated higher than ASL, although it should be noted that responses to both were in the neutral range. Signed English was rated "as having greater precision, more complete sentences, more consistently correct sign usage, grammar that is better, signs that are more functional, and a more complete message than ASL" (1989: 225). La Bue used a very different method from that employed by Ward Trotter, and carried out an ethnographic microanalysis focusing on the language practices of one hearing teacher in a middle school for deaf children. She discovered that, although this teacher was highly motivated and conscientious, her efforts at teaching reading and literature were continually undermined as she attempted to speak and sign simultaneously.

It is apparent that, compared to other individuals, teachers' perceptions are rather special. Teachers are in a position to directly impede a student's early success if they hold and act upon overly generalized views. It also follows that teachers are well placed to help students overcome the negative evaluations held by others. Both Ward Trotter and La Bue discuss the implications of their findings for the education of deaf students and teacher training. Both are in agreement that radical changes in the language practices of schools for deaf children are warranted and must include a shift in people's beliefs and attitudes about deaf people.

Studies of deaf school and college students' attitudes have typically identified a strong association between poor spoken language skills and inferior intelligence, between natural sign language and negative attributes of users, and between manual codes for spoken language and positive attributes of users (see Lentz, 1977; Berke, 1978; Curry and Curry, 1978; Meath-Lang et al., 1984; Kannapell, 1989; McDonnell, 1992). Kannapell (1989), for example, found that students at Gallaudet University associated the use of particular sign systems with the status of those who use them; i.e. ASL users are less-educated deaf people, PSE (contact sign) users are college educated, while MCE users are highly educated deaf people. McDonnell (1992) examined the attitudes of students at a residential school for deaf children in Ireland. He found that they placed great importance on the acquisition of oral language skills and almost two-thirds of them preferred placement in classes where oral communication was the only method used. More than half of all students believed that signing can have a negative impact on speech, although there was a considerable difference between the views of profoundly deaf and hard of hearing students. Significantly, despite the students' views, signing as a method of communication was prevalent among them.

The results of these studies highlight the ambivalence deaf people feel toward their language, as we discussed earlier. It has been demonstrated that even very young children are aware of language differences and that these differences have social consequences; yet, they continue to use their stigmatized variety because of its covert prestige (Giles and Coupland, 1991; Wardhaugh, 1998). Indeed, they may be well aware of what it means to change: "almost certain alienation from their peers without necessarily acceptance by social superiors" (Wardhaugh, 1998: 342). In a particularly interesting study, Sutcliffe (1975) investigated the relationship of group cohesiveness and communication preferences among deaf student leaders at Gallaudet University. Group cohesiveness was measured by the students' choice of eating area in the cafeteria at the university. He found that the student leaders (Student Body Government officers) tended to eat together in a specific area of the cafeteria, and shared the characteristics of being born deaf, learning sign language before the age of six, having deaf parents and/or siblings and having attended residential schools. Student assembly members' eating areas were scattered around the room. They preferred English-like signing, fewer than 75 percent had lost their hearing before age three, more than half had hearing parents and two-thirds had gone to residential schools. The study demonstrates how language influenced the social interaction of the students.

The last question, regarding the most appropriate language or variety for use in the classroom is perhaps the most salient of all. During the 1960s and 1970s, some research on language and education led to what became known as "verbal deprivation theory". Bernstein (1970), a British sociologist, whose research was prominent in the area, proposed that two kinds of English "code" could be distinguished: "elaborated code" and "restricted code". Elaborated code makes use of complex and grammatically accurate sentences, where meaning does not depend on the accompanying context. Restricted code employs short, grammatically simple sentences, and relies a great deal on accompanying context for its meaning. Bernstein held that everyone uses restricted code but, in order to achieve success at school, children must also acquire the elaborated code. In other words, those who have limited access to elaborated code (specifically lower working-class people and their children) are likely to experience failure at school where elaborated code is the medium of instruction. Linguists have criticized Bernstein's work and argued the fallacies of his theory. Perhaps best known is the work of William Labov (1969b; 1972a) on Black English (African American Vernacular English or AAVE) in the USA.

AAVE was widely perceived as a "deficient", and "illogical" form of Standard English. Many educators deduced that the consequence of this linguistic deficiency was cognitive deficiency, which led to proposals to teach African-American children the standard variety. Labov and other linguists argued that AAVE is systematic and rule governed like all natural speech (and sign) varieties. Their work, alongside the discontent felt among members of the

African-American community, led to efforts to change educational policy and legislation. In 1977, African-American parents in Ann Arbor, Michigan filed a suit against the school board for failure to take into account the linguistic background of their children. The parents had realized that their children's performance in reading and writing, both of which were assessed in Standard English, was significantly below that of their peers. They won their case, and the school board was directed to provide a program, which would give the children a better chance of educational success. One element of this program required by the judge was the provision of in-service workshops about language variation and AAVE for the teachers in the school district. Such training was aimed at raising the teachers' awareness of the minority variety and changing their attitudes toward it. In 1996, the Oakland Board of Education in California passed a resolution to officially recognize the use of AAVE in the classroom. The resolution did not, however, meet with widespread support and was eventually dropped. It now seems reasonable to believe that what Bernstein was describing was a language use style that is a natural outgrowth of dense-network social organization, and not a cognitive or linguistic deficit at all (Fasold, 1990). Nevertheless, today many minority languages and varieties, including AAVE, are still not considered suitable as a medium of education.

There are many parallels between the situation of AAVE and that of natural sign languages.[6] For over two centuries, the debate has raged, focusing on whether children who are deaf should be educated using natural sign language, speech and speech–reading, or a combination of speech and manual codes for expressing spoken language. Just as the use of AAVE has been stigmatized, natural sign languages have traditionally been treated as "restricted codes" by hearing educationalists and have not been considered appropriate as a medium of education. The education system has been designed to prepare the "special" deaf student for assimilation into the dominant hearing society, adopting its norms, values and traditions. The oral method emphasized immersion in a sound-based environment, arguing that any stimulation in a natural sign language can be detrimental to the development of listening skills. While there is no reason to believe that the intellectual abilities of deaf children are less than or different from their hearing peers (Moores, 1978; Kretschmer and Kretschmer, 1978; Gustason, 1983), many studies show that the overall level of achievement of deaf children is limited in oral communication, with low levels of attainment in reading and writing (Conrad, 1977; Quigley and Kretschmer, 1982; Allen, 1986; Bochner and Albertini, 1988). These disturbing findings have led proponents of a bilingual-bicultural approach to the education of deaf children to advocate that natural sign language be taught and accepted in the classroom. These issues are discussed in more detail in Chapter 6.

Changes in language attitudes

Language attitudes change over time: they are rarely static. Languages and language groups that were once stigmatized can become accepted and respected. Such a change in attitude can be influenced by the official recognition of a language by government, a nation's independence, increased autonomy, civil rights movements or institutions, such as parents, peers, community groups, school and the mass media. Historical, sociolinguistic, political and geolinguistic factors all may need to be considered. For a discussion of the key social psychological theories of attitude change, see Baker (1992).

Earlier, we referred to a study by Rubin carried out in Paraguay in the late 1960s, which found that attitudes to Guaraní were largely negative. By 1980, a study by Rhodes reported that attitudes toward the language had changed considerably. Guaraní had been officially recognized as a national language. The majority of Rhodes' informants thought it should be used as a language of instruction, that it should be preserved, and that ability to speak it is necessary in order to be considered a true Paraguayan. We also referred to the work of Lambert and his colleagues in Canada. The researchers' early work found that French speakers would evaluate English speakers more highly. From the 1970s, however, ratings of French Canadians in Quebec were higher, reflecting an increased political awareness after the Quiet Revolution and the increased self-esteem that came with it (Giles *et al.*, 1977; Veltman, 1996). Changes in attitude to Catalan are another example. Woolard and Gahng used the matched guise technique to collect data in 1980 and then again in 1987. During that time period, widespread changes affected institutional support for Catalan. The Linguistic Normalization Act was passed in 1983 giving Catalan co-official status with Castilian in government, legal affairs and education. As a result, the language was increasingly used in the press and publishing and on television and radio. These changes were reflected in Woolard and Gahng's results (Woolard and Gahng, 1990). At the time of their initial data collection, they found that Castilian judges gave high ratings to members of their own linguistic group speaking Castilian, but downgraded them significantly for speaking Catalan. By the late 1980s, Castilian judges no longer downgraded their in-group for speaking Catalan, and Catalan listeners were more favorably disposed to Castilians who accommodated them.

Attitudes toward sign languages have also been changing and becoming more positive. Fenn's (1992) study, which examined the attitudes of deaf students at Gallaudet University, is particularly optimistic. He found that ASL users were rated higher than users of either Signed English or contact signing on a bi-polar adjective list by most of his subjects. It is likely that a number of factors are responsible for the emergence of these more positive attitudes.

Within hours there seemed to emerge a new, calm, clear consciousness and resolution; a political body, two thousand strong, with a single will of its own. It was the astonishing swiftness with which this organisation emerged, the sudden precipitation from chaos, of a unanimous, communal mind, that astonished everyone who saw it. Sacks (1989: 135)

These are the words of Oliver Sacks as he describes the events that took place at Gallaudet University over a period of one week in March 1988. Gallaudet – the only university for deaf people in the world – is considered by many to be the "Mecca" of the Deaf community. However, in all its 124 years it had never had a deaf president. Following the resignation of Jerry C. Lee earlier that year, a hearing person who was both unable to sign and who was unfamiliar with the Deaf world, was selected as the new president over two deaf finalists. The university erupted into a week of protests which culminated with the resignation of the newly appointed president and the chairman of the Board of Trustees, the reconstitution of the board to contain a majority of deaf people, the selection of a deaf president (Dr. I. King Jordan), and the promise of no reprisals against the protesters (Gannon, 1989).

The issues around what happened at Gallaudet University are of fundamental importance not only in the USA, but also to Deaf communities worldwide. Taylor and Mason (1991) refer to the events as potentially the single most significant positive episode in deafness any of us alive today have ever witnessed. It offered encouragement to other Deaf communities because of its success. Organizations such as "Deaf Pride" and "Deaf Awareness" in the USA, the "National Union of the Deaf" in Britain, the "Irish Deaf Society" in Ireland and "Deux Langues Pour Une Education" in France were founded to encourage an appreciation of Deaf identity, and along with the various national organizations, intensified their lobbying for legislation to improve the status of natural sign languages, and to ensure deaf people's rights.

In North America and in Europe this lobbying has met with some success. In 1983, Sweden became the first country in the world to implement legislation legally recognizing their native sign language. A small number of other countries have since followed their lead. The Americans with Disabilities Act, 1990, created a precedent in terms of equal opportunities and equal rights. Although it does not directly refer to ASL, it does state that a person may not be discriminated against solely on the basis of their disability. In 1988, members of the European Parliament voted unanimously to pass a resolution on the official recognition of the sign languages of the member states. The resolution called on each state to abolish any remaining obstacles to the use of sign.

To date, no specific laws have been passed as a result of the European Parliament's resolution, and it was not until almost 10 years later, at the request of the European Union of the Deaf (EUD), that the Parliament funded a study to examine outcomes. This study (referred to above) found that within the 15 member countries of the European Union, and in Norway and Iceland, attitudes toward sign languages were generally more favorable than before. The research team noted that deaf people tend to be more optimistic about the extent of use of sign language in countries where the level of general awareness and provision is less than in countries where there is more. However, the overriding sentiment emerging from this report is that change has been limited and slow to come about, and that the views of deaf people continue to be different from those of hearing people (Kyle and Allsop, 1997).

Another extremely powerful force in bringing about change in people's attitudes to sign languages has been linguistic research.

We had read that sign language is "a collection of vague and loosely defined pictorial gestures"; that it is pantomime; that it is "much too much a depicting language, keeping the thinking slow"; that it is "much too concrete, too broken in pieces"; that "sign language deals mainly with material objects, dreads and avoids the abstract"; that "sign language has disadvantages, especially those of grammatical disorder, illogical systems, and linguistic confusion"; that sign language "has no grammar"; that it is a "universal" communication; that it is "derived from English, a pidgin form of English on the hands with no structure of its own". Klima and Bellugi (1979: 3)

Beginning with the work of Tervoort in Europe in the 1950s and Stokoe in the USA in the early 1960s, researchers from around the globe have gathered a significant body of data disputing these perceptions. Initially this research was treated with suspicion. Even at Gallaudet University, recognition that ASL was truly a language was slow to come about. Stokoe (1990: 2–3) recalls:

In 1960, when *Sign Language Structure* and *The Calculus of Structure* were published, the whole Gallaudet faculty in a special meeting denounced my sign language research. They charged me, in effect, with misappropriating funds; I was paid to teach English, they said, not to do research on sign language. They argued that paying attention to sign language could only interfere with the students' proper education.

Gradually, the collective power of this body of research brought about attitude change, not only in hearing society but also within the Deaf community itself.

By simply declaring that British Sign Language was a language, people's conceptions changed. Deaf people officially had something positive and attractive which made them equal to hearing people; deafness was not just viewed as being about the *loss* of something. Ladd (1988: 41)

The impact of linguistic research can be felt in a broad range of areas. Greater prominence has been given to grass-roots natural sign language users, especially deaf off-spring of deaf parents, rather than the previous models, who were people with good oral or spoken language (Ladd, 1988). Books and journals have been published. Dictionaries in print and compact disc format have been compiled. Conferences and lectures on sign language and other deafness related issues are frequently organized. Researchers in countries such as Sweden, Denmark and the USA have inspired and shared their expertise with their contemporaries in other countries where the study of sign language is in its infancy. The Deaf community in Ireland, for example, has benefited enormously from links with the Centre for Deaf Studies at Bristol, UK. Irish students have traveled to Bristol, and experts from there have made exchange visits to Ireland. Hearing people are now attending sign language classes in large numbers. Interpreter training courses have been established at colleges and universities. Programs for deaf people presented in sign language are broadcast on national television. Deaf characters using sign language have been portrayed on television and film. Advertisers have even used sign language to promote their goods. Anecdotal, as well as published evidence suggests, however, that natural sign languages continue to be very much in a position of inferiority compared to spoken languages. "In reality we have only won one battle. The war is not over – it has not yet begun!" (Bahan, 1989: 89).

Conclusions

Having explored the nature of language attitudes and how they have been studied, it is clear that there is a great need for further empirical research into attitudes toward sign languages and their users, and the consequences of these attitudes. Innovative methods of collecting and analyzing data that address the factors that have colored results in the past need to be developed. Language attitudes are never dormant: changes in language attitudes reflect changes in society and changes in attitudes toward language users. At the start of the twenty-first century, society is changing at a pace which is perhaps more rapid than at any other time in history. It remains to be seen what impact these changes and technological advancements, particularly with regard to the internet and the creation of a "global village", will have on attitudes toward sign languages and their users around the world.

Suggested readings

The reader is referred to Kannapell (1989), Ward Trotter (1989), Fenn (1992) and La Bue (1995) for examples of attitude studies, all investigating ASL. For a more international flavor, see Kyle and Allsop's (1997) survey of the status of sign languages in the European Union and Matthew's (1996) study of the Irish Deaf community. With regard to spoken language research, Fasold (1984), Romaine (1989), Bradac (1990), Giles and Coupland (1991) and Baker (1992) all provide very useful reviews of the classic studies and critiques of the various methodologies.

Exercises

1. Explore the role that your native language has in your life. Questions you might like to ask yourself could include: What does your language mean to you? Are you proud of it? Do you consider it to be an important part of your identity? Do you think there are better languages than yours? Write a short essay summarizing your thoughts.
2. "I knew that there was ASL, but somehow, I felt that I had to sign more the English way to show that I was smart." Discuss this quote from Esmé Farb in a collection of essays written by students at Gallaudet University. Explain why ambivalence is the key feature of the language attitudes of deaf people toward their own native sign languages.
3. Carry out a small number of interviews with people of a range of different ages. Ask your informants about their views on any minority language/variety that you choose. Decide what types of questions you want to ask. Do the informants' comments reflect attitudes toward the language group as well as toward the language/variety or not? Do any of the comments suggest a difference between covert and overt language attitudes? Once you have completed the interviews, pick out some important points of information that you have learnt from carrying them out. What were your problems? How could you solve them?
4. Write an essay on the roles of deaf and hearing sign language researchers focusing on the collection and interpretation of language attitude data. What are their common and different priorities, interests and presentation styles? What advice might you offer to a Deaf-Hearing team that is about to embark on a research project?
5. Refer to Bouchard Ryan et al.'s (1982: 40) two-dimensional model. Where would you plot the position of the indigenous sign language of your country on this model? Explain the factors you considered in making this judgment and evaluate how these factors interact with one another.
6. Refer to the "Friends First" advertisement below in Figure 7.2. Discuss how it uses sign language to publicize the company's change of name. Note the use of the terms: "perception", "communication", "identity" and "sign" in the text. How does the use of sign language in advertising reflect changing attitudes toward sign languages? Look for other references to deaf people in the print and broadcast media. What does your research tell you about current attitudes in your country?
7. How have attitudes toward sign language and deaf people changed during your lifetime? Present evidence of this change. At the start of the

Fig. 7.2   *What's in a name?: "Friends First" advertisement*

twenty-first century, hypothesize on likely further changes and developments, both positive and negative.

NOTES

1 Received Pronunciation (RP) is the accent associated with the best-educated and most prestigious members of English society. Also referred to as "the Queen's English", "Oxford English" and "BBC English", it is used by less than five percent of the British population. RP is essentially a social rather than a regional accent; the small number of speakers who use it do not identify themselves as coming from any particular geographical region. See Trudgill (1983) for further discussion.

2 According to a report by Dakic (1999), the following countries have constitutional references to sign language: Colombia, Czech Republic, Finland, Portugal, Slovak Republic, South Africa and Uganda. Countries which have legal references to sign language, apart from their constitution, include: Australia, Belarus, Canada, Denmark, France, Lithuania, Norway, Sweden, Switzerland, Ukraine, Uruguay and some states of the USA. Since Dakic's report was compiled, Thai Sign Language was officially recognized as the national language of the deaf people of Thailand in August 1999 and, in Ireland, ISL was mentioned in the Education Act of 1998. It is important to note that constitutional recognition does not guarantee full rights for deaf people, and service provision varies widely. Indeed, some countries, such as Sweden and Norway, which have not yet recognized sign language in their constitutions, enjoy a much more developed service than countries where sign language is officially recognized.

3 The type of signing that results from contact between natural sign language and spoken language has frequently been labeled Pidgin Sign Language (or Pidgin Sign English where the spoken language is English). Lucas and Valli (1989; 1991; 1992) have argued that it does not meet all the criteria of a pidgin and that it is more appropriately labeled contact signing.

4 There is a widespread perception in the Deaf community that individuals who have deaf parents or who were educated at a residential school are more competent users of natural sign language.

5 Deaf children, who are educated under an oral philosophy and are not officially "taught" sign language, typically create their own rudimentary sign system. Less than 10 percent of deaf children have deaf parents. At school, deaf children of hearing parents meet deaf children of deaf parents, and so schools, and particularly residential schools for deaf children, provide the institutional bases for the acquisition of sign language and Deaf culture. Deaf children encouraged to learn the majority spoken language differ significantly from the children of spoken language minority groups in that they do not have the same level of access to the majority language, and are therefore not as influenced to aspire to acquiring it.

6 It should be noted that there are also important differences between the situation of AAVE and natural sign languages. Natural sign languages are not dialects/varieties of a language; instead, they are full, autonomous languages with their own structure and grammatical rules. In addition, while AAVE is learned by African-American children from their parents in the home, natural sign languages are generally not passed down from parent to child but are passed from child to child at school.

Bibliography

Aarons, D. and P. Akach (1998) South African Sign Language: One language or many? *Stellenbosch Papers in Linguistics* 31. Stellenbosch, South Africa.

Aarons, D. and R. Morgan (1998) The linguistic structure of South African Sign Language after apartheid. Paper presented at the 6th International Conference on Theoretical Issues in Sign Language Research, Washington, DC.

Adegbija, E. (1994) *Language Attitudes in Sub-Saharan Africa.* Clevedon: Multilingual Matters.

Afolayan, A. (1988) Bilingualism and bilingual education in Nigeria. In C. Paulston (ed.), *International Handbook of Bilingualism and Bilingual Education.* New York: Greenwood Press, 345–358.

Agheyisi, R. and J. Fishman (1970) Language attitude studies: A brief survey of methodological approaches. *Anthropological Linguistics* 12, 137–157.

Ahlgren, I. (1990a) Deictic pronouns in Swedish and Swedish Sign Language. In S. Fisher and P. Siple (eds.), *Theoretical Issues in Sign Language Research 1: Linguistics.* Chicago, IL: University of Chicago Press, 167–174.

Ahlgren, I. (1990b) Swedish conditions: Sign language in Deaf education. In S. Prillwitz and T. Vollhaber (eds.), *Sign Language Research and Application: Proceedings of the International Congress on Sign Language Research and Application.* Hamburg: Signum, 91–94.

Akinnaso, F. (1989) One nation, four hundred languages: Unity and diversity in Nigeria's language policy. *Language Problems and Language Planning* 13, 133–146.

Akinnaso, F. and I. Ogunbiyi (1990) The place of Arabic in language education and language planning in Nigeria. *Language Problems and Language Planning* 14, 1–19.

Alexander, N. (1989) *Language Policy and National Unity in South Africa/Azania.* Cape Town: Buchu Books.

Allen, T.E. (1986) Patterns of academic achievements among hearing impaired students: 1974–1983. In A.N. Schildroth and M.A. Karchmer (eds.), *Deaf Children in America.* San Diego, CA: College Hill, 161–206.

Allport, G.W. (1935) Attitudes. In C. Murchison (ed.), *A Handbook of Social Psychology.* Worcester, MA: Clarke University Press.

Almond, B. (1993) Rights. In P. Singer (ed.), *A Companion to Ethics.* Oxford: Basil Blackwell, 259–269.

Altbach, P. (1984) The distribution of knowledge in the third world: A case study in neocolonialism. In P. Altbach and G. Kelly (eds.), *Education and the Colonial Experience,* 2nd revised edn. New Brunswick, NJ: Transaction, 229–251.

Anderson, L. (1979) A comparison of some American, British, Australian and Swedish Signs: Evidence on historical changes in signs and some family relationships of sign languages. Paper presented at First International Symposium on Sign Language, Stockholm, June.

Ann, J. (1998a) Contact between a sign language and a written language: Character Signs in Taiwan Sign Language. In C. Lucas (ed.), *Pinky Extension and Eye Gaze: Language Use in Deaf Communities*. Washington, DC: Gallaudet University Press, 59–99.

Ann, J. (1998b) Dialectal variation in Taiwan Sign Language: evidence from morphology, syntax and the lexicon. Paper presented at the 6th International Conference on Theoretical Issues in Sign Language Research, Washington, DC, November.

Ann, J. and L. Peng (2000) Optimality Theory and opposed handshapes in Taiwan Sign Language. *University of Rochester Working Papers in the Language Sciences* 1(2), 1–22.

Annamalai, E. (1986) Language rights and language planning. *New Language Planning Newsletter* 1, 1–3.

Anthony, D. (1971) *Seeing Essential English*. Anaheim, CA: Educational Services Division.

Antilla, A. (1997) Deriving variation from grammar. In F. Hinskens, R. van Hout and W. Leo Wetzels (eds.), *Variation, Change, and Phonological Theory*. Amsterdam: Benjamins, 35–68.

Aramburo, A. (1989) Sociolinguistic aspects of the Black Deaf community. In C. Lucas (ed.), *The Sociolinguistics of the Deaf Community*. New York: Academic Press, 103–122.

Asante, M. (1990) African elements in American English. In J. Holloway (ed.), *Africanism in American Culture*. Bloomington, IN: Indiana University Press, 19–23.

Austin, J. (1962) *How to Do Things with Words*. Oxford: Clarendon Press.

Baer, A.M. (1991) Tactility in the Deaf community. Paper presented at the Gallaudet University Department of Sign Communication Lecture Series. Washington, DC.

Bahan, B. (1989) The war is not over. Reprinted in S. Wilcox (ed.), *American Deaf Culture: An Anthology*. Burtonsville, MD: Linstok Press, 189–192.

Bahan, B. and S. Supalla (1995) Line segmentation and narrative structure: A study of eyegaze behavior and narrative structure in American Sign Language. In K. Emmorey and J. Reilly (eds.), *Language, Gesture, and Space*. Hillsdale, NJ: Lawrence Erlbaum, 171–191.

Bailey, G., T. Wikle, J. Tillery and L. Sand (1991) The apparent time construct. *Language Variation and Change* 3, 241–264.

Bailey, G., T. Wikle, J. Tillery and L. Sand (1993) Some patterns of linguistic diffusion. *Language Variation and Change* 5, 359–390.

Baker, C. (1977) Regulators and turntaking in American Sign Language. In L. Friedman (ed.), *On the Other Hand: New Perspectives on American Sign Language*. New York: Academic Press, 215–236.

Baker, C. (1992) *Attitudes and Language*. Clevedon: Multilingual Matters.

Baker, C. (1993) *Foundations of Bilingual Education and Bilingualism*. Clevedon: Multilingual Matters.

Baker, C. and D. Cokely (1980) *American Sign Language*. Silver Spring, MD: T.J. Publishers.

Baker, C. and C. Padden (1978) Focusing on the nonmanual components of American Sign Language. In P. Siple (ed.), *Understanding Language Through Sign Language Research*. New York: Academic Press, 59–90.

Ball, R. (1997) *The French-Speaking World: A Practical Introduction to Sociolinguistic Issues*. London: Routledge.

Banham, D. (1991) *Monasteriales Indicia: The Anglo-Saxon Monastic Sign Language*. London: Anglo-Saxon Books.

Barakat, R. (1987) Cistercian Sign Language. In J. Umiker-Sebeok and T. Sebeok (eds.), *Monastic Sign Languages*. Berlin: Mouton de Gruyter.

Baron, D. (1981) *Going native: The Regeneration of Saxon English*. American Dialect Society 69. University, AL: University of Alabama Press.

Baron, D. (1990) *The English-Only Question: An Official Language for Americans?* New Haven: Yale University Press.

Bateson, G. (1972) *Steps to an Ecology of Mind*. New York: Ballantine.

Battison, R. (1978) *Lexical Borrowing in American Sign Language*. Silver Spring, MD: Linstok Press.

Battison, R.M., H. Markowicz, and J.C. Woodward (1975) A good rule of thumb: Variable phonology in American Sign Language. In R.W. Fasold and R. Shuy (eds.), *Analyzing Variation in Language*. Washington, DC: Georgetown University Press.

Baugh, J. (1983) *Black Street Speech: Its History, Structure, and Survival*. Austin, TX: University of Texas Press.

Bayley, R. (1994a) Consonant cluster reduction in Tejano English. *Language Variation and Change* 6, 303–326.

Bayley, R. (1994b) Interlanguage variation and the quantitative paradigm: Past-tense marking in Chinese-English. In E. Tarone, S. Glass and A. Cohen (eds.), *Research Methodology in Second-Language Acquisition*. Hillsdale, NJ: Lawrence Erlbaum, 157–181.

Bayley, R. (1997) VARBRUL Analysis of Linguistic Variation. Workshop presented at the American Dialect Society Meeting, Chicago, January.

Bayley, R. and D.R. Preston (eds.) (1996) *Second Language Acquisition and Linguistic Variation*. Amsterdam and Philadelphia, PA: John Benjamins.

Bayley, R., C. Lucas and M. Rose (2000) Variation in American Sign Language: The case of DEAF. *Journal of Sociolinguistics* 4, 81–107.

Baynton, D. (1996) *Forbidden Signs: American Culture and the Campaign Against Sign Language*. Chicago, IL: University of Chicago Press.

Beer, W. and J. Jacob (eds.) (1985) *Language Policy and National Unity*. Totowa, NJ: Rowman and Allanheld.

Benson, A. (1979) An attitude study. *Teaching English to the Deaf*, 6(1), 10–14.

Benson, P., P. Grundy, H. Itakura, and T. Skutnabb-Kangas (eds.) (in press) *Access to Language Rights*. Amsterdam: John Benjamins.

Bergman, E. (1976) Deaf students speak up: how they feel about the teaching and teachers of English. *Teaching English to the Deaf* 3(1), 4–14.

Bergman, B. (1979) *Signed Swedish*. Stockholm: National Swedish Board of Education.

Bergmann, R. (1994) Teaching sign language as the mother tongue in the education of deaf children in Denmark. In I. Ahlgren and K. Hyltenstan (eds.), *Bilingualism in Deaf Education*. Hamburg: Signum, 83–90.

Berke, L. (1978) Attitudes of deaf high school students toward American Sign Language. In *Proceedings of the Second National Symposium on Sign Language Research and Teaching*. Silver Spring, MD: National Association of the Deaf.

Bernstein, B. (1970) Social class, language and socialisation. Reprinted in P. Giglioli (ed.) (1972) *Language and Social Context*. Harmondsworth: Penguin, 157–178.

Beukes, A. (1991) The politics of language in formal education: The position of Afrikaans. *Journal for Language Teaching* 25, 64–77.

Biber, D. and E. Finegan (eds.) (1993) *Sociolinguistic Perspectives on Register*. Oxford: Oxford University Press.

Blattberg, S., L. Byers, E. Lockwood and R. Smith (1995) Sociolinguistic variation in American Sign Language: Phonological variation by age group in fingerspelling. In L. Byers, J. Chaiken and M. Mueller (eds.), *Communication Forum 1995*. Washington, DC: Gallaudet University Department of ASL, Linguistics, and Interpretation, 157–182.

Bloomfield, L. (1933) *Language*. London: George Allen and Unwin.

Bochner, J.H. and J.A. Albertini (1988) Language varieties in the deaf population. In M. Strong (ed.), *Language, Learning and Deafness*. Cambridge: Cambridge University Press, 3–48.

Bord na Gaeilge, An Coiste Comharleach Pleanála (1989) *The Irish Language in a Changing Society*. Dublin: Bord na Gaeilge.

Bornstein, H. (ed.) (1990) *Manual Communication: Implications for Education*. Washington, DC: Gallaudet University Press.

Bornstein, H., L. Hamilton, K. Saulnier and H. Roy (eds.) (1975) *The Signed English Dictionary for Pre-school and Elementary Levels*. Washington, DC: Gallaudet College Press.

Bouchard Ryan, E., H. Giles and R.J. Sebastian (1982) An integrative perspective for the study of attitudes towards language variation. In E. Bouchard Ryan and H. Giles (eds.), *Attitudes Towards Language Variation: Social and Applied Contexts*. London: Edward Arnold.

Bouvet, D. (1990) *The Path to Language: Bilingual Education for Deaf Children*. Clevedon: Multilingual Matters.

Boyes-Braem, P. (1985) Studying sign language dialects. In W. Stokoe and V. Volterra (eds.), *SLR 1983: Proceedings of the III International Symposium on Sign Language Research, Rome, 22–26 June 1983*. Silver Spring, MD: Linstok Press, 247–253.

Bradac, J.J. (1990) Language attitudes and impression formation. In H. Giles and W.P. Robinson (eds.) *Handbook of Language and Social Psychology*. London: John Wiley, 387–412.

Bragg, B. (1990) Communication and the Deaf community. In M. Garretson (ed.), *Eyes, Hands and Voices: Communication Issues Among Deaf People. A Deaf American Monograph*. Silver Spring, MD: National Association of the Deaf.

Branson, J. and D. Miller (1993) Sign language, the deaf and the epistemic violence of mainstreaming. *Language and Education* 7, 21–41.

Branson, J. and D. Miller (1998a) Achieving human rights: Educating deaf immigrant students from non-English-speaking families in Australia. In A. Weisel (ed.), *Issues Unresolved: New perspectives on Language and Deaf Education*. Washington, DC: Gallaudet University Press, 88–100.

Branson, J. and D. Miller (1998b) Nationalism and the linguistic rights of deaf communities. *Journal of Sociolinguistics* 2, 3–34.

Branson, J., D. Miller and I.G. Marsaja, with the assistance of I.W. Negara (1996) Everyone here speaks sign language, too: A deaf village in Bali, Indonesia. In C. Lucas (ed.), *Multicultural Aspects of Sociolinguistics in Deaf Communities*. Washington, DC: Gallaudet University Press, 39–57.

Bridges, B. (1993) Gender variation with sex signs. Unpublished manuscript, Gallaudet University Department of ASL, Linguistics, and Interpretation, Washington, DC.

Brien, D. (ed.) (1992) *Dictionary of British Sign Language/English*. London: Faber and Faber.

Brien, D and M. Brennan (1995) Sign language dictionaries: Issues and developments. In H. Bos and T. Schermer (eds.), *Sign Language Research*. Hamburg: Signum, 313–336.

Brown, P. and S.C. Levinson (1987) *Politeness: Some Universals in Language Usage*. Cambridge: Cambridge University Press.

Bruce, J. (1993) A comparative study of backchanneling signals between an African American Deaf speaker and African American and White Deaf speakers. In E. Winston (ed.), *Communication Forum, Vol. 2*. Washington, DC: School of Communication Student Forum, 1–10.

Bucholtz, M. (1999) "Why be normal?": Language and identity practices in a community of nerd girls. *Language in Society* 28, 203–223.

Budding, C., R. Hoopes, M. Mueller and K. Scarcello (1995) Identification of foreign sign language accents by the deaf. Student Forum, Gallaudet University Department of ASL, Linguistics and Interpretation, Washington DC, 1–16.

Bullivant, B. (1981) *The Pluralist Dilemma in Education: Six Case Studies*. Sydney: George Allen and Unwin.

Bulwer, J. (1644) *Chirologia; Or the Natural Language of the Hand*. London: R. Whitaker.

Burns, S.E. (1998) Irish Sign Language: Ireland's second minority language. In C. Lucas (ed.), *Pinky Extension and Eye Gaze: Language Use in Deaf Communities*. Washington, DC: Gallaudet University Press, 233–273.

Calvet, L.J. (1998) *Language Wars and Linguistic Politics*. New York: Oxford University Press.

Cameron, R. (1993) Ambiguous agreement, functional compensation, and non-specific *tu* in the Spanish of San Juan, Puerto Rico and Madrid, Spain. *Language Variation and Change* 5, 305–335.

Cameron, R. (1998) A variable syntax of speech, gesture and sound effect: Direct quotations in Spanish. *Language Variation and Change* 10, 43–83.

Campos de Abreu, A. (1994) The deaf social life in Brazil. In C. Erting *et al.* (eds.), *The Deaf Way*. Washington, DC: Gallaudet University Press, 114–116.

Carranza, M.A. and E.B. Ryan (1975) Evaluative reactions of bilingual Anglo and Mexican American adolescents toward speakers of English and Spanish. *International Journal of the Sociology of Language* 6, 83–104.

Cedergren, H. and D. Sankoff (1974) Variable rules: Performance as a statistical reflection of competence. *Language* 50, 233–255.

Celo, P. (1996) Pragmatic aspects of the interrogative form in Italian Sign Language. In C. Lucas (ed.), *Multicultural Aspects of Sociolinguistics in Deaf Communities*. Washington, DC: Gallaudet University Press, 132–151.

Chambers, J.K. (1995) *Sociolinguistic Theory: Linguistic Variation and its Social Significance*. Oxford: Blackwell.

Chao, Chien-Min, Chu Hsi-Hsiung and Liu Chao-Chung (1988) *Taiwan Ziran ShouYu [Taiwan Natural Sign Language]*. Taipei, Taiwan: Deaf Sign Language Research Association.

Chen, C. (1993) Attention getting strategies used by a Deaf adult with Deaf children. In E. Winston (ed.), *Gallaudet University Communication Forum, Vol. 2*. Washington, DC: Gallaudet University School of Communication Student Forum. 11–19.

Chen, P. (1999) *Modern Chinese: History and Sociolinguistics*. Cambridge: Cambridge University Press.

Christian, D. (1988) Language planning: The view from linguistics. In F. Newmeyer (ed.), *Linguistics: The Cambridge survey, Vol. 4*. Cambridge: Cambridge University Press, 193–209.

Cluver, A. (1993) *A Dictionary of Language Planning Terms*. Pretoria: University of South Africa.

Cobarrubias, J. (1983a) Ethical issues in status planning. In J. Cobarrubias and J. Fishman (eds.), *Progress in Language Planning*. Berlin: Mouton, 41–85.

Cobarrubias, J. (1983b) Language planning: The state of the art. In J. Cobarrubias and J. Fishman (eds.), *Progress in Language Planning*. Berlin: Mouton, 3–26.

Cobarrubias, J. and J. Fishman (eds.) (1983) *Progress in Language Planning: International Perspectives*. Berlin: Mouton.

Cokely, D. (1983) When is a pidgin not a pidgin? An Alternative Analysis of the ASL-English contact situation. *Sign Language Studies* 38, 1–24.

Cokely, D. and R. Gawlik (1973) A position paper on the relationship between manual English and sign. *The Deaf American*, 7–11.

Collins, S. and K. Petronio (1998) What happens in Tactile ASL? In C. Lucas (ed.), *Sociolinguistics in Deaf Communities, Vol. 4: Pinky Extension and Eye Gaze: Language Use in Deaf Communities*. Washington, DC: Gallaudet University Press, 18–37.

Collins-Ahlgren, M. (1990) Word formation processes in New Zealand Sign Language. In S. Fischer and P. Siple (eds.), *Theoretical Issues in Sign Language Research, Vol. 1: Linguistics*. Chicago, IL: University of Chicago Press, 279–312.

Conrad, R. (1977) The reading ability of deaf school-leavers. *British Journal of Educational Psychology* 47: 138–148.

Cooper, R. (1989) *Language Planning and Social Change*. Cambridge: Cambridge University Press.

Cooper, R. and J. Fishman (1974) The study of language attitudes. *International Journal of the Sociology of Language* 3, 5–19.

Corson, D. (1999) *Language Policy in Schools: A Resource for Teachers and Administrators*. Mahwah, NJ: Lawrence Erlbaum.

Coulombe, P. (1993) Language rights, individual and communal. *Language Problems and Language Planning* 17, 140–152.

Coulter, G. (ed.) (1992) *Phonetics and Phonology, Vol. 3: Current Issues in ASL Phonology*. San Diego, CA: Academic Press.

Coupland, N. and A. Jaworski (1997) *Sociolinguistics: A Reader and Coursebook*. London: Macmillan.

Covington, V. (1976) Problems for a sign language planning agency. *International Journal of the Sociology of Language* 11, 85–106.

Crawford, J. (1992a) *Hold Your Tongue: Bilingualism and the Politics of "English only"*. Reading, MA: Addison-Wesley.

Crawford, J. (ed.) (1992b) *Language Loyalties: A Source Book on the Official English Controversy*. Chicago, IL: University of Chicago Press.

Crystal, D. (1997) *The Cambridge Encyclopaedia of Language*. 2nd edition. Cambridge University Press.

Crystal, D. and E. Craig (1978) Contrived sign language. In I.M. Schlesinger and L. Namir (eds.), *Sign Language of the Deaf: Psychological, Linguistic and Sociological Perspectives*. New York: Academic Press, 141–168.

Cummins, J. and M. Swain (1986) *Bilingualism in Education: Aspects of Theory, Research and Practice*. London: Longman.

Curry, J. and R. Curry (1978) Deaf students can use their fluency in American Sign Language to develop English competency. In *Proceedings of the Second National Symposium on Sign Language Research and Teaching*. Silver Spring, MD: National Association of the Deaf.

Dakic, A. (1999) Report on sign languages in the constitution and in other governmental branches to the Deaf Association of Munich and surrounding area, and the German Deaf Association. Munich: German Deaf Association.

Davis, J. (1989) Distinguishing language contact phenomena in ASL interpretation. In C. Lucas (ed.), *The Sociolinguistics of the Deaf Community*. San Diego, CA: Academic Press, 85–102.

Day, L. (1995) Sign language acquisition of deaf adults in deaf and hearing families. Unpublished video dissertation at University of Bristol.

Dede, K. (1999) The ablative postposition in the Xining dialect. *Language Variation and Change* 11, 1–17.

De Francis, J. (1984) *The Chinese Language: Fact and Fantasy*. Honolulu, HI: University of Hawaii Press.

Degenaar, J. (1987) Nationalism, liberalism, and pluralism. In J. Butler, R. Elphick and D. Walsh (eds.), *Liberalism in South Africa*. Cape Town: David Philip, 236–249.

de la Zerda, N. and R. Hopper (1979) Employment interviewers' reactions to Mexican American speech. *Communication Monographs* 46, 126–134.

DeMatteo, A. (1977) Visual imagery and visual analogues in American Sign Language. In L. Friedman (ed.), *On the Other Hand*. New York: Academic Press.

DeSantis, S. (1977) Elbow to hand shift in French and American Sign Languages. Paper presented at the New Ways of Analyzing Variation (NWAV) conference, Georgetown University, Washington, DC.

Deuchar, M. (1980) Language planning and treatment of BSL: Problems for research. In I. Ahlgren and B. Bergman (eds.), *Papers from the First International Symposium on Sign Language Research*. Stockholm: Swedish National Association of the Deaf, 109–119.

Deuchar, M. (1984) *British Sign Language*. London: Routledge and Kegan Paul.

Dively, V. (1998) Conversational repairs in ASL. In C. Lucas (ed.), *Pinky Extension, Eye Gaze, and Other Sign Language Intricacies: Language Use in Deaf Communities*. Washington, DC: Gallaudet University Press, 137–169.

Djité, P. (1990) Les langues africaines dans la nouvelle francophonie. *Language Problems and Language Planning* 14, 20–32.

Djité, P. (1991) Langues et développement en Afrique. *Language Problems and Language Planning* 15, 121–138.

Dogançay-Aktuna, S. (1995) An evaluation of the Turkish language reform after 60 years. *Language Problems and Language Planning*, 19, 221–249.

Eastman, C. (1983) *Language Planning: An Introduction.* San Francisco, CA: Chandler and Sharp.

Eastman, G. (1974) *Sign Me Alice: A Play in Sign Language.* Washington, DC: Gallaudet College Bookstore.

Ebbinghaus, H. and J. Hessman (1996) Signs and words: Accounting for spoken language elements in German Sign Language. *International Review of Sign Linguistics* 1(1) 23–56.

Eckert, P. (1989) The whole woman: Sex and gender differences in variation. *Language Variation and Change* 1, 245–267.

Eckert, P. (2000) *Linguistic Variation as Social Practice: The Linguistic Construction of Identity in Belten High.* Oxford: Blackwell.

Eckert, P. and S. McConnell-Ginet (1999) New generalizations and explanations in language and gender research. *Language in Society* 28, 185–201.

Eco, U. (1995) *The Search for the Perfect Language.* Oxford: Blackwell.

Edwards, J. (1984a) Irish: Planning and preservation. *Journal of Multilingual and Multicultural Development* 5, 267–275.

Edwards, J. (ed.) (1984b) *Linguistic Minorities, Policies and Pluralism.* London: Academic Press.

Edwards, J. (1985) *Language, Society and Identity.* Oxford: Blackwell.

Edwards, J. (1999) Refining our understanding of language attitudes. *Journal of Language and Social Psychology* 18, 101–110.

Edwards, V. (1978) Language attitudes and under-performance in West Indian children. *Educational Review* 30, 51–58.

Edwards, V. (1983) *Language in Multicultural Classrooms.* London: Batsford.

Edwards, V. and P. Ladd (1983) British Sign Language and West Indian Creole. In J. Kyle and B. Woll (eds.), *Language in Sign.* London: Croom Helm, 147–158.

Ellis, R. (1986) *Understanding Second Language Acquisition.* New York: Oxford University Press.

Emenanjo, E. (ed.) (1990) *Multilingualism, Minority Languages and Language Policy in Nigeria.* Agbor, Nigeria: Center Books, in collaboration with the Linguistic Association of Nigeria.

Emmorey, K. and B. Falgier (1999) Talking about space with space: Describing environments in ASL. In E. Winston (ed.), *Storytelling and Conversation: Discourse in Deaf Communities.* Washington, DC: Gallaudet University Press, 3–26.

Emmorey, K. and J. Reilly (eds.) (1995) *Language, Gesture, and Space.* Hillsdale, NJ: Lawrence Erlbaum.

Engberg-Pedersen, E. (1995) Point of view expressed through shifters. In K. Emmorey and J. Reilly (eds.), *Language, Gesture, and Space.* Hillsdale, NJ: Lawrence Erlbaum, 133–154.

Eriksson, P. (1998) *The History of Deaf People.* Örebro: Daufr.

Erting, C. (1978) Language policy and deaf ethnicity in the United States. *Sign Language Studies* 19, 139–152.

Erting, C. (1982) Deafness, communication and social identity: An anthropological analysis of interaction among parents, teachers, and deaf children in a preschool. Unpublished doctoral dissertation, American University, Washington, DC.

Erting, C.J. (1994) *Deafness, Communication, Social Identity: Ethnography in a Pre-school for Deaf Children*. Burtonsville, MD: Linstok Press.

Ethnologue database (1996) collected by the Summer Institute of Linguistics. Available at www.sil.org/ethnologue.

Fairclough, N. (1989) *Language and Power*. London: Longman.

Fasold, R. (1984) *The Sociolinguistics of Society*. Oxford: Blackwell.

Fasold, R. (1990) *The Sociolinguistics of Language*. Oxford: Blackwell.

Fenn, A. (1992) A pilot study on sign language attitudes. Unpublished thesis, Gallaudet University, Washington, DC.

Ferguson, C.A. (1959) Diglossia. *Word* 15, 325–340.

Ferguson, C.A. (1973) Language problems of variation and repertoire. *Daedalus* 102, 37–46.

Fischer, J. (1958) Social influences on the choice of a linguistic variant. *Word* 14, 47–56.

Fischer, R. and H. Lane (eds.) (1993) *Looking Back: A Reader on the History of Deaf Communities and their Sign Languages*. Hamburg: Signum.

Fischer, S. (1978) Sign Language and Creoles. In P. Siple (ed.), *Understanding Language through Sign Language Research*. New York: Academic Press, 309–331.

Fischer, S. (1996) By the numbers: Language-internal evidence for creolization. *International Review of Sign Linguistics* 1, 1–22.

Fishman, J.A. (1968) Nationality-nationalism and nation-nationism. In J.A. Fishman, C.A. Ferguson and J. Das Gupta (eds.), *Language Problems of Developing Nations*. New York: Wiley, 39–52.

Fishman, J. (1971) *Advances in the Sociology of Language*. The Hague: Mouton.

Fishman, J. (1991) *Reversing Language Shift*. Clevedon: Multilingual Matters.

FitzPatrick, T. (1993) Attention getting strategies used by a Deaf adult with deaf children. In E. Winston (ed.) *Gallaudet University Communication Forum, Vol. 2*. Washington, DC: Gallaudet University School of Communication, 37–50.

Fleetwood, E. and M. Metzger (1998) *Cued Language Structure: An Analysis of Cued American English Based on Linguistic Principles*. Silver Spring, MD: Calliope Press.

Flynn, J. (1984) *No Longer by Gaslight: The First 100 Years of the Adult Deaf Society of Victoria*. Melbourne: Adult Deaf Society of Victoria.

Fodor, I. and C. Hagège (eds.) (1983/84) *Language Reform: History and Future*, 3 vols. Hamburg: Buske Verlag.

Fodor, I. and C. Hagège (eds.) (1990) *Language Reform: History and Future, Vol. 5*. Hamburg: Buske Verlag.

Fok, A. and U. Bellugi (1986) The acquisition of Visual Spatial Script. In H.S.R. Kao, G.P. van Galen, R. Hoosain (eds.), *Graphonomics: Contemporary Research in Handwriting*. North Holland: Elsevier, 329–355.

Fok, A., U. Bellugi, K. van Hoek and E. Klima (1988) The formal properties of Chinese languages in space. In Mao Liu, Hsuan-Chih Chen and May Jane Chen (eds.), *Cognitive Aspects of the Chinese Language*. Hong Kong: Asian Research Service, 187–205.

Foster, S. (1986) Employment experiences of Deaf RIT graduates. Occasional Papers of the National Technical Institute of the Deaf, Rochester, NY.

Frender, R. and W. Lambert (1973) Speech style and scholastic success: The tentative relationships and possible implications for lower social class children. In R. Shuy (ed.), *Georgetown Round Table on Languages and Linguistics, 1972*. Washington, DC: Georgetown University Press, 237–272.

Frishberg, N. (1975) Arbitrariness and iconicity: Historical change in American Sign Language. *Language* 51, 696–719.

Fromkin, V. and R. Rodman (1998) *An Introduction to Language*. 6th edn. Fort Worth, TX: Harcourt Brace Jovanovich.

Gannon, J.R. (1989) *The Week the World Heard Gallaudet*. Washington, DC: Gallaudet University Press.

Gardner, R.C. (1985) *Social Psychology and Second Language Learning: The Role of Attitudes and Motivation*. London: Edward Arnold.

Gardner, R.C. and W.E. Lambert (1972) *Attitudes and Motivation in Second Language Learning*. Rowley, MA: Newbury House.

Garfinkel, H. (1967) *Studies in Ethnomethodology*. Englewood Cliffs, NJ: Prentice-Hall.

Garfinkel, H. (1974) On the origins of the term "ethnomethodology". In R. Turner (ed.), *Ethnomethodology*. Harmondsworth: Penguin, 15–18.

Garretson, M.D. (ed.) (1990) *Eyes, Hands, Voices: Communication Issues Among Deaf People*. Silver Spring, MD: National Association of the Deaf.

Garrett, P., N. Coupland and A. Williams (1999) Evaluating dialect in discourse: Teachers' and teenagers' responses to young English speakers in Wales. *Language in Society* 28, 321–354.

Gauchat, L. (1905) L'unité phonétique dans le patois d'une commune. *Aus Romanischen Sprachen und Literaturen: Festschrift Heinrich Mort*. Halle: Max Niemeyer, 175–232.

Gee, J. (1986) Units in the production of narrative discourse. *Discourse Processes* 9, 391–422.

Gee, J. and J. Kegl (1983) Narrative/Story structure, pausing, and American Sign Language. *Discourse Processes* 6, 243–258.

Genesee, F. (1988) The Canadian second language immersion program. In C. Paulston (ed.), *International Handbook of Bilingualism and Bilingual Education*. New York: Greenwood Press, 163–183.

Giles, H. (1970) Evaluative reactions to accents. *Educational Review* 22, 211–227.

Giles, H. (1973) Accent mobility, a model and some data. *Anthropological Linguistics* 15, 87–105.

Giles, H., R. Bourhis and D. Taylor (1977) Towards a theory of language in ethnic group relations. In H. Giles (ed.), *Language, Ethnicity and Inter-group Relations*. London: Academic Press, 307–349.

Giles, H. and N. Coupland (1991) *Language: Contexts and Consequences*. Milton Keynes: Open University Press.

Giles, H. and P.F. Powesland (1975) *Speech Style and Social Evaluation*. London: Academic Press.

Giles, H., P. Wilson and T. Conway (1981) Accent and lexical diversity as determinants of impression formation and employment selection. *Language Sciences* 3, 92–103.

Glaser, M. (1999) Affect, emphasis, and comment in text telephone conversations. In E. Winston (ed.), *Storytelling and Conversation: Discourse in Deaf Communities.* Washington, DC: Gallaudet University Press, 83–106.

Godfrey, E. and S. Tagliamonte (1999) Another piece of the verbal -*s* story: Evidence from Devon in southwest England. *Language Variation and Change* 11, 87–121.

Goffman, E. (1974) *Frame Analysis.* New York: Harper and Row.

Goffman, E. (1981) *Forms of Talk.* Philadelphia, PA: University of Pennsylvania Press.

Gomes de Matos, F. (1985) The linguistic rights of language learners. *Language Planning Newsletter* 11, 1–2.

Gregory, S. (1992) The language and culture of deaf people: Implications for education. *Language and Education* 6, 183–197.

Gregory, S. and G. Hartley (eds.) (1991) *Constructing Deafness.* London: Pinter Publishers, in association with the Open University.

Gregory, S. and D. Miles (1991) *BSL, Communication and Deafness, Unit 3: Issues in Deafness.* Milton Keynes: The Open University.

Grice, H.P. (1957) Meaning. *Philosophical Review* 67, 377–388.

Grice, H.P. (1968) Utterer's meaning, sentence-meaning, and word-meaning. *Foundations of Language* 4, 1–18.

Grice, H.P. (1975) Logic and conversation. In P. Cole and J. Morgan (eds.), *Syntax and Semantics, Vol. 3: Speech Acts.* New York: Academic Press, 41–58.

Griffey, N. (1994) *From Silence to Speech.* Dublin: Dominican.

Groce, N. (1985) *Everyone Here Spoke Sign Language.* Cambridge, MA: Harvard University Press.

Grosjean, F. (1982) *Life with Two Languages: An Introduction to Bilingualism.* Cambridge, MA: Harvard University Press.

Grosjean, F. (1992) The bilingual and the bicultural person in the hearing and in the deaf world. *Sign Language Studies* 77, 307–320.

Grosjean, F. (1998) Living with two languages and two cultures. In I. Parasnis (ed.), *Cultural and Language Diversity and the Deaf Experience.* New York: Cambridge University Press, 20–37.

Gudschinsky, S. (1956) The ABC's of lexicostatistics (glottochronology). *Word* 12, 175–210.

Guggenheim, L. (1993) Ethnic variation in ASL: The signing of African Americans and how it is influenced by conversational topic. In E. Winston (ed.), *Communication Forum 1993.* Washington, DC: Gallaudet University Department of ASL, Linguistics, and Interpretation, 51–76.

Gustason, G. (1983) Manual English and American Sign Language: Where do we go from here? In J. Kyle and B. Woll (eds.), *Language in Sign.* London: Croom Helm, 163–172.

Gustason, G. and J. Woodward (eds.) (1973) *Recent Developments in Manual English.* Washington, DC: Department of Education, Gallaudet College.

Gustason, G., D. Pfetzing and E. Zawolkow (1975) *Signing Exact English.* Los Alamitos, CA: Modern Signs Press.

Gustason, G., D. Pfetzing and E. Zawolkow (1980) *Signing Exact English.* Los Alamitos, CA: Modern Signs Press.

Gutiérrez, P. (1994) A preliminary study of deaf educational policy. *Bilingual Research Journal* 18, 85–113.

Guy, G.R. (1980) Variation in the group and in the individual: The case of final stop deletion. In W. Labov (ed.), *Locating Language in Time and Space*. New York: Academic Press, 1–36.

Guy, G.R. (1981) Linguistic variation in Brazilian Portuguese: Aspects of the phonology, syntax, and language history. Unpublished doctoral dissertation. University of Pennsylvania, Philadelphia, PA.

Guy, G.R. (1991) Explanation in variable phonology: An exponential model of morphological constraints. *Language Variation and Change* 3, 1–2.

Guy, G.R. (1997) Violable is variable: Optimality theory and linguistic variation. *Language Variation and Change* 9, 333–347.

Guy, G.R. and R. Bayley (1995) On the choice of relative pronouns in English. *American Speech* 70, 148–162.

Haas, C., E. Fleetwood and M. Ernest (1995) An analysis of ASL variation within Deaf-Blind interaction: Question forms, backchanneling, and turn-taking. In L. Byers, J. Chaiken and M. Mueller (eds.), *Communication Forum 1995*. Washington, DC: Gallaudet University Department of ASL, Linguistics, and Interpretation, 103–140.

Halliday, M.A.K. and R. Hasan (1976) *Cohesion in English*. London: Longman.

Hansen, B. (1990) Trends in the progress towards bilingual education for deaf children in Denmark. In S. Prillwitz and T. Vollhaber (eds.), *Sign Language Research and Application: Proceedings of the International Congress on Sign Language Research and Application*. Hamburg: Signum, 51–62.

Harries, L. (1983) The nationalisation of Swahili in Kenya. In C. Kennedy (ed.), *Language Planning and Language Education*. London: George Allen and Unwin, 118–128.

Hartshorne, K. (1987) Language policy in African education in South Africa, 1910–1985, with particular reference to the issue of medium of instruction. In D. Young (ed.), *Bridging the Gap Between Theory and Practice in English Second Language Teaching: Essays in Honour of L.W. Lanham*. Cape Town: Maskew Miller Longman, 62–81.

Hartshorne, K. (1992) *Crisis and Challenge: Black Education, 1910–1990*. Cape Town: Oxford University Press.

Haugen, E. (1966) *Language Conflict and Language Planning: The Case of Modern Norwegian*. Cambridge, MA: Harvard University Press.

Haugen, E. (1971) Linguistics and language planning. In W. Bright (ed.), *Sociolinguistics: Proceedings of the UCLA Sociolinguistics Conference, 1964*. The Hague; Mouton, 50–71.

Henry, A. (1995) *Belfast English and Standard English: Dialect Variation and Parameter Setting*. Oxford: Oxford University Press.

Herriman, M. and B. Burnaby (eds.) (1996) *Language Policies in English-Dominant Countries*. Clevedon: Multilingual Matters.

Hess, M.C. (1997) On the Notion of Accent. Unpublished manuscript, Gallaudet University, Washington, DC.

Heugh, K. (1985) The relationship between nationalism and language in education in the South African context. In D. Young (ed.), *UCT papers in Language Education*. Cape Town: University of Cape Town, Language Education Unit, Department of Education, 35–70.

Heugh, K. (1987) Trends in language medium policy for a post-apartheid South Africa. In D. Young (ed.), *Language: Planning and Medium in Education.* Rondebosch: Language Education Unit (UCT) and SAALA, 206–220.

Hindley, R. (1990) *The Death of the Irish Language.* London: Routledge.

Hinnebusch, T. (1979) Swahili. In T. Shopen (ed.), *Languages and their Status.* Philadelphia, PA: University of Pennsylvania Press, 209–293.

Hirson, B. (1981) Language in control and resistance in South Africa. *African Affairs* 80, 219–237.

Holmes, J. (1992) *An Introduction to Sociolinguistics.* New York: Longman.

Hooghe, L. (1991) *A Leap in the Dark: Nationalist Conflict and Federal Reform in Belgium.* Western Societies Program, Occasional Paper No. 27, Cornell University, Ithaca, NY.

Hoopes, R. (1998) A preliminary examination of pinky extension: Suggestions regarding its occurrence, constraints and function. In C. Lucas (ed.), *Sociolinguistics in Deaf Communities, Vol. 4: Pinky Extension and Eye Gaze: Language Use in Deaf Communities.* Washington, DC: Gallaudet University Press, 3–17.

Hoopes, R., M. Rose, R. Bayley, C. Lucas, A. Wulf, K. Petronio and S. Collins (2001) Analyzing variation in sign languages: Theoretical and methodological issues. In V. Dively, M. Metzger, S. Taub and A.M. Baer (eds.), *Signed Languages: Discoveries from International Research.* Washington, DC: Gallaudet University Press.

Houston, A. (1991) A grammatical continuum for (ING). In P. Trudgill and J.K. Chambers (eds.), *Dialects of English: Studies in Grammatical Variation.* London: Longman, 241–257.

Hymes, D. (1972) Models of the interaction of language and social life. In J. Gumperz and D. Hymes (eds.), *Directions in Sociolinguistics: The Ethnography of Communication.* New York: Holt, Rinehart and Winston, 35–71.

Jacobs, L. (1980) *A Deaf Adult Speaks Out.* Washington, DC: Gallaudet University Press.

Janton, P. (1993) *Esperanto: Language, Literature, and Community.* Albany, NY: State University of New York Press.

Jensen, S.E. (1995) Television to video. In *Proceedings of Equal Partnership in the Media: A Seminar Organised by the Irish Deaf Society and the European Union of the Deaf.* Dublin, 10–11 November 1995.

Jepson, J. (1991) Urban and rural sign language in India. *Language in Society* 20, 37–57.

Jernudd, B. (1977) Linguistic sources for terminological innovation: Policy and opinion. In J. Rubin, B. Jernudd, J. Das Gupta, J. Fishman and C. Ferguson (eds.), *Language Planning Processes.* The Hague: Mouton, 209–293.

Jernudd, B. and M. Shapiro (eds.) (1989) *The Politics of Language Purism.* Berlin: Mouton de Gruyter.

Johnson, R.C. (1990) The publication and early aftermath of 'Unlocking the Curriculum'. *Sign Language Studies* 69, 295–325.

Johnson, R.E. (1994a) Sign language and the concept of deafness in a traditional Yucatec Mayan village. In C. Erting, R. Johnson, D. Smith and B. Snider (eds.), *The Deaf Way: Perspectives from the International Conference on Deaf Culture.* Washington, DC: Gallaudet University Press, 102–109.

Johnson, R.E. (1994b) The structure of fingerspelling. Fifth International Teleclass: Waubonsee Community College, Chicago, IL.

Johnson, R.E. and C. Erting (1989) Ethnicity and socialization in a classroom for Deaf children. In C. Lucas (ed.), *The Sociolinguistics of the Deaf Community*. San Diego, CA: Academic Press, 41–83.

Johnson, R., S. Liddell and C. Erting (1989) *Unlocking the Curriculum: Principles for Achieving Access in Deaf Education*. Gallaudet Research Institute Working Paper 89–3. Washington, DC: Gallaudet University.

Johnston, L. (1993) Conversational analysis of ASL in a second-language classroom: Modeling a discourse repair. In E. Winston (ed.), *Gallaudet University Communication Forum, Vol. 2*. Washington, DC: Gallaudet University School of Communication, 77–85.

Johnston, T. (1989) *AUSLAN Dictionary: A Dictionary of the Sign Language of the Australian Deaf Community*. Petersham, NSW: Deafness Resources Australia.

Johnston, T. (1991) Autonomy and integrity in sign languages. *Signpost*. Spring, 2–5.

Jones, L. and G. Pullen (1990) *Inside We are All Equal: A Social Policy Survey of Deaf People in the European Community*. London: European Community Regional Secretariat of the World Federation of the Deaf.

Joseph, J. and T. Taylor (eds.) (1990) *Ideologies of Language*. London: Routledge.

Kachru, B. (1992) *The Other Tongue: English Across Cultures*. 2nd edition. Chicago, IL: University of Illinois Press.

Kalin, R. and D. Rayko (1980) The social significance of speech in the job interview. In R.N. St Clair and H. Giles (eds.), *The Social and Psychological Contexts of Language*. Hillsdale, NJ: Erlbaum, 39–50.

Kannapell, B. (1982) Inside the Deaf community. *The Deaf American* 34, 23–26.

Kannapell, B. (1989) An examination of deaf college students' attitudes toward ASL and English. In C. Lucas (ed.), *The Sociolinguistics of the Deaf Community*. San Diego, CA: Academic Press.

Kannapell, B. (1991 [1985]) *Language Choice: Identity Choice*. Burtonsville, MD: Linstok Press. Originally doctoral dissertation (1985), Georgetown University, Washington, DC.

Kaplan, R. and R. Baldauf (1997) *Language Planning: From Practice to Theory*. Clevedon: Multilingual Matters.

Kegl, J., A. Senghas and M. Coppola (1999) Creation through contact: Sign language emergence and sign language change in Nicaragua. In M. DeGraff (ed.), *Language Creation and Language Change: Creolization, Diachrony, and Development*. Cambridge, MA: MIT Press.

Kelly, A.B. (1995) Fingerspelling interaction: A set of Deaf parents and their Deaf daughter. In C. Lucas (ed.), *Sociolinguistics in Deaf Communities, Vol. 1*. Washington, DC: Gallaudet University Press, 62–73.

Kendon, A. (1988) *Sign Languages of Aboriginal Australia: Cultural, Semiotic and Communicative Perspectives*. Cambridge: Cambridge University Press.

Kennedy, C. (ed.) (1983) *Language Planning and Language Education*. London: George Allen and Unwin.

Kerr, D. (1976) *Educational Policy: Analysis, Structure, and Justification*. New York: David McKay.

Khalid, A. (1977) *The Liberation of Swahili from European Appropriation*. Nairobi: East Africa Literature Bureau.

Khubchandani, L. (1983) *Plural Languages, Plural Cultures*. Honolulu, HI: University of Hawaii Press.

King, K. (1999) Inspecting the unexpected: Language status and corpus shifts as aspects of Quichua language revitalization. *Language Problems and Language Planning* 23, 109–132.

Kiparsky, P. (1982) *Explanation in Phonology.* Dordrecht: Foris.

Kisch, S. (in preparation) Deafness among a Bedouin tribe in southern Israel. MA Thesis, Tel-Aviv University.

Kleinfeld, M. and N. Warner (1996) Variation in the Deaf community: Gay, lesbian, and bisexual signs. In C. Lucas (ed.), *Sociolinguistics in Deaf Communities, Vol. 2: Multicultural Aspects of Sociolinguistics in Deaf Communities.* Washington, DC: Gallaudet University Press, 3–35.

Klima, E. and U. Bellugi (1979) *The Signs of Language.* Cambridge, MA: Harvard University Press.

Kretschmer, R. and L. Kretschmer (1978) *Language Development and Intervention in the Hearing Impaired.* Baltimore, MD: University Park Press.

Kroch, A. (1978) Toward a theory of social dialect variation. *Language in Society* 7, 17–36.

Kuo, E.C.Y. and B.H. Jernudd (1994) Balancing macro- and micro-sociolinguistic perspectives in language and management: The case of Singapore. In T. Kandiah and J. Kwan-Terry (eds.), *English and Language Planning: A Southeast Asian Contribution.* Singapore: Times Academic Press, 70–91.

Kuschel, R. (1973) The silent inventor: The creation of a sign language by the only deaf-mute on a Polynesian island. *Sign Language Studies* 2, 1–28.

Kyle, J. (ed.) (1987) *Sign and School: Using Signs in Deaf Children's Development.* Clevedon: Multilingual Matters.

Kyle, J. and L. Allsop (1997) *Sign in Europe: A Study of Deaf People and Sign Language in the European Union.* Bristol: Centre for Deaf Studies, University of Bristol.

Kyle, J. and B. Woll (1983) *Language in Sign.* London: Croom Helm.

Kyle, J.G. and B. Woll (1985) *Sign Language: The Study of Deaf People and Their Language.* Cambridge: Cambridge University Press.

Labov, W. (1963) The social motivation of a sound change. *Word* 19, 273–307.

Labov, W. (1966a) The linguistic variable as a structural unit. *Washington Linguistics Review* 3, 4–22.

Labov, W. (1966b) *The Social Stratification of English in New York City.* Washington, DC: Center for Applied Linguistics.

Labov, W. (1969a) Contraction, deletion, and inherent variability of the English copula. *Language* 45, 715–762.

Labov, W. (1969b) The logic of nonstandard English. Reprinted in P.P. Giglioli (ed.) (1972) *Language and Social Context.* Harmondsworth: Penguin, 179–215.

Labov, W. (1972a) *Language in the Inner City: Studies in the Black English Vernacular.* Philadelphia, PA: University of Pennsylvania.

Labov, W. (1972b) *Sociolinguistic Patterns.* Philadelphia, PA: University of Pennsylvania.

Labov, W. (1984) Field methods of the project on language change and variation. In J. Baugh and J. Sherzer (eds.), *Language in Use: Readings in Sociolinguistics.* Englewood Cliffs, NJ: Prentice Hall, 28–53.

Labov, W. (1989) The child as linguistic historian. *Language Variation and Change* 1, 85–97.

Labov, W. (1990) The intersection of sex and social class in the course of linguistic change. *Language Variation and Change* 2, 205–244.

Labov, W. (1994) *Principles of Linguistic Change, Vol. 1: Internal Factors.* Oxford: Blackwell.

Labov, W. (1997) Resyllabification. In F. Hinskens, R. van Hout and L. Wetzels (eds.), *Variation, Change and Phonological Theory.* Amsterdam: John Benjamins, 145–179.

Labov, W., P. Cohen, C. Robins and J. Lewis (1968) *A Study of the Non-standard English of Negro and Puerto Rican Speakers in New York City.* Cooperative Report 3288. Philadelphia, PA: US Regional Survey.

La Bue, M.A. (1995) Language and learning in a deaf education classroom: Practice and paradox. In C. Lucas (ed.), *Sociolinguistics in Deaf Communities.* Washington, DC: Gallaudet University Press, 164–220.

Ladd, P. (1988) The modern deaf community. In D. Miles (ed.), *British Sign Language: A Beginner's Guide.* London: BBC, 27–43.

Lambert, R. (1990) *Language Policy: An International Perspective.* Washington, DC: National Foreign Language Center, Johns Hopkins University.

Lambert, W.E., R. Hodgson, R.C. Gardner and S. Fillenbaum (1960) Evaluational reactions to spoken languages. *Journal of Abnormal and Social Psychology* 60, 44–51.

Lane, H. (1984) *When the Mind Hears: A History of the Deaf.* New York: Random House.

Lane, H. (1985) On Language, power and the Deaf. Unpublished manuscript, Convention of the Registry of Interpreters for the Deaf, Boston, MA.

Lane, H. (1992) *The Mask of Benevolence: Disabling the Deaf Community.* New York: Alfred A. Knopf.

Lane, H., R. Hoffmeister and B. Bahan (1996) *A Journey into the Deaf-world.* San Diego, CA: Dawn Sign Press.

Lane, H. and F. Philip (1984) *The Deaf Experience: Classics in Language and Education.* Cambridge, MA: Harvard University Press.

Language Plan Task Group (1996) *Towards a National Language Plan for South Africa: Final Report of the Language Plan Task Group (LANGTAG).* Pretoria: Government Printer.

Lawrence, S. (1998) Sign language interpreters' effect on audience perception of deaf speaker's credibility. Unpublished Master's thesis, California State University, Hayward, CA.

Lawson, L. (1981) The role of sign in the structure of the Deaf community. In B. Woll, J. Kyle and M. Deuchar (eds.), *Perspectives on BSL and Deafness.* London: Croom Helm.

Leben, W. (1996) Tonal feet and the adaptation of English borrowings into Hausa. *Studies in African Linguistics* 25, 139–154.

Lee, D.M. (1982) Are there really signs of diglossia? Reexamining the Situation. *Sign Language Studies* 35, 127–152.

Le Master, B. and J. Dwyer (1991) Knowing and using female and male signs in Dublin. *Sign Language Studies* 73, 361–396.

Lentz, E. (1977) Informing deaf people about the structure of American Sign Language. In *Proceedings of the First National Symposium on Sign Language Research and Teaching.* Silver Spring, MD: National Association of the Deaf.

Lentz, E., K. Mikos and C. Smith (1988) *Signing Naturally: Teacher's Curriculum Guide, Level I*. San Diego, CA: Dawn Sign Press.

LePage, R. and A. Tabouret-Keller (1985) *Acts of Identity: Creole-Based Approaches to Language and Ethnicity*. Cambridge: Cambridge University Press.

Levinson, S. (1983) *Pragmatics*. Cambridge: Cambridge University Press.

Lewis, J. (1996) Parallels in communication styles of hearing and deaf African Americans. Unpublished manuscript, Gallaudet University, Washington, DC.

Lewis, J., C. Palmer and L. Williams (1995) Existence of and attitudes toward black variations of sign language. In L. Byers, J. Chaiken and M. Mueller (eds.), *Communication Forum 1995*. Washington, DC: Gallaudet University Department of ASL, Linguistics, and Interpretation, 17–48.

Liddell, S. (1980) *American Sign Language Syntax*. The Hague: Mouton.

Liddell, S. (1984) THINK and BELIEVE: Sequentiality in American Sign Language signs. *Language* 60, 372–399.

Liddell, S. (1992) Holds and positions: Comparing two models of segmentation in ASL. In G. Coulter (ed.), *Phonetics and Phonology, Vol. 3: Current Issues in ASL Phonology*. San Diego, CA: Academic Press, 189–211.

Liddell, S. (1995) Real, surrogate, and token space: Grammatical consequences in ASL. In K. Emmorey and J. Reilly (eds.), *Language, Gesture, and Space*. Hillsdale, NJ: Lawrence Erlbaum, 19–42.

Liddell, S. and M. Metzger (1998) Gesture in sign language discourse. *Journal of Pragmatics* 30, 657–697.

Liddell, S. and R.E. Johnson (1989) American Sign Language: The phonological base. *Sign Language Studies* 64, 195–278.

Lippi-Green, R. (1997) *English with an Accent*. London: Routledge.

Llewellyn-Jones, P., J. G. Kyle and B. Woll (1979) Sign language communication. Paper presented at International Conference on Social Psychology of Language, Bristol.

Locker McKee, R. (1992) Footing shifts in American Sign Language lectures. Unpublished doctoral dissertation, University of California, Los Angeles, CA.

Louw, J. (1983/84) The development of Xhosa and Zulu as languages. In I. Fodor and C. Hagège (eds.), *Language Reform, Vol. 2*. Hamburg: Buske Verlag, 371–392.

Lucas, C. (ed.) (1989) *The Sociolinguistics of the Deaf Community*. San Diego, CA: Academic Press.

Lucas, C. (ed.) (1995) *Sociolinguistics in Deaf Communities*. Washington, DC: Gallaudet University Press.

Lucas, C. (ed.) (1996) *Multicultural Aspects of Sociolinguistics in Deaf Communities*. Washington, DC: Gallaudet University Press.

Lucas, C. (ed.) (1998) *Pinky Extension and Eye Gaze: Language Use in Deaf Communities*. Washington, DC: Gallaudet University Press.

Lucas, C. and C. Valli (1989) Language contact in the American Deaf community. In C. Lucas (ed.), *The Sociolinguistics of the Deaf Community*. San Diego, CA: Academic Press, 11–40.

Lucas, C. and C. Valli (1991) ASL or contact signing: Issues of judgement. *Language and Society* 20, 201–216.

Lucas, C. and C. Valli (1992) *Language Contact in the American Deaf Community*. San Diego, CA: Academic Press.

Lucas, C., R. Bayley and C. Valli (2001) *Sociolinguistics in Deaf Communities, Vol. 7: Sociolinguistic Variation in ASL.* Washington, DC: Gallaudet University Press.

Lucas, C., R. Bayley, M. Rose and A. Wulf (in press). Location variation in American Sign Language. *Sign Language Studies.*

Luetke-Stahlman, B. (1988) The benefit of oral English-only as compared with signed input to hearing-impaired students. *Volta Review* 90, 349–361.

Machabée, D. (1995) Description and status of initialized signs in Québec Sign Language. In C. Lucas (ed.), *Sociolinguistics in Deaf Communities, Vol. 1.* Washington, DC: Gallaudet University Press.

Machabée, D. and C. Dubuisson (1995) Initialized signs in (or outside of?) Québec Sign Language. In H. Bos and T. Schermer (eds.), *Sign Language Research.* Hamburg: Signum, 211–229.

Maclagan, M., E. Gordon and G. Lewis (1999) Women and sound change: Conservative and innovative behavior by the same speakers. *Language Variation and Change* 11, 19–41.

Maclean, J. (1896) *Canadian Savage Folk: The Native Tribes of Canada.* Toronto: William Briggs, 486–495.

MacMillan, M. (1982) Henri Bourassa on the defence of language rights. *Dalhousie Review* 62, 413–430.

Maguire, G. (1991) *Our Own Language: An Irish Initiative.* Clevedon: Multilingual Matters.

Mahshie, S.N. (1995) *Educating Deaf Children Bilingually.* Washington, DC: Gallaudet University Pre-College Programs.

Malloy, C. and J. Doner (1995) Variation in ASL discourse: Gender differences in the use of cohesive devices. In L. Byers, J. Chaiken and M. Mueller (eds.), *Communication Forum 1995.* Washington, DC: Gallaudet University Department of ASL, Linguistics, and Interpretation, 183–205.

Mansfield, D. (1993) Gender differences in ASL: A sociolinguistic study of sign choices by Deaf native signers. In E. Winston (ed.), *Communication Forum 1993.* Washington, DC: Gallaudet University Department of ASL, Linguistics, and Interpretation, 86–98.

Marivate, C. (1993) Language and education, with special reference to the mother-tongue policy in African schools. *Language Matters: Studies in the Languages of Southern Africa* 24, 91–105.

Mar-Molinero, C. (1997) *The Spanish-Speaking World: A Practical Introduction to Sociolinguistic Issues.* London: Routledge.

Martinez, L. (1993) Eye gaze as an element in Filipino Sign Language discourse. In E. Winston (ed.), *Gallaudet Communication Forum, Vol. 2.* Washington, DC: Gallaudet University School of Communication, 99–102.

Martinez, L. (1995) Turn-taking and eye gaze in sign conversations between Deaf Filipinos. In C. Lucas (ed.), *Sociolinguistics in Deaf Communities.* Washington, DC: Gallaudet University Press, 272–306.

Mas, C. (1994) Bilingual education for the deaf in France. In I. Ahlgren and K. Hyltenstan (eds.), *Bilingualism in Deaf Education.* Hamburg: Signum, 71–81.

Mather, S. (1987) Eye gaze and communication in a deaf classroom. *Sign Language Studies* 54, 11–30.

Mather, S. (1989) Visually oriented teaching strategies with deaf preschool children. In C. Lucas (ed.), *The Sociolinguistics of the Deaf Community.* San Diego, CA: Academic Press, 165–187.

Mather, S. (1990) Home and classroom communication. In D. Moores and K. Meadow-Orleans (eds.), *Educational and Developmental Aspects of Deafness.* Washington, DC: Gallaudet University Press, 232–254.

Mather, S. (1991) The discourse marker OH in typed telephone conversations among deaf typists. Unpublished doctoral dissertation, Georgetown University, Washington, DC.

Mather, S. (1994) Adult-Deaf toddler discourse. In B.D. Snider (ed.), *Post-Milan-ASL and English Literacy: Issues, Trends, and Research.* Washington, DC: Gallaudet University College for Continuing Education, 283–297.

Mather, S. (1996) Initiation in visually constructed dialogue: Reading books with three-to-eight year old students who are deaf and hard of hearing. In C. Lucas (ed.), *Pinky Extension, Eye Gaze, and Other Sign Language Intricacies: Language Use in Deaf Communities.* Washington, DC: Gallaudet University Press, 109–131.

Mather, S. and E. Winston (1998) Spatial mapping and involvement in ASL storytelling. In C. Lucas (ed.), *Pinky Extension, Eye Gaze, and Other Sign Language Intricacies: Language Use in Deaf Communities.* Washington, DC: Gallaudet University Press, 170–182.

Mathur, G., C. Rathman and G. Mirus (1998) Why not 'GIVE-US': An articulatory constraint in signed languages. Paper presented at the 6th International Conference on Theoretical Issues in Sign Language Research, Washington, DC, November 1998.

Matthews, P. (1996) *The Irish Deaf Community: Survey Report, History of Education, Language and Culture, Vol. 1.* Dublin: Linguistic Institute of Ireland.

Mazrui, A. and A. Mazrui (1998) *The Power of Babel: Language and Governance in the African Experience.* Oxford: James Currey.

McCagg, W. (1993) Some problems in the history of Deaf Hungarians. In J.V. van Cleve (ed.), *Deaf History Unveiled,* Washington, DC: Gallaudet University Press, 252–271.

McDonnell, P. (1992) *Patterns of Communication Among Deaf Pupils.* Dublin: Sociological Association of Ireland, National Rehabilitation Board.

McDonnell, P. and H. Saunders (1993) Sit on your hands. In R. Fischer and H. Lane (eds.), *Looking Back.* Hamburg: Signum, 255–260.

McGroarty, M. (1996) Language attitudes, motivation and standards. In S.L. McKay and N.H. Hornberger (eds.), *Sociolinguistics and Language Teaching.* Cambridge: Cambridge University Press.

McKay, S. (1993) *Agendas for Second Language Literacy.* Cambridge: Cambridge University Press.

McKee, D. and G. Kennedy (1998) Lexical comparisons of signs from American, Australian, British and New Zealand sign languages. Paper presented at the 6th International Conference on Theoretical Issues in Sign Language Research, Washington, DC, November 1998.

McNeill, D. (1992) *Hand and Mind: What Gestures Reveal about Thought.* Chicago, IL: University of Chicago Press.

McRae, K. (1978) Bilingual language districts in Finland and Canada: Adventures in the transplanting of an institution. *Canadian Public Policy* 4, 331–351.

Meath-Lang, B. (1978) A comparative study of experienced and non-experienced groups of deaf college students: Their attitude toward language learning. *Teaching English to the Deaf* 5, 9–13.

Meath-Lang, B., F. Caccamise and J. Albertini (1984) Deaf people's views on English language learning: educational and sex implications. In R. Hoeman and R. Wilbur (eds.), *Interpersonal Communication and Deaf People*. Working Papers No. 5. Washington, DC: Gallaudet College.

Metzger, M. (1993) Pronoun variation in formal and informal discourse. In E. Winston (ed.), *Communication Forum 1993*. Washington, DC: Gallaudet University Department of ASL, Linguistics, and Interpretation, 132–149.

Metzger, M. (1995) Constructed dialogue and constructed action in American Sign Language. In C. Lucas (ed.), *Sociolinguistics in Deaf Communities*. Washington, DC: Gallaudet University Press, 255–271.

Metzger, M. (1999) *Sign Language Interpreting: Deconstructing the Myth of Neutrality*. Washington, DC: Gallaudet University Press.

Milroy, J. (1992) *Linguistic Variation and Change*. Oxford: Blackwell.

Milroy, J. and L. Milroy (1978) Belfast: Change and variation in an urban vernacular. In P. Trudgill (ed.), *Sociolinguistic Patterns in British English*. London: Edward Arnold, 19–36.

Milroy, L. (1987a) *Language and Social Networks*. 2nd edition. Oxford: Blackwell.

Milroy, L. (1987b) *Observing and Analyzing Natural Language*. Oxford: Blackwell.

Mirzoeff, N. (1995) *Silent Poetry: Deafness, Sign and Visual Culture in Modern France*. Princeton, NJ: Princeton University Press.

Mohanan, K.P. and T. Mohanan (1987) The lexical phonology of Malayalee English: Structure formation in transplanted second language systems. Unpublished manuscript, Stanford University, Stanford, CA.

Moores, D.F. (1978) *Educating the Deaf*. Boston, MA: Houghton Mifflin.

Morgan, G. (1999) Event packaging in British Sign Language discourse. In E. Winston (ed.), *Storytelling and Conversation: Discourse in Deaf Communities*. Washington, DC: Gallaudet University Press, 27–58.

Mori, S. (1996) JSL Phonology from comparative study between JSL and ASL. Poster session at Theoretical Issues in Sign Language Research, University of Quebec at Montreal and McGill University, Montreal, Quebec, Canada.

Mottez, B. (1977) La diglossia à l'interieur de la langue des signes. *Rééducation Orthophonique* 15, 415–418.

Mulrooney, K. (2001) Gender variation in fingerspelling in American Sign Language. Paper presented at the American Dialect Society, Washington, D.C., Jan. 6. (to appear in *Sociolinguistics in Deaf Communities, Vol. 8*, C. Lucas ed., Washington, D.C., Gallaudet University Press).

Nagy, N. and B. Reynolds (1997) Optimality theory and variable word-final deletion in Faetar. *Language Variation and Change* 9, 37–56.

Nahir, M. (1977) The five aspects of language planning. *Language Problems and Language Planning* 1, 107–124.

Nahir, M. (1988) Language planning and language acquisition: The 'great leap' in the Hebrew revival. In C. Paulston (ed.), *International Handbook of Bilingualism and Bilingual Education*. New York: Greenwood Press, 275–295.

Namir, L., I. Sella, M. Rimor and I.M. Schlesinger (1979) *Dictionary of Sign Language of the Deaf in Israel*. Jerusalem: Ministry of Social Welfare.

Nash, J. (1987) Policy and practice in the American Sign Language community. *International Journal of the Sociology of Language* 68, 7–22.

Neidle, C., J. Kegl, D. McLaughlin, R. Lee and B. Bahan (2000) *The Syntax of American Sign Language: Functional Categories and Hierarchical Structure*. Cambridge, MA: MIT Press.

Nover, S. (1995) Politics and language: American Sign Language and English in Deaf education. In C. Lucas (ed.), *Sociolinguistics in Deaf Communities, Vol. 1*. Washington, DC: Gallaudet University Press, 109–163.

Nover, S. and J. Andrews (1998) *Critical Pedagogy in Deaf Education: Bilingual Methodology and Staff Development*. Santa Fe, New Mexico: New Mexico School for the Deaf.

Nuessel, F. (2000) *The Esperanto Language*. New York: Legas.

Nwachukwu, P. (1983) *Towards an Igbo Literary Standard*. London: Kegan Paul.

O'Huallacháin, C. (1991) *The Irish Language in Society*. Coleraine: University of Ulster.

O'Huallacháin, C. (1994) *The Irish and Irish: A Sociolinguistic Analysis of the Relationship Between a People and their Language*. Baile Átha Cliath: Irish Franciscan Provincial Office.

Ó Murchú, H. (1994) 'There are more things in heaven and earth, Horatio . . .' Paper presented at the international conference of the Irish Association for Applied Linguistics: Language Education and Society in a Changing World, Dublin, Ireland, June 1994.

Ong, W. (1982) *Orality and Literacy: The Technologising of the Word*. London: Routledge.

Ó Riagáin, P. (1997) *Language Policy and Social Reproduction: Ireland, 1893–1993*. Oxford: Clarendon Press.

Ó Riagáin, P. and M. Ó Gliasáin (1984) *The Irish language in the Republic of Ireland 1983: Preliminary Report of a National Survey*. Dublin: Institiúid Teangeolaíochta Éireann.

Ó Riagáin, P. and M. Ó Gliasáin (1994) *National Survey on Languages 1993: Preliminary Report*. Dublin: Institiúid Teangeolaíochta Éireann.

Osgood, C.A., G.J. Suci and P.H. Tannenbaum (1957) *The Measurement of Meaning*. Urbana, IL: University of Illinois Press.

Oviedo, A. (1996) Bilingual deaf education in Venezuela: Linguistic comments on the current situation. In C. Lucas (ed.), *Multicultural Aspects of Sociolinguistics in Deaf Communities*. Washington, DC: Gallaudet University Press.

Padden, C. (1987) American Sign Language. In J. van Cleve (ed.), *Gallaudet Encyclopaedia of Deaf People and Deafness*. London: McGraw-Hill.

Padden, C. (1988) *Interaction of Morphology and Syntax in American Sign Language*. New York: Garland.

Padden, C. (1990) Rethinking fingerspelling. *Signpost* 4, 2–4.

Padden, C. (1991) Rethinking fingerspelling: Part two. *Signpost*. Winter, 2–4.

Padden, C. (1998) From the cultural to the bicultural: The modern Deaf community. In I. Parasnis (ed.), *Cultural and Language Diversity and the Deaf Experience*. Cambridge: Cambridge University Press, 79–98.

Padden, C. and T. Humphries (1988) *Deaf in America: Voices from a Culture*. Cambridge, MA: Harvard University Press.

Paget, L.G. and P. Gorman (1976) *The Paget–Gorman Sign System*. London: Association for Experiment in Deaf Education.

Paget, R. (1951) *The New Sign Language.* London: Wellcome Foundation.

Pakir, A. (1994) Education and invisible language planning: The case of English in Singapore. In T. Kandiah and J. Kwan-Terry (eds.), *English and Language Planning: A Southeast Asian Contribution.* Singapore: Times Academic Press, 158–181.

Parasnis, I. (ed.) (1998) *Cultural and Language Diversity and the Deaf Experience.* Cambridge: Cambridge University Press.

Patrick, P. (1999) *Urban Jamaican Creole.* Amsterdam: John Benjamins.

Patrick, P. and M. Metzger (1996) Sociolinguistic factors in sign language research. In J. Arnold, R. Blake, B. Davidson, S. Schwenter and J. Solomon (eds.), *Sociolinguistic Variation: Data, Theory, and Analysis.* Selected papers from New Ways of Analyzing Variation (NWAV) 23. Stanford, CA: Center for the Study of Language and Information, 229–240.

Patrie, C.J. and R.E. Johnson (in preparation) *Fingerspelled Word Recognition: A Rapid Serial Visual Processing Approach.* San Diego, CA: Dawn Sign Press.

Paul, P. and D. Jackson (1993) *Toward a Psychology of Deafness: Theoretical and Empirical Perspectives.* Boston, MA: Allyn and Bacon.

Paul, P. and S. Quigley (1990) *Education and Deafness.* New York: Longman.

Pedersen, L., S. Leas, G. Bailey and M. Bassett (1981) *LAGS: The Basic Materials.* Ann Arbor, MI: University Microfilms.

Pelissier, M. (1856) *Des Sourds-Muets.* Paris: Paul Dupont.

Peltz, R. (1991) Ethnic identity and aging. In J.R. Dow (ed.), *Language and Ethnicity: Focusschrift in Honour of J.A. Fishman, Vol 2.* Amsterdam: Benjamins, 183–205.

Peng, L. and J. Ann (2001) Stress and duration in three varieties of English. *World Englishes* 20(1).

Penn, C. (ed.) (1992–94) *Dictionary of Southern African Signs.* 5 vols. Pretoria: Human Sciences Research Council and the South African National Council for the Deaf.

Penn, C. and T. Reagan (1990) How do you sign 'apartheid'? The politics of South African Sign Language. *Language Problems and Language Planning* 14, 91–103.

Penn, C. and T. Reagan (1991) Toward a national policy for deaf education in the 'new' South Africa. *South African Journal of Communication Disorders* 38, 19–24.

Penn, C. and T. Reagan (1994) The properties of South African Sign Language: Lexical diversity and syntactic unity. *Sign Language Studies* 85, 319–327.

Penn, C. and T. Reagan (1995) On the other hand: Implications of the study of South African Sign Language for the education of the deaf in South Africa. *South African Journal of Education* 15, 92–96.

Penn, C. and T. Reagan (1999) Linguistic, social and cultural perspectives on sign language in South Africa. *Indian Journal of Applied Linguistics* 25, 49–69.

Pennycook, A. (1994) *The Cultural Politics of English as an International Language.* London: Longman.

Pennycook, A. (1998) *English and the Discourses of Colonialism.* London: Routledge.

Perlmutter, D. (1992) Sonority and syllable structure in American Sign Language. In G. Coulter (ed.), *Phonetics and Phonology, Vol. 3: Current Issues in ASL Phonology.* San Diego, CA: Academic Press, 227–261.

Phillipson, R. (1992) *Linguistic Imperialism.* Oxford: Oxford University Press.

Phillipson, R., M. Rannut and T. Skutnabb-Kangas (1995) Introduction. In T. Skutnabb-Kangas and R. Phillipson, in conjunction with M. Rannut (eds.), *Linguistic Human Rights: Overcoming Linguistic Discrimination.* Berlin: Mouton de Gruyter, 1–22.

Pizzuto, E. and V. Volterra (1996) Sign language lexicon: Cross-linguistic and cross-cultural comparisons. Report prepared for the Commission of the European Communities, Human Capital and Mobility Programme Project: Intersign: Multi professional study of sign language and the deaf community in Europe (Network).

Poplack, S. (1979) Function and process in a variable phonology. Unpublished Ph.D. dissertation, University of Pennsylvania, Philadelphia, PA.

Poplack, S. (1980) 'Sometimes I'll start a sentence in Spanish and TERMINO EN ESPAÑOL': Towards a typology of code-switching. *Linguistics* 18, 581–618.

Poplack, S. and S. Tagliamonte (1989) There's no tense like the present: Verbal *-s* inflection in early Black English. *Language Variation and Change* 1, 47–84.

Poulin, C. and C. Miller (1995) On narrative discourse and point of view in Québec Sign Language. In K. Emmorey and J. Reilly (eds.), *Language, Gesture, and Space.* Hillsdale, NJ: Lawrence Erlbaum, 117–131.

Quay, S. (1998) Monastic sign language in the Far East. Paper presented to the 12th Sociolinguistics Symposium, London, March 1998.

Quigley, S. and P.E. Kretschmer (1982) *The Education of Deaf Children.* London: Edward Arnold.

Radutzky, E. (1990) The changing handshape in Italian Sign Language. In W.H. Edmondson and F. Karlsson (eds.), *SLR 1987: Papers from the Fourth International Symposium on Sign Language Research.* Hamburg: Signum.

Radutzky, E. (1992) *Dizionario bilingue elementare della lingua italiana dei segni.* Roma: Edizioni Kappa.

Rampton, B. (1997) *Crossing: Language and Ethnicity Among Adolescents.* London: Longman.

Ramsey, C.L. (1989) Language planning in deaf education. In C. Lucas (ed.), *The Sociolinguistics of the Deaf Community.* San Diego, CA: Academic Press, 123–146.

Ramsey, C.L. (1993) A description of classroom language and literacy learning among deaf children in a mainstreaming program. Unpublished PhD dissertation, University of California, Berkeley, CA.

Ramsey, C.L. (1997) *Deaf Children in the Public Schools.* Washington, DC: Gallaudet University Press.

Reagan, T. (1983) The economics of language: Implications for language planning. *Language Problems and Language Planning* 7, 148–161.

Reagan, T. (1984) Language policy, politics and ideology: The case of South Africa. *Issues in Education* 2, 155–164.

Reagan, T. (1985) The deaf as a linguistic minority: Educational implications. *Harvard Educational Review* 55, 265–277.

Reagan, T. (1986) 'Language ideology' in the language planning process: Two African case studies. *South African Journal of African Languages* 6, 94–97.

Reagan, T. (1987) The politics of linguistic apartheid: Language policies in black education in South Africa. *Journal of Negro Education* 56, 299–312.

Reagan, T. (1988) Multiculturalism and the deaf: An educational manifesto. *Journal of Research and Development in Education* 22, 1–6.

Reagan, T. (1989) Nineteenth century conceptions of deafness: Implications for contemporary educational practice. *Educational Theory* 39, 39–46.

Reagan, T. (1990) The development and reform of sign languages. In I. Fodor and C. Hagège (eds.), *History and Future, Vol. 5: Language Reform.* Hamburg: Buske Verlag, 253–267.

Reagan, T. (1991) Responding to linguistic diversity in South Africa: The contribution of language planning. *South African Journal of Linguistics* 8, 178–184.

Reagan, T. (1995a) Language planning and language policy in South Africa: A perspective on the future. In R. Mesthrie (ed.), *Language and Social History: Studies in South African Sociolinguistics.* Cape Town: David Philip, 319–328.

Reagan, T. (1995b) Neither easy to understand nor pleasing to see: The development of manual sign codes as language planning activity. *Language Problems and Language Planning* 19, 133–150.

Reagan, T. (1997) When is a language not a language? Challenges to 'linguistic legitimacy' in educational discourse. *Educational Foundations* 11, 5–28.

Reagan, T. (in press) Language rights and the deaf: Compensatory and empowerment approaches in language policy. In P. Benson, P. Grundy, H. Itakura and T. Skutnabb-Kangas (eds.), *Access to Language Rights.* Amsterdam: John Benjamins.

Reagan, T. and C. Penn (1997) Language policy, South African Sign Language, and the deaf: Social and educational implications. *Southern African Journal of Applied Language Studies* 5, 1–13.

Rée, J. (1999) *I See a Voice: Deafness, Language and the Senses: A Philosophical History.* New York: Metropolitan Books.

Reilly, J. and M. McIntire (1980) American Sign Language and Pidgin Sign English: What's the difference? *Sign Language Studies* 27, 151–192.

Rhodes, N. (1980) Attitudes toward Guaraní and Spanish: A survey. *Linguistic Reporter* 22, 4–5.

Ricento, T. and B. Burnaby (eds.) (1998) *Language and Politics in the United States and Canada: Myths and Realities.* Mahwah, NJ: Lawrence Erlbaum.

Richey, M. (2000) Interactional aspects in a religious setting. Unpublished manuscript, Gallaudet University, Washington, DC.

Roberts, C., E. Davies and T. Jupp (1992) *Language and Discrimination: A Study of Communication in Multi-Ethnic Workplaces.* London: Longman.

Roberts, J. (1997) Acquisition of variable rules: A study of (-*t, d*) deletion in preschool children. *Journal of Child Language* 24, 351–372.

Romaine, S. (1989) *Bilingualism.* Oxford: Blackwell.

Rosenthal, M. (1974) The magic boxes: Pre-school children's attitudes toward Black and Standard English. *Florida Foreign Language Reporter* 12, 55–62, 92–93.

Roush, D. (1999) *Indirectness in American Sign Language: Requests and Refusals.* Department of ASL, Linguistics and Interpretation Working Papers 1999. Washington, DC: Gallaudet University.

Rousseau, P. and D. Sankoff (1978) Advances in variable rule methodology. In D. Sankoff (ed.), *Linguistic Variation: Models and Methods.* New York: Academic Press, 57–69.

Roy, C. (1989a) A sociolinguistic analysis of the interpreter's role in the turn exchanges of an interpreted event. Unpublished doctoral dissertation, Georgetown University, Washington DC.

Roy, C. (1989b) Features of Discourse in an American Sign Language Lecture. In C. Lucas (ed.), *The Sociolinguistics of the Deaf Community.* San Diego: Academic Press, 231–251.

Rubin, D.L. (1992) Non-language factors affecting undergraduates' judgements of non-native English-speaking teaching assistants. *Research in Higher Education* 33, 511–531.

Rubin, D.L. and K.A. Smith (1990) Effects of accent, ethnicity and lecture topic on undergraduates' perceptions of non-native English-speaking teaching assistants. *International Journal of Intercultural Relations* 14, 337–353.

Rubin, J. (1968) *National Bilingualism in Paraguay.* The Hague: Mouton.

Rubin, J. and B. Jernudd (eds.) (1971) *Can Language be Planned? Sociolinguistic Theory and Practice for Developing Nations.* Honolulu, HI: University Press of Hawaii.

Ryazanova-Clarke, L. and T. Wade (1999) *The Russian Language Today.* London: Routledge.

Sacks, H., E. Schegloff and G. Jefferson (1974) A simplest systematics for the organization of turntaking in conversation. *Language* 50, 696–735.

Sacks, O. (1989) *Seeing Voices: A Journey into the World of the Deaf.* Berkeley, CA: University of California Press.

Sáenz-Badillos, A. (1993) *A History of the Hebrew Language.* Cambridge: Cambridge University Press.

Safford, P. and E. Safford (1996) *A History of Childhood and Disability.* New York: Teachers College Press.

Sandler, W. (1992) Linearization of phonological tiers in ASL. In G. Coulter (ed.), *Phonetics and Phonology, Vol. 3: Current Issues in ASL Phonology.* San Diego, CA: Academic Press, 103–129.

Sanheim, L. (2000) Turn exchange in an interpreted medical encounter. Unpublished manuscript, Gallaudet University, Washington, DC.

Sankoff, D. (1988) Variable rules. In U. Ammon, N. Dittmar and K. J. Mattheier (eds.), *Sociolinguistics: An International Handbook of the Science of Language and Society, Vol. 2.* Berlin: de Gruyter, 984–997.

Sankoff, D. and P. Rousseau (1978) Advances in variable rule methodology. In D. Sankoff (ed.), *Linguistic Variation: Models and Methods.* New York: Academic.

Santa Ana, O. (1992) Chicano English and the exponential hypothesis. *Language Variation and Change* 4, 275–288.

Sarnoff, I. (1970) Social attitudes and the resolution of motivational conflict. In M. Jahoda and N. Warren (eds.), *Attitudes.* Harmondsworth: Penguin.

Saville-Troike, M. (1989) *The Ethnography of Communication.* 2nd edn. Oxford: Blackwell.

Schaller, S. (1991) *A Man Without Words.* Berkeley, CA: University of California Press.

Schecter, S. and R. Bayley (1997) Language socialization practices and cultural identity: Case studies of Mexican-descent families in California and Texas. *TESOL Quarterly* 31, 513–541.

Schegloff, E. (1972) Sequencing in conversational openings. In J. Gumperz and D. Hymes (eds.), *Directions in Sociolinguistics.* New York: Holt, Rinehart and Winston, 346–380.

Schegloff, E., G. Jefferson and H. Sacks (1977) The preference for self-correction in the organization of repair in conversation. *Language* 53, 361–382.

Schegloff, E. and H. Sacks (1973) Opening up closings. *Semiotica* 7, 289–327.

Schein, J.D. (1984) *Speaking the Language of Sign: The Art and Science of Signing.* New York: Doubleday.

Schein, J.D. (1987) The demography of deafness. In P.C. Higgins and J. Nash (eds.), *Understanding Deafness Socially.* Springfield, IL: Thomas, 3–28.

Schein, J.D. (1989) *At Home Among Strangers: Exploring the Deaf Community in the United States.* Washington, DC: Gallaudet University Press.

Schein, J.D. and M.T. Delk (1974) *The Deaf Population of the United States*. Silver Spring, MD: National Association for the Deaf.

Schein, J.D. and D. Stewart (1995) *Language in Motion: Exploring the Nature of Sign*. Washington, DC: Gallaudet University Press.

Schermer, T. (1990) *In Search of Language: Influences from Spoken Dutch on Sign Language of the Netherlands*. Delft: Eburon.

Schiffman, H. (1996) *Linguistic Culture and Language Policy*. London: Routledge.

Schiffrin, D. (1987) *Discourse Markers*. Cambridge: Cambridge University Press.

Schiffrin, D. (1994) *Approaches to Discourse Analysis*. Cambridge: Blackwell.

Schilling-Estes, N. (1999) Situated ethnicities: Constructing and reconstructing identity in the sociolinguistic interview. *University of Pennsylvania Working Papers in Linguistics* 6(2), 137–151.

Schmaling, C. (2000) *Maganar Hannu: Language of the Hands: A Descriptive Analysis of Hausa Sign Language*. Hamburg: Signum.

Schuchman, J. (1988) *Hollywood Speaks: Deafness and the Film Entertainment Industry*. Urbana, IL: University of Illinois Press.

Scott D.A., R. Carmi, K. Elbedour, S. Yosefsberg, E.M. Stone and V.C. Sheffield (1996) An autosomal recessive nonsyndromic-hearing-loss locus identified by DNA pooling using two inbred Bedouin kindreds. *American Journal of Human Genetics* 59, 385–391.

Searle, J. (1962) What is a speech act? In M. Black (ed.), *Philosophy in America*. Ithaca, NY: Cornell University Press, 221–239.

Searle, J. (1969) *Speech Acts*. Cambridge: Cambridge University Press.

Seligman, C., G.R. Tucker and W.E. Lambert (1972) The effects of speech style and other attributes on teachers' attitudes toward pupils. *Language in Society* 1, 131–142.

Serpell, R. and M. Mbewe (1990) Dialectal flexibility in sign language in Africa. In C. Lucas (ed.), *Sign Language Research*. Washington, DC: Gallaudet University Press, 275–287.

Shapiro, E. (1993) Socioeconomic variation in American Sign Language. In E. Winston (ed.), *Communication Forum 1993*. Washington, DC: Gallaudet University Department of ASL, Linguistics, and Interpretation, 150–175.

Shapiro, J. (1993) *No Pity: People with Disabilities Forging a New Civil Rights Movement*. New York: Times Books.

Shorish, M. (1984) Planning by decree: The Soviet language policy in Central Asia. *Language Problems and Language Planning* 8, 35–49.

Shroyer, E. and S. Shroyer (1984) *Signs Across America: A Look at Regional Differences in American Sign Language*. Washington, DC: Gallaudet College Press.

Shuy, R., W. Wolfram and W. Riley (1968) *Linguistic Correlates of Social Stratification in Detroit Speech*. Washington, DC: US Office of Education Final Report No. 6–1347.

Sibayan, B. (1974) Language policy, language engineering and literacy in the Philippines. In J. Fishman (ed.), *Advances in Language Planning*. The Hague: Mouton, 221–254.

Skutnabb-Kangas, T. (1994) Linguistic human rights: A prerequisite for bilingualism. In I. Ahlgren and K. Hyltenstam (eds.), *Bilingualism in Deaf Education*. Hamburg: Signum, 139–159.

Skutnabb-Kangas, T. (2000) *Linguistic Genocide in Education: Or Worldwide Diversity and Human Rights?* Mahwah, NJ: Lawrence Erlbaum.

Skutnabb-Kangas, T. and R. Phillipson (eds.) (1995) *Linguistic Human Rights: Overcoming Linguistic Discrimination.* Berlin: Mouton de Gruyter.

Smith, D. (1993) Conversational analysis of American Sign Language in a second language classroom. In E. Winston (ed.), *Gallaudet University Communication Forum, Vol. 2.* Washington, DC: Gallaudet University School of Communication Student Forum, 176–188.

Smith, W. (1977) A history of the development of education of the deaf in the Republic of China. Unpublished manuscript, California State University, Northridge, CA.

Smith, W. (1989) The Morphological Characteristics of Verbs in Taiwan Sign Language. Unpublished dissertation, Indiana University, Bloomington, IN.

Smith, W. and L. Ting (1979) *Shou Neng Shen Chyau [Your Hands can Become a Bridge], Vol. 1.* Taipei: Deaf Sign Language Research Association of the Republic of China.

Smith, W. and L. Ting (1984) *Shou Neng Shen Chyau [Your Hands can Become a Bridge], Vol. 2.* Taipei: Deaf Sign Language Research Association of the Republic of China.

Srivastava, R. (1988) Societal bilingualism and bilingual education: A study of the Indian situation. In C. Paulston (ed.), *International Handbook of Bilingualism and Bilingual education.* New York: Greenwood Press, 247–274.

Stachlewitz, J. and B. Rundfunk (1995) German television programmes for the Deaf and its viewers' reactions and developments. In *Proceedings of Equal Partnership in the Media.* A Seminar Organised by the Irish Deaf Society and the European Union of the Deaf, Dublin, November.

Stevenson, P. (1997) *The German-Speaking World: A Practical Introduction to Sociolinguistic Issues.* London: Routledge.

Steyn, J. (1980) *Tuiste in Eie Taal [At Home in One's Language].* Cape Town: Tafelberg.

Stokoe, W. (1960) *Sign Language Structure: An Outline of Visual Communication Systems of the American Deaf.* Studies in Linguistics: Occasional Paper No. 8. Buffalo, NY: University of Buffalo.

Stokoe, W. (1969) Sign language diglossia. *Studies in Linguistics* 21, 27–41.

Stokoe, W. (1990) An historical perspective on sign language research: A personal view. In C. Lucas (ed.), *Sign Language Research: Theoretical Issues.* Washington, DC: Gallaudet University Press.

Stokoe, W. (1994) A sign language dictionary. In C. Erting, R. Johnson, D. Smith and B. Snider (eds.), *The Deaf Way: Perspectives from the International Conference on Deaf Culture.* Washington, DC: Gallaudet University Press.

Stokoe, W., D.C. Casterline and C.G. Croneberg (1965) *A Dictionary of American Sign Language on Linguistic Principles.* Silver Spring, MD: Linstock Press.

Stubbs, M. (1983) *Discourse Analysis.* Chicago, IL: University of Chicago Press.

Sutcliffe, R. (1975) *A Study of Language as a Determinant of Group Cohesiveness.* Unpublished Master's thesis, University of Maryland, College Park, MD.

Sutton, V. (1999) Available on the internet at: http://www.signwriting.org

Sutton-Spence, R. (1998) Grammatical constraints on fingerspelled English verb loans in BSL. In C. Lucas (ed.), *Pinky Extension and Eye Gaze: Language Use in Deaf Communities.* Washington, DC: Gallaudet University Press, 41–58.

Sutton-Spence, R. and B. Woll (1999) *The Linguistics of British Sign Language.* Cambridge: Cambridge University Press.

Swadesh, M. (1972) *The Origin and Diversification of Language.* London: Routledge and Kegan Paul.

Swisher, M.V. and D. McKee (1989) The sociolinguistic situation of natural sign language. *Applied Linguistics* 10, 294–312.

Tabouret-Keller, A. (1997) Language and identity. In F. Coulmas (ed.), *The Handbook of Sociolinguistics.* London: Blackwell.

Tai, J. (1988) Bilingualism and bilingual education in the People's Republic of China. In C. Paulston (ed.), *International Handbook of Bilingualism and Bilingual Education.* New York: Greenwood Press, 185–201.

Tannen, D. (1984) *Conversational Style: Analyzing Talk Among Friends.* Norwood, NJ: Ablex.

Tannen, D. (1986) *That's Not What I Meant.* New York: Ballantine.

Tannen, D. (1989) *Talking Voices: Repetition, Dialogue and Imagery in Conversational Discourse.* Cambridge: Cambridge University Press.

Tannen, D. (1993) What's in a frame? Surface evidence for underlying expectations. In Tannen (ed.), *Framing in Discourse.* New York: Oxford University Press, 14–56.

Taylor, G. and C. Mason (1991) *Deaf Futures.* Milton Keynes: The Open University.

Tennant, R. and M. Brown (1998) *The American Sign Language Handshape Dictionary.* Washington, DC: Clerc Books, Gallaudet University Press.

Tervoort, B. (1978) Bilingual Interference. In I.M. Schlesinger and L. Namir (eds.), *Sign Language of the Deaf: Psychological, Linguistic and Sociological Perspectives.* New York: Academic Press, 169–239.

Thibeault, A. (1993) Overlap in Filipino Sign Language discourse. In E. Winston (ed.), *Gallaudet University Communication Forum, Vol. 2.* Washington, DC: Gallaudet University School of Communication Student Forum, 207–218.

Thomas, L. (1999) Attitudes to language. In L. Thomas and S. Wareing (eds.), *Language, Society and Power: An Introduction.* London: Routledge.

Todd, L. (1984) *Modern Englishes: Pidgins and Creoles.* London: Basil Blackwell.

Tollefson, J. (1991) *Planning Language, Planning Inequality: Language Policy in the Community.* London: Longman.

Tomkins, W. (1969) *Indian Sign Language.* New York: Dover Publications.

Trudgill, P. (1974) *The Social Differentiation of English in Norwich.* Cambridge: Cambridge University Press.

Trudgill, P. (1983) *Sociolinguistics: An Introduction to Language and Society.* Revised edition. Harmondsworth: Penguin.

Trudgill, P. (1999) *The Dialects of England.* Oxford: Blackwell.

Turner, G. (1995) Contact signing and language shift. In H. Bos and T. Schermer (eds.), *Sign Language Research 1994.* Hamburg: Signum, 211–229.

Turner, G.H., M. Brennan, D. Brien, F.A. Elton and J.M. Collins (1998) Sociolinguistic issues in the making of 'The Dictionary of BSL/English'. In M.K. Vermon (ed.), *Sociolinguistics, Language and Society.* London: Sage.

Valli, C. (1994) Poetics of American Sign Language poetry. Unpublished doctoral dissertation, Union Institute, Cincinnati, OH.

Valli, C. (1995) *ASL poetry: Selected works of Clayton Valli.* (Video) San Diego, CA: Dawn Sign Press.

Valli, C. (1996) Poetics of ASL poetry. In *Visions of the Past, Visions of the Future: Proceedings of the 4th Gallaudet University College for Continuing Education Deaf Studies Conference, April 1995*. Washington, DC: Gallaudet University, 253–264.

Valli, C. and C. Lucas (1992) *ASL PAH! Deaf Students' Perspectives on their Language*. Burtonsville, MD: Linstok Press.

Valli, C. and C. Lucas (2000) *Linguistics of American Sign Language: An Introduction*. 3rd edition. Washington, DC: Gallaudet University Press. 1st edition 1992; 2nd edition 1995.

van Cleve, J. (ed.) (1993) *Deaf History Unveiled: Interpretations from the New Scholarship*. Washington, DC: Gallaudet University Press.

van Dijk, T. (1995) Discourse analysis as ideology analysis. In C. Schäffner and A. Wenden (eds.), *Language and Peace*. Aldershot: Harwood Academic Publishers, 17–33.

van Dijk, T. (1997a) *Discourse Studies: A Multidisciplinary Introduction, Vol. 1: Discourse as Structure and Process*. London: Sage.

van Dijk, T. (1997b) *Discourse Studies: A Multidisciplinary Introduction, Vol. 2: Discourse as Social Interaction*. London: Sage.

van Hoek, K. (1992) Conceptual spaces and pronominal reference in American Sign Language. *Nordic Journal of Linguistics* 15, 183–199.

van Hoek, K. (1996) Conceptual locations for reference in American Sign Language. In G. Fauconnier and E. Sweetser (eds.), *Spaces, Worlds, and Grammar*. Chicago, IL: University of Chicago Press, 334–350.

van Hoek, K., F. Norman and L. O'Grady (1989) Development of spatial and nonspatial referential cohesion in American Sign Language narrative. Unpublished paper presented at Stanford Child Research Forum, Stanford, CA.

van Uden, A. (1986) Sign languages of Deaf people and psycholinguistics: A critical evaluation. Reprinted in S. Gregory and G. Hartley (eds.) (1991) *Constructing Deafness*. Milton Keynes: The Open University, 192–199.

van Zijl, J. (1987) Teacher education for a multi-cultural society: Seven strategies. *South African Journal of Education* 7, 187–190.

Veltman, C. (1996) The English language in Québec, 1940–1990. In J.A. Fishman, A. Rubal-Lopez and A.W. Conrad (eds.), *Post-imperial English: Status Changes in Former British and American Colonies, 1940–1990*. Amsterdam: Mouton de Gruyer, 232–233.

Voegelin, C. and F. Voegelin (1977) *Classification and Index of the World's Languages*. New York and Oxford: Elsevier.

Walworth, M., D. Moores and T.J. O'Rourke (eds.) (1992) *A Free Hand: Enfranchising the Education of Deaf Children*. Silver Spring, MD: T.J. Publishers.

Wardhaugh, R. (1998) *An Introduction to Sociolinguistics*. 3rd edn. Oxford: Blackwell.

Ward Trotter, J. (1989) An examination of language attitudes of teachers of the deaf. In C. Lucas (ed.), *The Sociolinguistics of the Deaf Community*. San Diego, CA: Academic Press, 211–228.

Washabaugh, W. (1981) The Deaf of Grand Cayman, British West Indies. *Sign Language Studies* 31, 117–133.

Washabaugh, W. (1986) *Five Fingers for Survival*. Ann Arbor, MI: Karoma.

Wassink, A.B. (1999) Historic low prestige and seeds of change: Attitudes toward Jamaican Creole. *Language in Society* 28, 57–92.

Weinberg, J. (1992) *The History of the Residential School for Jewish Deaf Children*. London: Reunion of the Jewish Deaf School Committee.

Weinreich, U., W. Labov and M. Herzog (1968) Empirical foundations for a theory of language change. In W. Lehmann and Y. Malkiel (eds.), *Directions for Historical Linguistics: A Symposium*. Austin, TX: University of Texas Press, 95–188.

Weinstein, B. (1980) Language planning in francophone Africa. *Language Problems and Language Planning* 4, 55–77.

Weinstein, B. (ed.) (1990) *Language Policy and Political Development*. Norwood, NJ: Ablex.

Wilbur, R. (1979) *American Sign Language and Sign Systems*. Baltimore, MD: University Park Press.

Wilcox, S. (ed.) (1988) *Academic Acceptance of American Sign Language*. Special issue of *Sign Language Studies* 59. Burtonsville, MD: Linstok Press.

Wilcox, S. and P. Wilcox (1997) *Learning to See: American Sign Language as a Second Language*. 2nd edn. Washington, DC: Gallaudet University Press.

Wilkinson, W. (1875) *Eleventh Report of the Board of Directors and Officers of the California Institution for the Education of the Deaf and Blind*. Sacramento, CA: D.W. Gelwicks, State printer.

Williams, F. (1973) Some research notes on dialect, attitudes and stereotypes. In R. Shuy and R. Fasold (eds.), *Language Attitudes: Current Trends and Prospects*. Washington, DC: Georgetown University Press, 113–128.

Williams, F. (1974) The identification of linguistic attitudes. *International Journal of the Sociology of Language* 9, 43–47.

Williams, G. (1992) *Sociolinguistics: A Sociological Critique*. London: Routledge.

Wilson, J. (1996) The tobacco story: Narrative structure in an ASL story. In C. Lucas (ed.), *Multicultural Aspects of Sociolinguistics in Deaf Communities*. Washington, DC: Gallaudet University Press, 152–180.

Wilson, J. and A. Henry (1998) Parameter setting within a socially realistic linguistics. *Language in Society* 27, 1–22.

Winefield, R. (1987) *Never the Twain Shall Meet: Bell, Gallaudet, and the Communications Debate*. Washington, DC: Gallaudet University Press.

Winston, E. (1991) Spatial referencing and cohesion in an American Sign Language text. *Sign Language Studies* 73, 397–410.

Winston, E. (1992) Space and involvement in an American Sign Language lecture. In J. Plant-Moeller (ed.), *Expanding Horizons: Proceedings of the 12th National Convention of the Registry of Interpreters for the Deaf*. Silver Spring, MD: RID Publications, 93–105.

Winston, E. (1993) Spatial mapping in comparative discourse frames in an ASL lecture. Unpublished doctoral dissertation, Georgetown University, Washington, DC.

Winston, E. (1994) Space and reference in ASL. In B. Johnstone (ed.), *Repetition in Discourse*. Norwood, NJ: Ablex.

Winston, E. (1995) Spatial mapping in comparative discourse frames. In K. Emmorey and J. Reilly (eds.), *Language, Gesture, and Space*. Hillsdale, NJ: Lawrence Erlbaum, 87–114.

Winston, E. (1998) Contextualizing prosody in ASL. Unpublished paper presented at Theoretical Issues in Sign Language Research (TISLR) 6. Washington, DC: Gallaudet University.

Winston, E. (ed.) (1999) *Storytelling and Conversation: Discourse in Deaf Communities.* Washington, DC: Gallaudet University Press.

Wolfram, W. (1969) *A Sociolinguistic Description of Detroit Negro Speech.* Washington, DC: Center for Applied Linguistics.

Wolfram, W. (1989) Structural variability in phonological development: Final nasals in vernacular Black English. In R.W. Fasold and D. Schiffrin (eds.), *Language Change and Variation.* Amsterdam: John Benjamins, 301–332.

Wolfram, W. (1991) *Dialects and American English.* Englewood Cliff, NJ and Washington, DC: Prentice Hall and Center for Applied Linguistics.

Wolfram, W. (1993) Identifying and interpreting variables. In D. Preston (ed.), *American Dialect Research.* Amsterdam and Philadelphia, PA: John Benjamins, 193–221.

Wolfram, W. (1997) Dialect in society. In F. Coulmas (ed.), *The Handbook of Sociolinguistics.* Oxford: Blackwell, 107–126.

Wolfram, W. and D. Christian (1976) *Appalachian Speech.* Arlington, VA: Center for Applied Linguistics.

Wolfram, W. and R. Fasold (1974) *The Study of Social Dialects in the United States.* Englewood Cliffs, NJ: Prentice Hall.

Wolfram, W. and N. Schilling-Estes (1998) *American English.* Oxford: Blackwell.

Wolfram, W., C. Dannenberg and N. Schilling-Estes (2000) Constructing ethnolinguistic identity in a tri-ethnic context. Paper presented at the annual meeting of the Linguistic Society of America, Chicago, IL.

Wolfson, N. (1979) The conversational historical present alternation. *Language* 55, 168–182.

Woll, B. (1991) *Variation and Recent Change in British Sign Language.* Final report to Economic and Social Research Council. University of Bristol: Centre for Deaf Studies.

Woll, B. (1994) The influence of television on the Deaf community in Britain. In I. Ahlgren, B. Bergman and M. Brennan (eds.), *Perspectives on Sign Language Usage: Papers from the 5th International Symposium on Sign Language Research, Vol. 2.* Durham: University of Durham, Deaf Studies Research Unit: The International Sign Linguistics Association.

Woodward, J.C. (1972) Implications for sociolinguistic research among the Deaf. *Sign Language Studies* 1, 1–7.

Woodward, J.C. (1973a) Implicational lects on the deaf diglossic continuum. Unpublished doctoral dissertation, Georgetown University, Washington, DC.

Woodward, J.C. (1973b) Interrule implication in American Sign Language. *Sign Language Studies* 3, 47–56.

Woodward, J.C. (1973c) Some characteristics of Pidgin Sign English. *Sign Language Studies* 3, 39–46.

Woodward, J.C. (1976) Black southern signing. *Language in Society* 5, 211–218.

Woodward, J.C. (1978) Historical bases of American Sign Language. In P. Siple (ed.), *Understanding Language through Sign Language Research.* New York: Academic Press, 333–348.

Woodward, J.C. (1982) *How You Gonna Get to Heaven if You Can't Talk with Jesus: On Depathologizing Deafness.* Silver Spring, MD: T.J. Publishers.

Woodward, J.C. (1987) Sociolinguistics. In J. van Cleve (ed.), *Gallaudet Encyclopedia of Deaf People and Deafness, Vol. 3.* London: McGraw-Hill, 152–157.

Woodward, J. C. and S. DeSantis (1977a) Negative incorporation in French and American Sign Language. *Language in Society* 6(3), 379–388.

Woodward, J. C. and S. DeSantis (1977b) Two to one it happens: Dynamic phonology in two sign languages. *Sign Language Studies* 17, 329–346.

Woodward, J.C. and H. Markowicz (1975) Some handy new ideas of pidgins and creoles: Pidgin sign languages. Unpublished paper presented at the Conference on Pidgin and Creole Languages, Honolulu, HI.

Woodward, J. C. and H. Markowicz (1980) Pidgin sign languages. In W.C. Stokoe (ed.), *Sign and Culture: A Reader for Students of American Sign Language.* Silver Spring, MD: Linstok Press, 55–76.

Woodward, J. C., C. Erting and S. Oliver (1976) Facing and hand(1)ing variation in American Sign Language. *Sign Language Studies* 10, 43–52.

Woodward, R. (1978) Historical bases of ASL. In P. Siple (ed.), *Understanding Language through Sign Language Research.* London: Academic Press.

Woolard, K.A. (1985) Catalonia: The dilemma of language rights. In N. Wolfson and J. Manes (eds.), *Language of Inequality.* Berlin: Mouton, 91–109.

Woolard, K.A. and T.J. Gahng (1990) Changing language policies and attitudes in autonomous Catalonia. *Language in Society* 19, 311–330.

Woolley, M. (1981) Deaf broadcasting campaign. Reprinted in R. Lee (ed.) (1992), *Deaf Liberation: A Selection of National Union of the Deaf papers, 1976–1986.* Feltham, UK: National Union of the Deaf.

World Federation of the Deaf (1975) *Gestuno: International Sign Language of the Deaf.* Carlisle: The British Deaf Association.

World Federation of the Deaf (1993) The WFD report on the status of sign languages. Helsinki: World Federation of the Deaf.

Wrigley, O. (1997) *The Politics of Deafness.* Washington, DC: Gallaudet University Press.

Wulf, A., P. Dudis, R. Bayley and C. Lucas (1999) Null subject variation in ASL narratives. Paper presented at New Ways of Analyzing Variation (NWAV) conference, Toronto.

Yau, S. and J. He (1990) How do deaf children get their name signs during their first month in school? In W.H. Edmondson and F. Karlsson (eds.), *SLR 1987: Papers from the Fourth International Symposium on Sign Language Research, Lappeenranta, Finland, 15–19 July 1987.* Hamburg: Signum Press, 243–254.

Young, D. (1988) Bilingualism and bilingual education in a divided South African society. In C. Paulston (ed.), *International Handbook of Bilingualism and Bilingual Education.* New York: Greenwood Press, 405–428.

Young, R. and R. Bayley (1996) VARBRUL analysis for second language acquisition research. In R. Bayley and D.R. Preston (eds.), *Second Language Acquisition and Linguistic Variation.* Amsterdam and Philadelphia, PA: John Benjamins, 253–306.

Zentella, A.C. (1997) *Growing Up Bilingual: Puerto Rican Children in New York.* Oxford: Blackwell.

Zeshan, U. (forthcoming 2001): *Gebärdensprachen des indischen Subkontinents.* Munich: LINCOM Europa.

Index

Aarons, D. 14–15
acquisition 51, 202–3
Adegbija, E. 204
adjacency pairs 123
advertisements 204, 212, 214*f*
Africa 30, 215 n2
African American signing 87
African American Vernacular English (AAVE)
    65, 70–3, 207–8, 215 n6
age 61, 95, 96
agent–beneficiary directionality 82, 89
Akach, P. 14–15
Allport, G.W. 183
Allsop, L. 24, 192, 195, 211, 212
Almond, B. 165
Altbach, P. 147
American Sign Language (ASL)
  age differences 61
  code switching 64, 192–3
  cohesion 135–6
  constructed dialogue and action 133–5
  creolization 57
  DEAF 61–2, 85, 101–4, 103*f*, 106, 107, 124
  Deaf attitudes towards 197
  definition of 16–17, 23
  diachronic variation 83–4
  dictionaries 6, 78, 79–80, 152
  discourse 86
  discourse markers 132–3
  and fingerspelling 50–1, 85–6
  as 'foreign language' 168
  influences on 10, 23, 29
  internationalization 163
  lexical variation 80, 84
  linguistic factors 61–2
  and manual sign codes 154–5, 175 n5
  morphological and syntactic variation 82–3
  mouthing 54
  negative incorporation 82, 89
  NOW/NOW-THAT 132
  phonological variation 80–2, 84–5, 97–9,
    98*f*, 106, 107

  and Pidgin Sign English 56
  politeness in 122
  recognition of 151, 168–9, 215 n2
  regional variation 61
  repair strategies 130
  research on variation 77–86, 89, 97–109
  sermons 142
  social attitude 17
  status 102, 104, 169, 206, 209
  syntactic variation 64
  teaching and learning 202
  see also African American signing; Tactile
    ASL
Anderson, L. 25–7, 26*f*, 27*f*
Ann, J. 54
Anthony, D. 153
Aramburo, A. 87
ASL *see* American Sign Language
Auslan *see* Australian Sign Language
Austin, J. 117
Australian Sign Language (Auslan) 16, 23, 28,
    152, 215 n2
  see also Warlpiri sign language

back-channeling 86, 142
Baer, A.M. 128
Bahan, B. 140–1, 168, 212
Bailey, G. *et al.* 74, 75
Baker, C. 125, 127–8, 129, 182, 184,
    193, 209, 212
Baldauf, R. 173
Bali 10–11, 40–1
Banham, D. 9
Barakat, R. 9
Baron, D. 149, 174 n2
Bateson, G. 118
Battison, R. 50, 59, 100
Battison, R.M. 93
Bayley, R. 61, 62, 64, 73, 74, 85, 96, 97,
    101–4, 106, 107, 108, 109,
    124, 125
Belgium 23, 24, 36

249